BUSINESS ACTION IN A CHANGING WORLD

BUSINESS ACTION IN A CHANGING WORLD

Public Administration Service.
Publication no. 127

BUSINESS ACTION IN A CHANGING WORLD

Edited by

HENRY C. THOLE and CHARLES C. GIBBONS

CONTRIBUTORS

C. Canby Balderston

Francis Bello

R. E. Brooker

J. Douglas Brown

Gilbert Burck

Joel Dean

John Diebold

Peter F. Drucker

Arthur P. Felton

Curtis H. Gager

Charles C. Gibbons

John J. Hopkins

Joseph M. Juran

Charles H. Kline

Douglas M. McGregor

Robert P. Neuschel

Sanford Parker

Keith Powlison

Robert V. Roosa

Erwin H. Schell

Sumner H. Slichter

Henry C. Thole

Samuel M. Wilson

PUBLIC ADMINISTRATION SERVICE
1313 East Sixtieth Street
Chicago 37, Illinois

List price $5.00

PAS Publication Number 127
Library of Congress Catalog Card Number: 56-13383

Acknowledgments

THE editors express their appreciation to the organizations and individuals who generously gave permission for reprinting the selections in this volume. In each case, credit has been given to the author and publisher of the material.

Dr. Harold C. Taylor, director of the W. E. Upjohn Institute for Community Research, gave encouragement to the project and assisted in the preparation of the Introduction. Dr. Ernest Dale, of Ernest Dale Associates, read the manuscript and made valuable suggestions regarding the selection of articles and the organization of the book.

Henry C. Thole

Kalamazoo, Michigan

Charles C. Gibbons

THE W. E. UPJOHN INSTITUTE FOR
COMMUNITY RESEARCH

THE Institute is a privately sponsored nonprofit research organization. It is an activity of the W. E. Upjohn Unemployment Trustee Corporation, which was established in 1932 by the late Dr. W. E. Upjohn for research on the causes and effects of unemployment and on measures for the alleviation of unemployment.

The interest of the Institute in problems of employment and unemployment is centered at the community level, as distinguished from the national or international level. While broader influences have not been ignored, the emphasis has been on what can be done by local businessmen and community leaders to maintain a high level of business activity and employment. The Institute is equally concerned with what can be done locally to adjust to the broader economic changes which are national in scope.

Since its establishment in 1945, the Institute has conducted research on economic, industrial, and community problems related to employment and unemployment. Recognizing that job opportunities depend upon the success of business enterprise, the Institute has focused its attention on research dealing with investment and the establishment of enterprise, the management of enterprise, and the community setting for enterprise.

v

Contents

III. MANAGEMENT ACTION IN SPECIFIC AREAS

IV. THE GUARANTEED ANNUAL WAGE AND BUSINESS STABILIZATION

Survival and Growth of the Individual Firm in a Dynamic Economy

AN INTRODUCTORY STATEMENT BY THE EDITORS

The Process of Change

THE economic and social climate in which businessmen operate is changing constantly. Changes within the economic system that affect business firms include new products and services, technological improvements, business cycles, changes in costs, and changes resulting from action by competitors. External factors such as wars, threats of war, and inflationary or deflationary action by the government also influence the operation of business firms.

These changes present problems of adjustment to every business firm. Instability in the economy causes instability in the individual firm. A period of rapid growth means that most firms must increase sales, obtain new capital and facilities, increase production, and employ more workers. A period of contraction means that most firms must curtail expenditures, decrease production, and lay off workers. While such changes are commonly associated with booms and depressions, they are actually occurring all the time. New products, new methods, and new ideas appear continually; and the competition they foster, the failures they cause, are part of the never-ending process of change.

Change as such is not new, of course; the world has always been changing. It is only that the pace of change is now increasing so rapidly. Big opportunities that formerly occurred perhaps once in a lifetime may now confront a business manager any day. And if the chance of big success comes often, the chance "to miss the boat," and thus to fail, comes equally often.

Dynamic Planning

Dynamic planning is planning that anticipates the future, and is constantly revised to meet changing conditions. Planning is not a function

1

which can be performed once and then be forgotten. Competition and change in the economic weather demand constant planning and revision of plans.

There is a current trend for management planning to become more long range in character. One of the important factors contributing to this trend is the growth of the economy. Increasing population and rising standards of living mean that there will be a greater demand for products in the future. Managers are motivated to increase or at least to maintain their share of the market. Long-range requirements for buildings, equipment, and manpower must be established. Advertising and pricing plans aimed at expanding the market must be made long before they are put into effect. Decisions on such matters are likely to commit men, money, and machines for long periods into the future.

Another factor that makes long-range planning necessary is that most manufacturing businesses require large capital outlays. Automation and increasing labor costs tend to make it profitable to increase capital expenditures still further. Recovery of these costs must be spread over a long period of time, and it is therefore necessary to plan far ahead.

If firms are to meet successfully labor's demands for a guaranteed annual wage, they must plan for increased stability in sales and production. Interruptions in mass production have always been costly. Guaranteed annual wages or supplementary unemployment benefits are simply additional factors that make irregular operations costly.

In planning, the manager must pay constant attention to the possibility of emergencies. In a dynamic economy there is always the possibility of sudden change. Sharp increases in demand may result from war or from sudden shifts in consumer preferences. Managers must also be prepared for sudden decreases in demand which may result from economic readjustments or competitive conditions. Extra sales effort that may be desperately needed during such an emergency cannot be organized over night. The new products needed to stimulate sales must be ready when sales start to decline. A company whose management skills include dynamic planning will be more likely to be ready for emergencies of all kinds.

A Program of Action

Decisions on important matters must be made as they arise; the majority of them cannot be postponed without jeopardizing the welfare of the company. If a firm is to grow, expenditures for new plant and equipment must be made in spite of possible losses due to obsolescence or decline in demand; sales effort must be expanded in the face of shifts in population, changing consumer tastes, and competitors' price changes; and research on new products and processes must be carried out without assurance that it will be fruitful or that the company will obtain the desired result before competitors do.

Let us now consider some of the requirements for sound management action under changing conditions. First, management must develop better techniques for recognizing important changes affecting its business. In a free economy the majority of firms are striving for an increased share of the market. This means that many firms are contributing to the process of economic change by looking for new ways to satisfy consumer wants and by producing and merchandising new products. It is one of management's major responsibilities to be aware of such changes.

Having discerned as well as possible the direction of change, management must then adapt soundly and swiftly to such change. Changing conditions necessitate revision of present plans and policies and creation of new ones to meet the new problems effectively. Even though management is aware of basic trends and changes in the economy, failure to adapt company plans and actions to these new conditions may result first in loss of competitive position, and eventually in failure.

While adaptive action is important, it alone will not assure success. It is necessary for management to be creative in its planning and operating activities. Not only must a firm adapt to changes in competitors' actions and to changes in the economic weather, but it must create new products and services, new customers, and better management methods in order to survive.

Successful operation in a dynamic economy depends, finally, on management's ability to visualize the business as a whole and to manage the entire operation as an integrated unit. Each function of the business is dependent on the others, and changes in any one part affect all the others. It is not enough for management to be excellent in one or two areas of the business. If one part of the business becomes inefficient, the entire organization is in danger of failure. All functions must be kept efficient.

There have been many examples of firms which, despite excellence in some phases of management, have suffered competitively because of poor performance in other areas of the business. The classic example is the Ford Motor Company which in the late 1920's was outstanding in its manufacturing skill, but failed to recognize the importance of design and sales appeal. Consumer preferences were not given sufficient weight. The result for Ford was loss of industry leadership to General Motors. Such instances will multiply as the pace of change accelerates.

The Caliber of Management

It must be apparent from what we have already said that a company's greatest resource for survival and growth in a changing world is its management personnel. Most of the resources which a company needs to carry on its operations are available to all on the open market. Buildings, machines, and materials are available to all who have the necessary cash or credit. This is not true to the same extent of management men. A smoothly functioning management team cannot be purchased at any price. It is a resource which must be developed over a period of years. Once developed, however, a good management group will contribute more than anything else toward a company's success in a changing world.

Because the future survival and growth of a company will depend upon its leadership in the future, today's managers can contribute most to the long-run success of their companies by developing the men who will manage their companies in the future. The best corporate managers of today cannot accurately foresee the problems of tomorrow. The decisions of today will have to be discarded or modified to permit successful operation in the world of tomorrow. The future success of a company will depend upon having men at the top who can make wise decisions.

Managing for Tomorrow

It is apparent that this is, in general, a book about good management. Since there are already many excellent books on the subject of business management, perhaps we should state the contribution that we hope this book will make.

In recent years, some excellent material has been written with regard to management action to meet changing conditions. We have collected these contributions from the several journals and books in which they originally appeared so that they may be readily available to business managers and others interested in the problems of managing a business in a changing world.

The readings in this book focus on some of the major trends and issues facing the manager of tomorrow and on the techniques which are likely to be most useful in managing a business during a period of rapid change. Special emphasis is placed on measures necessary to assure healthy growth and on measures necessary to prepare for periods of emergency, such as inflation or recession. There are selections on management planning and action which enable a company to influence to some extent the conditions under which it operates. Other selections deal with management's role in adapting to economic changes over which it has little control.

Ordinarily when we refer to good management we mean doing today's jobs better: better selling today; better production efficiency today; better product development today. For most firms, doing today's jobs better is a great challenge and a source of profit. Managing for today is a great challenge, but there is even greater challenge in managing for tomorrow. This book is about managing for tomorrow. While the subject matter of the selections included in this volume may seem superficially to be quite traditional, their focus is on tomorrow; and that focus is the reason for bringing them together.

As the pace of change increases, some qualities will be at a premium; and, as the careful reader will note, these qualities are underscored by most of the materials in this book. *Creativity* will be at a premium. Since tomorrow will be different from today, there will be a high place for *foresight*. And finally, since no one can shape the future or foresee it completely, there is need for *flexibility* to meet the future no matter what it may bring. Managing for tomorrow will require managers who possess the qualities of creativity, foresight, and flexibility. We hope that this volume will assist business managers in developing these necessary qualities as they prepare for the days that lie ahead.

I. CHANGES FACING THE MANAGER OF TOMORROW

1 The Changing Role of Management*

By Douglas M. McGregor

About the time the sit-down strikes occurred in Detroit, I entered the field of human relations in industry. Some of you may remember back to those trying days. During the almost 20 years since then, I think it is fair to say that there has been a major revolution in the thinking, the practices, and the philosophy of American management.

This is not true, of course, of all management. It is most apparent today at the top of organizations, although it is filtering down through lower levels too. Most of us have been so close to the day-by-day problems that it is hard to realize how much change has occurred in the time of which I am speaking. Let us consider, for a little while, some of the changes that have occurred in the period of the last 20 years.

It is easy to list certain developments that have occurred in the management field. Many new programs and practices of management have come along, to be sure. However, I am looking for something more than this. What are the broad changes in point of view that have affected management's role as it has operated in American industry? What are the significant threads that are gradually making a pattern in the fabric of our industrial life? There are several of these, and I propose to talk about three which seem to me to be especially significant.

The first thread I would like to mention is the realization that the successful operation of an industrial organization, in a free enterprise system, requires the *willing* collaboration of the people who comprise the organization. We have not always believed this to be so. In fact, this idea wasn't at all common even 20 years ago. The prevalent notion in management thinking in those days was that if the work was to get done, people had to be made to do it. The basic concept of motivation we relied on was that of

* Reprinted from the *Technology Review*, April 1955, edited at the Massachusetts Institute of Technology.

fear. Fear of loss of employment and other forms of economic punishment was what management used to keep people at work.

Throughout these last 20 years and more, we have discovered that force in human affairs—as in physics—breeds counterforce. We have discovered the degree of ingenuity that human beings can exercise against management in such forms as restriction of output, all kinds of subtle sabotage, militant unionism, and the like. We have begun to learn that, if we attempt to use force, the counterforces will tend to defeat the purpose we are trying to achieve. Therefore, most of us have come to the realization that it is management's task to create the kind of conditions that lead people to want to do the job, and to collaborate willingly in achieving organizational goals.

In looking back, I think evidence is to be seen of the growth of this conception in management's thinking. Consider, for a moment, the developments in wage and salary administration over the past 20 years. Certainly these have served one important purpose—that of helping to convince people that their wages and salaries are set on a fair basis, and that they need not be concerned about arbitrary action. If people are convinced that their earnings are equitably established, perhaps they will be more willing to collaborate with management.

In most companies the basic climate in which union-management negotiations occur has changed very remarkably in the past two decades. We still read about an occasional difficult conflict situation in the newspapers. But close study and examination (such as the National Planning Association has given in recent years) to bargaining in companies where the relationship has settled down and become "healthy," indicates an entirely different pattern than was formerly characteristic. Today we see the pattern of people working across the table from each other, trying to find the reasonable and fair way to resolve their differences so that all will be willing to work toward a stated goal or objective.

The development of the personnel administration function has helped to create willingness in the organization. For example, consider the importance we place, today, on good communications in an organization. Throughout the entire organization we strive to let people know what is going on, to help them understand the changes that are about to take place, and therefore to be more willing to adjust to the circumstances they have to face.

And finally, consider the general emphasis which today's management places on the whole structure of motivation. We have been shifting around from the negative emphasis on fear, to the search for positive incentives which will lead people to collaborate willingly toward organizational objectives.

To a large extent these changes have resulted from trial and error. One company discovers something useful, or a university conducts some research that leads a management to try out a new method. If the new technique works out well, other companies copy or adopt it. We like to "keep up with the Jones's" in this field as we do in other respects. Gradually a lot of changes occur. Finally, out of the details of improved practice and the gradual day-by-day shift in our attitude or policy, something emerges that is broader and deeper than any of the contributing factors. We are becoming genuinely conscious of the fact that the willing collaboration of everybody in the organization, from the Board of Directors to the janitor, is essential if we are going to get the output—and the economic results and the human results—we desire.

The second thread involves another matter of attitudes. This is a growing feeling of confidence, on the part of management, in the potentialities of people. We no longer hear management talking about employees as "hands." Labor is no longer seen solely as a commodity. We are beginning to regard people as individuals—whole human beings—who have remarkable potentialities. By and large we have not yet tapped these potentialities in industry, up to now.

"Potentiality" may lead you to think in terms of productivity. However, I am not concerned with productivity in the narrow sense of the word—of how many ergs of energy a man develops, or how many units of effort per hour (or per day) he expends, or whatever else is usually meant by productivity. Productivity is important, of course, but sometimes we tend to overemphasize it. What I am concerned with is the potentiality which we sense when we become aware of what ingenious, creative minds can do when there is encouragement, under the proper circumstances, to help make the enterprise a more successful one.

Ingenuity is a cornerstone of our civilization. It is characteristic of the janitor and the bench hand, as well as of the director of research and the vice-president. Only now are we beginning to recognize these potentialities. I have a feeling that 20 years from now we may look back on our present attempts as clumsy and inept ones, but there are signs that we are groping in the right direction.

One example of present groping is that whole area which is practically a fad today in management thinking: decentralization and the delegation of authority. This topic would not be emphasized if we did not have increased confidence in people. We don't talk so much today about the concept of span of control—that one man can supervise from five to seven other persons—even though this topic is still treated in textbooks. The reason for this is that we have begun to change our conception of supervision, particularly at higher managerial levels. We realize that it isn't necessary to "breathe down the neck" of every man who is reporting to us, to control his actions.

The concept of decentralization means, in effect, that we have enough confidence in men to outline the broad range of their responsibility and authority, and then to turn them loose to find a way to do the job—without supervision in the narrow sense, but with full expectation that their efforts will produce the desired results.

This kind of relaxation of control is possible only because we have come to have a genuine confidence in people and what they can do. Firms, such as Sears, Roebuck and Company, and Johnson and Johnson have demonstrated some remarkable achievements along the lines of delegated authority.

In the last two or three years the same concept has been carried still lower in the organization, and today we hear about job enlargement. To be sure, in part, job enlargement has been accelerated by the process of automation. The people in an automatized organization must exercise a different and higher level of judgment than those in firms where automatization has not yet appeared. People are upgraded for their higher level of judgment, as they have been in the oil industry, which has largely gone through the automation process. Today we recognize that the worker is capable of exercising judgment, and so job enlargement is coming to replace excessive specialization, which has been characteristic of the last few years.

The concept of participation is bandied around a great deal today in industry. It represents, in one more way, a growth in management's confidence in people and their potentialities. When the idea of participation was first introduced, 10 or 15 years ago, it came with the idea that we needed more "democracy" in industry. However, the rather naïve idea that democracy implies that everyone is going to decide everything is not the core of the concept of participation.

There is quite another characteristic of democracy which is relevant to participation. It is this: If people are freed from the restraints of rigid authoritarian control, then—given proper circumstances and motivation—they will help to create a better society. This is the concept of participation which we are gradually exploring and finding to be very fruitful.

The work of my colleague, Joseph N. Scanlon, lecturer in the Department of Economics and Social Science at M.I.T., has led to the adoption of the participation idea harnessed and utilized in a special manner—the Scanlon Plan—in a number of industries. Most of the companies which have adopted the plan are showing remarkable economic achievements, above anything that would have been predicted.

We have a great deal more to learn about the limits of participation and about its potentialities, but the point I wish to make is simply this: Management would not be experimenting at all with the idea if some fundamental attitudes had not shifted. Management has, today, a new confidence in people and what they are capable of doing.

The field of executive development provides still another illustration of changes in managerial thinking. Instead of seeking personnel for top management posts in a very small stratum of our industrial society, we are recognizing that potentialities, latent in many people, can be developed so that they can become capable of top management responsibility.

A year and a half ago, I had the experience of attending a 13-nation European conference on the subject of executive development. It was interesting to see how our European friends were only just beginning to grasp the importance of this concept which, after 15 or 20 years, is now quite familiar to us. For generations Europeans have attempted to draw their managers from a very narrow segment of society on the assumption that this segment contained the only people with the necessary capacity. It was only when this small group could no longer supply the growing need that attempts were made to look lower down in the organization for potential leaders.

Finally, in this connection, I refer again to our current emphasis on communications. When, through programs of communicating with employees, we attempt to tell them what we are about, we do so because we have confidence in their good sense. Otherwise we would not bother to tell them.

Not long ago one big company developed a series of films intended to enhance the economic education of its employees. It was designed to show people how their company operated, what its philosophy was, and how it fitted into the general economy. After this set of films was shown to people throughout the organization, I was talking with one of the executives about the problem of evaluating its effect. I was interested to find that the executive was not planning any "before and after" measure of attitude. Instead, he was trying to develop a method that his firm could use to indicate whether, as a result of seeing and discussing the film, people would take more variables into account as they considered the complex problems of our economy. You don't talk as that executive did unless you have a pretty high level of confidence in the common sense and intellectual ability of the average person. He was saying, in effect: "People are bright enough, smart enough, and sensible enough so that they are likely to arrive at wise answers if they only recognize how many variables there are. I don't argue that they ought to arrive at the same answers I do."

This development—this thread of a growing confidence in people and their potentialities—has not been a logical, planned result of management action. It is emerging out of trial-and-error experience in dealing with people. As a result, instead of defining management as the direction and control of the elements of production—machines, money, processes (and, incidentally, people)—we are defining it today as the conservation, the development, and the utilization of the human resources of industry. The emphasis is on people as a resource.

The third and last thread in the picture that I want to talk about today is that of management's self-confidence in itself. The dominant characteristic of top management in our society 40 years ago was probably arrogance. The executives were on top of the heap, and they knew it.

During the thirties, management came under severe attack from many quarters, and became understandably insecure and defensive. But today, it seems to me, management has begun to achieve a genuine self-confidence. Executives display the kind of confidence characteristic of a respected profession, including a concern for ethics, and genuine humility.

Perhaps some of you have seen Adolf Berle's new book on the American capitalist.[1] It is the second one he has written in which he has pointed to the power that big corporations have in our economy. However, there is an interesting change in his point of view in this book as compared to the one he wrote a few years back. The change is simply that he can see very little evidence that the managements of our big corporations have exercised their power in ways detrimental to society. They have exercised self-restraint. This is a facet of the self-confidence that is making management a real profession today.

There are two or three other symptoms of management's emerging self-confidence which deserve mention. First, I would mention management's growing willingness to exercise authority in the real sense of that term, with readiness to accept the consequences.

During the depression and post-depression days, when management was facing the tremendous problems of militant unionism, there was a swing away from an authoritarian concept of authority to what almost

---

[1] Adolf A. Berle, *20th Century Capitalist Revolution* (New York: Harcourt Brace and Company, 1954).

amounted to anarchy. In many instances, management simply abdicated. We have come back to a balanced middle position in which management is willing to make decisions, to absorb the uncertainties which go into making them, and to accept the inevitable hostility that goes with the exercise of authority. No important decision pleases all.

Incidentally, the personal pattern of adjustment to authority turns up frequently as significant in the research on leadership behavior. The adjustment pattern involves authority in several directions. First, how does the individual deal with authority above him? Is he too submissive to it or, on the other hand, is he too resentful of it? Can he live with it in a comfortable fashion? Second, how does he handle his own authority? Does he grab it too quickly; does he exercise it like the new "cop" on the beat? Or, on the other hand, does he try to avoid it? Does he try to evade consequences of exercising authority? Or does he accept the more difficult position of living with the responsibility, the anxiety, and the consequences of his actions and decisions?

The second symptom of management's developing self-confidence is the acceptance of the fact that conflict and disagreement in human organizations are inevitable. We have gone through a long period of searching for sweetness and light. We have hoped for that blessed state in which everyone will agree with everybody, everyone will love everybody, and no one will quarrel with anybody about anything. The simple fact is that if we had organizations like that, they would be completely "dead on their feet."

It is only in those organizations where people disagree, where new ideas can come up and be knocked down and be fought about, where people can differ sharply and sincerely about important issues, that we find growth and development and vitality. To seek for peace as a condition of health is basically nonsense.

I have recently talked with a management concerned with the problems created by a rigid policy of promotion from within. This group was raising such questions as these: Are we getting enough new blood into the organization? Are we permitting the capable person—who happens to be a "porcupine"—to grow, to develop, and to climb in the organization? If we create a mold in which we all think alike, in which everyone agrees all the time, are we going to be able to meet the kind of problems that will surely face us a little farther down the road?

One more evidence of management's self-confidence is the fact that the line manager is coming to accept full responsibility for human relations and for personnel administration. For a long time there was a consistent attempt to get rid of this type of responsibility. In fact, part of the impetus to the development of the field of personnel administration was an attempt of line management to slough off the responsibility of dealing with people.

Management was not too busy: it simply wanted to avoid difficult, complex, and sometimes frightening problems. We know now that we can't operate an organization successfully by neglecting problems in human relations. The staff has its function—and it is an important one—but it is not its function to be solely responsible for dealing with people.

Let me summarize. I have talked about three significant threads in the fabric of our industrial life which seem to be emerging as a pattern. These threads are all elements of basic attitude and philosophy on the part of management. The first is the belief that the willing collaboration of people is the only sound way to achieve the objectives of a free enterprise system. The second is the growing confidence in the abilities and the potentialities of the ordinary man. The third is the emerging genuine self-confidence that includes a good measure of humility and a genuine social conscience.

These attitudes are not, of course, characteristic of all managements, nor of all individuals within any given management. The three points of view, as are summarized above, get built into a system only gradually, but I think they are beginning to have a profound importance in our free enterprise system. Over the next 15 or 20 years we will see unsuspected new developments resulting from these changes in management philosophy.

For many years Clinton S. Golden—one of the great statesmen in the labor movement—has been saying that, by and large and in the long run, management gets the kind of labor relations it deserves. I think one can extend his statement and say that, by and large and in the long run, management also gets the kind of organizational effectiveness that it deserves.

I feel that management in this country is beginning to build a new, a healthier, and a more realistic relationship with the people who comprise our industrial organizations. As you can see, I am optimistic for the future.

2 The Manager of Tomorrow*

By Peter F. Drucker

The demands on the skill, knowledge, performance, responsibility and integrity of the manager have doubled in every generation during the past half century. Things which in the twenties only a few pioneers in top management were aware of we now expect young men straight out of school to be able to do. Daring innovations of yesterday—market research, product planning, human relations, or trend analysis, for instance—have become commonplace. Operations Research is fast becoming so. Can we expect this almost explosive increase in the demands on the manager to continue? And what can we expect to be demanded of the manager of tomorrow?

We have repeatedly referred to the new pressures, the new demands on the manager. Let me refer again briefly to the most important ones:

The new technology will demand the understanding of the principles of production and their consistent application by all managers. It will require that the entire business be seen, understood and managed as an integrated process. Even if distribution of the product is carried on in physical separation from production and by a legally distinct and independent distributor, it will have to be considered an integral part of the process. And the same applies to raw-materials procurement or to customer service.

This process requires a maximum of stability and of ability to anticipate future events. Hence it must be based on careful objectives and on long-range decisions in all key areas. But it also requires great internal flexibility and self-guidance. Hence managers on all levels must be able to make decisions which adapt the whole process to new circumstances,

* Reprinted from *The Practice of Management* by Peter F. Drucker (Harper & Brothers, 1954, pages 370-378), by permission of the author.

changes in the environment and disturbances, and yet maintain it as a going process.

In particular the new technology demands that management create markets. Management can no longer be satisfied with the market as it exists, it can no longer see in selling an attempt to find a purchaser for whatever it is that the business produces. It must create customers and markets by conscious and systematic work. Above all, it must focus continuously on creating mass purchasing power and mass purchasing habits.

Marketing itself is affected by the basic concepts of the new technology. We have, on the whole, discussed Automation as if it were exclusively a principle of production. It is, however, a principle of work in general. Indeed, the new methods of mass marketing may require greater application of the principles of Automation than the automatic factory, even though not one single automatic machine or electronic relay may be used. Marketing itself is becoming an increasingly integrated process. And increasingly it requires close integration with all other phases of the business. Instead of putting the emphasis on selling the individual customer, marketing centers more and more in product and market planning, product design and styling, product development and customer service. Instead of the individual sale, the creation of mass demand will be the pay-off. Television advertising is as much Automation, in other words, as is a mechanized machine feed. And the technological changes in distribution and marketing have as much impact as the technological changes in production.

This will demand that tomorrow's managers, regardless of their level and function, understand the marketing objectives and policies of their company, and know what they have to contribute to them. Business management will have to be able to think through long-range market objectives and to plan and build a long-range marketing organization.

The new technology will make new demands for innovation. Not only must the chemist, designer or engineer work closely with production and marketing men, but there will have to be the kind of systematic approach to innovation that Sears, Roebuck, for instance, applies to its merchandise planning and its development of suppliers. Innovation will have to be managed by objectives that reflect long-term market goals. It will also have to attempt much more systematically to foresee the inherent possibilities of technological and scientific development and to shape manufacturing and marketing policies accordingly.

The new technology will result in greater competition. True, it will broaden the market and raise the level of production and consumption, but these new opportunities will also demand consistent efforts to do better on the part of the enterprise and its managers.

Both because the new technology requires it and because social pressures demand it, the manager of tomorrow will have to make it possible to anticipate employment and to maintain it as close to stability as possible. At the same time, as today's semi-skilled machine operator becomes tomorrow's highly trained maintenance man, and today's skilled worker tomorrow's individual professional contributor, labor will become a more expensive resource—a capital investment of the business rather than a current cost. And its performance will have a much greater impact on the performance of the whole business.

Finally, the manager will have to acquire a whole new set of tools —many of which he will have to develop himself. He needs to acquire adequate yardsticks for performance and results in the key areas of business objectives. He needs to acquire economic tools to make meaningful decisions today for a long-range tomorrow. He will have to acquire the new tools of the decision-making process.

The New Tasks

We can summarize by saying that the new demands require that the manager of tomorrow acquit himself of *seven new tasks:*

1. He must manage by objectives.

2. He must take more risks and for a longer period ahead. And risk-taking decisions will have to be made at lower levels in the organization. The manager must therefore be able to calculate each risk, to choose the most advantageous risk-alternative, to establish in advance what he expects to happen and to "control" his subsequent course of action as events bear out or deny his expectations.

3. He must be able to make strategic decisions.

4. He must be able to build an integrated team each member of which is capable of managing and of measuring his own performance and results in relation to the common objectives. And there is a big task ahead in developing managers equal to the demands of tomorrow.

5. He will have to be able to communicate information fast and clearly. He will have to be able to motivate people. He must, in other words, be able to obtain the responsible participation of other managers, of the professional specialists and of all other workers.

6. Traditionally a manager has been expected to know one or more functions. This will no longer be enough. The manager of tomorrow must be able to see the business as a whole and to integrate his function with it.

7. Traditionally a manager has been expected to know a few products or one industry. This, too, will no longer be enough. The manager of tomorrow will have to be able to relate his product and industry to the total environment, to find what is significant in it and to take it into account in his decisions and actions. And increasingly the field of vision of tomorrow's manager will have to take in developments outside his own market and his own country. Increasingly he will have to learn to see economic, political and social developments on a world-wide scale and to integrate world-wide trends into his own decisions.

But No New Man

But there will be no new men to do these staggering tasks. The manager of tomorrow will not be a bigger man than his father was before him. He will be possessed of the same endowments, beset by the same frailties and hedged in by the same limitations. There is no evidence that the human being has altered much in the course of recorded history, certainly none that he has grown in intellectual stature or emotional maturity. The Bible is still the fullest measure of man's nature, Aeschylus and Shakespeare still the best textbooks of psychology and sociology, Socrates and St. Thomas Aquinas still the high-water marks of human intellect.

How then can we accomplish these new tasks with the same men?

There is only one answer: the tasks must be simplified. And there is only one tool for this job: to convert into system and method what has been done before by hunch or intuition, to reduce to principles and concepts what has been left to experience and "rule of thumb," to substitute a logical and cohesive pattern for the chance recognition of elements. Whatever progress the human race has made, whatever ability it has gained to tackle new tasks has been achieved by making things simple through system.

The manager of tomorrow will not be able to remain an intuitive manager. He will have to master system and method, will have to conceive patterns and synthesize elements into wholes, will have to formulate general concepts and to apply general principles. Otherwise he will fail. In small business and in large, in general management and in functional management, a manager will have to be equipped for the Practice of Management.

To find the necessary general concepts, to develop the right principles, to formulate the appropriate system and method and to show basic patterns has, of course, been the main purpose here. It has been based on the premise that in our management of today we have the experience out of which we can distill valid methods and general conclusions for the management task of tomorrow.

The Preparation of Tomorrow's Manager

If a man is to manage by concepts, patterns and principles, if he is to apply system and methods he can, however, also prepare himself for the job. For concepts and principles can be taught as can system, method and the formulation of patterns. Indeed, perhaps the only way to acquire them is by systematic learning. At least I have never heard of anyone acquiring those basic patterns, the alphabet and the multiplication table, by experience.

Tomorrow's manager will actually need two preparations rather than one. Some things a man can learn before he becomes a manager; he can acquire them as a youth or as he goes along. Others he can learn only after he has been a manager for some time; they are adult education.

One does not have to have been a manager to learn reading and writing. Indeed, these skills are best acquired in one's youth.

It can be said with little exaggeration that of the common college courses being taught today the ones most nearly "vocational" as preparation for management are the writing of poetry and of short stories. For these two courses teach a man how to express himself, teach him words and their meaning and, above all, give him practice in writing. It can also be said that nothing would help so much to prepare young men for management as a revival of the honorable practice of the oral defense of one's "thesis"—only it should be made a frequent, normal, continuing part of college work rather than something that happens once, at the end of formal schooling.

In one's youth one can also most easily acquire knowledge and understanding of logic and of its analytical and mathematical tools. A young man can also learn the basic understanding of science and scientific method which the manager of tomorrow will need. He can acquire the ability to see the environment and to understand it through history and the political sciences. He can learn economics and acquire the analytical tools of the economist.

To prepare himself to be a manager, a young man can, in other words, acquire a general education. He may acquire it through formal schooling. Or, as so many of the best have always done, he may educate himself. But all these things together constitute what has always been considered the general knowledge and discipline of the educated man.

I do not mean to imply that what the young man needs to prepare himself for management is incompatible with specific business or engineering training. On the contrary, there is no reason why the required general education should not be an integral part of the business-school or engineering-school curriculum (as is indeed being recognized increasingly by our engineering schools). I also do not mean that there is no value to specific business or engineering subjects. On the contrary; they give a man ability to perform functional work with some degree of workmanship. And it is not only still important that everyone in an enterprise possess the ability to do functional work—at least on the journeyman's level—but it is crucial that every manager acquire the respect for workmanship which only a technical or craft skill can give. The young man who only acquires functional skills, however, and only learns specific business or engineering subjects, is not being prepared to be a manager. All he is being prepared for is to get his first job.

Indeed, the demands that tomorrow will make on the manager may well force us to create anew what we have all but lost: the liberal education for use. It will be very different (at least in outward appearance) from what our grandfathers knew by that name. But it will again have strict method and real standards, especially of self-discipline and of ethics, instead of the abandonment of method and standards that characterizes so much of today's so-called "progressive education." It will again have a unified focus rather than be fragmented departmentally. And, like every living liberal education in the past, it will be preparation for work as an adult and citizen rather than merely "general culture."

One needs experience in management as well as maturity, however, to learn to manage by objectives, to analyze the company's business, to learn to set objectives and to balance them, to learn to harmonize the needs of immediate and long-range future. Without experience as a manager—or at least as an adult—one can learn to recite these things; but one cannot learn to do them.

One needs experience as a manager to learn how to assess and to take risks. One needs experience to learn how to exercise judgment and make decisions. One needs experience to see the business in society, to assess the impact of the environment on the business and to decide what management's public responsibilities are.

One cannot, as a young man, learn what managing managers means, nor managing worker and work. Nothing is as futile or as pathetic as the young man who has learned "personnel management" in a business school and then believes himself qualified to manage people. And no one can do quite as much harm—or as little good.

The specific work of the manager makes sense only to men who have set objectives, organized, communicated and motivated, measured performance and developed people. Otherwise it is formal, abstract and lifeless. But to a manager who can put the flesh of his own experience on these bones, the terms can become extremely meaningful. Their classification can become a tool by means of which he can organize his own work, examine his own performance and improve his own results. For young people who have no management experience this classification appears the way French irregular verbs appear to a schoolboy in rural Idaho: an assignment to be learned mechanically. All they can do is to parrot: "The sixteen principles of control are . . ."; this may get them a good mark in an examination but it is of little meaning to them in their work. The experienced manager, however, can be brought to see and to use these classifications the way a mature French poet would use the study of the same irregular verbs: as a tool to gain greater insight into his language, greater skill as a writer and greater depth as a thinker.

To discharge tomorrow's management tasks we therefore will need advanced education for people already in management. We have already made the first steps in this direction, as witness the countless "advanced management programs" that have come into being in this country in the last ten years. And it is a fairly safe bet that the focus in education for management will increasingly shift to advanced work for the adult, experienced manager.

The business manager's need for a systematic attempt at his own advanced education is a new development; but it is not unprecedented. All armies have what is called in this country the "Command and General Staff School," for professional training in the specific work of a senior officer. All armies have learned that this training cannot be given to young men learning to be officers but only to mature men with considerable experience in actual command and performance of military duties. Similarly, the oldest elite corps, the Jesuit Order, does not subject its men to training in advanced theology and philosophy until they have had many years of practical experience in the study of such lay subjects as medicine, sociology or meteorology, in teaching and in administrative work. It has found that the most advanced, the really professional training for being a Jesuit, does not "take" until a man has acquired the actual experience in the work that his advanced studies organize, make meaningful, appraise and focus.

In fact, that management has a need for advanced education—as well as for systematic manager development—means only that management today has become an institution of our society.

But Central Will Always Be: Integrity

Yet intellectual and conceptual education alone will not enable the manager to accomplish the tasks of tomorrow.

The more successfully tomorrow's manager does his work, the greater will be the integrity required of him. For under the new technology the impact on the business of his decisions, their time-span and their risks, will be so serious as to require that he put the common good of the enterprise above his own self-interest. Their impact on the people in the enterprise will be so decisive as to demand that the manager put genuine principles above expediency. And their impact on the economy will be so far-reaching that society itself will hold the manager accountable. Indeed, the new tasks demand that the manager of tomorrow root every action and decision in the bedrock of principles, that he lead not only through knowledge, competence and skill but through vision, courage, responsibility and integrity.

No matter what a man's general education or his adult education for management, what will be decisive above all, in the future even more than in the past, is neither education nor skill; it is integrity of character.

3 Basic Industrial Trends and Their Challenge to Management*

By ERWIN H. SCHELL

THE structure of change in industry, as elsewhere, is stratified. As the Gulf Stream underlies the tide, the ground swell, the wave and the ripple, so there are deep and fundamental changes which form the basic layer of movement in the stream of industrial affairs.

These deepest of all movements have qualities which distinguish them from lesser changes. First, they are characteristically world-wide phenomena. Second, they do not contain blameworthy elements, as they arise more from changing conditions or circumstances than from the accomplishments or failures of any individual or group of individuals. Third, their influence extends over the longest swing of time of any industrial trend. Finally, they have a quality common to all changes in that they bring both difficulty and opportunity. Able management avoids the former and capitalizes upon the latter.

It is not easy to discern these Gulf Streams of industry. The chief obstacle is the natural tendency of the observer to attribute to dramatic events which are quite ephemeral in nature a basic, long-term characteristic which they actually do not possess. Again, it is easy to build a facade of logic that may be imposing and yet misleading.

Five such fundamental movements seem to merit a critical survey. These will be first discussed in terms of the difficulties they represent, after which the reaction of industry to them as opportunities will be considered.

* Reprinted from *The Basis of Production Planning*. Production Series No. 182 (1949), by permission of the American Management Association, copyright holder.

Five Areas of Change

1. *Changing Industrial Obsolescence Rates*

Rates of obsolescence in industrial equipment, processes, methods, and products give evidence of steady and rapid increase. We need not seek far for a plausible explanation. During the war years many new and radical changes in manufacturing output were called for by the government. Accompanying these requests were the promise of ample financial resources, priority advantages in relation to materials, equipment and labor and other perquisites which permitted the wartime manufacturer to adventure and to experiment under conditions of unusual security in terms of corporate expenditure or risk. Furthermore, pressures of extreme emergency drove human ingenuity to heights of accomplishment far above normal rates of creative advance. Once again, the truth of the adage that necessity is the mother of invention was affirmed.

The Research Specialist. A component factor in this acceleration has been the advancing state of the art of creativeness in industry. The old-time inventor who was viewed as a sporadic sort of genius has long since been superseded by the trained research specialist, and there is hardly a company of reasonable size today without its corps of professionally disciplined investigators who are speeding obsolescence in the plant in which they work.

Organized Research and Development. During the last world conflict a new technique—that of organized developmental activities—was initiated. Through this technique it is possible to establish nicely interrelated creative sequences involving the work of many specialists, thereby greatly speeding the birth rate of new industrial products, processes and procedures. It is now safe to prophesy that this new organizational device may further radically increase the present obsolescence rates in industry.

Public Receptivity to Change. In the United States, at least, the public has been unusually receptive to this increasing rate of change. The concept of the annual model, the introduction of the style factor into ever-widening areas of consumer goods, together with enlarged purchasing power among major sectors of our population, all have encouraged the industrialist to participate in more creative undertakings.

Competitive Security. Of equal if not greater stimulus has been the discovery that competitive security based on advantages in point of time (to be "six months ahead of the field," as one industrialist put it) is perhaps the surest form of safety which may be enjoyed in this changing world.

Accelerating Obsolescence Rates. The satisfactions of more rapid progress appear to assure accelerating obsolescence rates in the future; and there is evidence that this is a world-wide, long-term trend.

2. Changing Influence of Financial Incentives

It was not many years ago that the old rule, "If you want some one to do something, pay him for it" could be safely relied upon, although it was not too long before the disagreeable job received such undue premiums that the wage structure became badly unbalanced. Then came the wave of executive dependence upon the working principle that "the more the output the more the pay." Today it is becoming clear that the financial incentive in part at least has given way in the eyes of the worker to other desiderata which have joint if not equal appeal.

Waning Influence of Money. The waning influence of the dollar, the pound or the franc, may be readily explained. Undoubtedly rationing was a major influence in lessening the public's homage to the coin of the realm, for it was the little pink square of paper that made the purchase possible and the wherewithal to pay for it became of secondary importance. More recently, the marked declines in the purchasing power of money have leached away its significance in the eyes of the consumer. The workman's wife who exclaims, "Take ten dollars into town and see what you can get!" echoes the prevailing distrust of the potency of the weekly pay envelope.

Payroll Deductions. Not least among the corrosive influences affecting financial incentives has been the growing multiplicity of payroll deductions. Over-all salary or wage figures have lost their earlier significance in view of the marked divergence between gross and net worker income. A further weakening factor has been the disalignment of wage rates occasioned by the exigencies of war. When speed was of the essence, the price paid for human effort frequently bore little relationship to the skill or experience required, and ghosts of these wartime inequalities still haunt many of our factory payrolls.

Lessening Prestige Value of Riches. It may be argued that all these influences are of temporary significance and that financial incentives will shortly return to their former preeminence as stimulants of effort; but there is another element which seems of longer-term significance and which militates against the renaissance of money as a prime work incentive. This is the clearly lessening prestige value of riches as such. Time was when the man of means was the man of standing, but today wealth is an object of criticism rather than of praise. It is true that this point of view may have little significance to the man who lives on his weekly pay envelope. Yet the spirit of the times cannot but dull ambition to amass even a moderate saving when it appears that the world tomorrow will place higher values on other accomplishments.

Lowered Potency of Financial Incentives. It is difficult to escape the conclusion that the lessening potency of financial incentives marks a world-wide movement and reveals a fundamental and lasting change in worker psychology and attitude.

3. Changing Nature of Executive Authority

The industrial administrator aims as far as possible to maintain control over all elements affecting the success of his enterprise. To put it another way, he tries to establish a ring of control around his business. This he has rarely been able to do. In earlier times, the market at least resisted control and remained in the area of persuasion. Since the war, persuasion has replaced control in several other zones. For example, postwar relationships with the government continue to be a sort that do not permit decisions hitherto within the control of the industrialist in many aspects of his prewar activities. Continuing shortages, whether they be of equipment, materials, supplies, or transportation facilities, inevitably remove controls from the manager and require him to use persuasive techniques to assure effective joint action.

Lessening Fears over Unemployment. It is improbable that labor will ever again be subject to the same type of control that was exercised in the years prior to the depression. In this earlier period, fear of unemployment exerted a powerful influence upon employee behavior in response to executive order. With the provision by the government of unemployment benefits, the American workman no longer was completely dependent upon industry for his income; and with this transfer of dependency the ultimatum "do it—or else" has lost much of its earlier potency.

Decline of Coercive Control. Little by little over the years, in many countries there appears to have been a lessening of opportunity for the exercise of what may be called coercive control in industry, and if current trends are read aright, this underlying trend shows no signs of lessening.

4. Changing Relations with the Public

It has been said that after every great war, pestilence or famine, the status of the common people always rises, and present developments tend to support this statement. It can be argued that such gains in relative position result from the inevitable shortages of the products of labor following upon such disasters, upon the subsequent shortage of labor itself, and upon the ensuing public attitude toward the veterans or other survivors who lived through these difficulties.

Short-Term Public Attitude. A second influence heightens the public's evaluative attitude toward industry. The people of any country are ordinarily willing to endure a degree of economic hardship if they have faith in a long-term incremental advance. However, in the face of wide disillusionment as to the probability of world harmony, people tend to become concerned over immediate advantages during the interims of peace.

Growing Power of Public Opinion. It also appears that public opinion has risen to inordinate heights of importance as a result of the wide application of opinion-poll techniques until today our congressmen give more attention to the ground-swells of popular opinion than to the statesmanlike determination of the appropriate national policy. The principle that public opinion does not always reflect the public welfare was one of the fundamental tenets basing our republican form of government, but it has been submerged under the flood of telegrams which daily inundates thought in Washington.

Increasing Competition for Loyalty. The public has discovered new mass potentialities via the vote as well as via mass influence upon its governmental representatives, and it now finds itself in position to dictate in no small measure industry's future. As a result, industry must win public approval no less than public acceptance, and the business administrator currently finds himself in competition with organized labor leaders on the one hand, and government representatives on the other, for a proper share of the loyalty and support of his employees and of his community.

Growth in Importance of Public Relations. A new and largely uncharted responsibility is being placed upon the shoulders of industrial leaders. The ability to gain and to hold active public approbation is still in its infancy. It is an activity which seems destined to grow in global importance as the years pass, if industry is to maintain its place of influence and appropriate prestige in today's and tomorrow's world of affairs.

5. *Changing Price of National Security*

All over the world the peacetime price of a nation's security is rising. Whether the organizations for peaceful adjudication of differences or the protective machinery of modern warfare is to be employed in building a safe place in which to live, the price to be paid will inevitably rise in every country if past and present world trends are to be logically interpreted. These costs will unquestionably find their way in large measure into industrial tax levies; and business administrators everywhere face the presence in their financial calculations of a growing sector of gross income which is to be signed over to their respective governments as their payment on the franchise for national security.

Rise in the Year-to-Year Cost of Peace. To view this trend as ephemeral is to permit the wish to father the thought. While recessions from the abnormally high taxes of wartime may occur, the year-to-year cost of peace with security seems bound to rise. To meet these additive demands for funds and still maintain satisfactory cost-price relationships with existing consumer purchasing power, thus insuring adequate commercial flow and dependably active rates of turnover, is the prime problem facing the manufacturer today in every country.

Summary

The acceleration of industrial obsolescence, the waning potency of financial incentives, the swing from controlling to collaborative executive techniques, the growth of public interest and influence in industry, and the rising price of peace constitute five fundamental, long-term industrial tendencies which carry for administrators a measure of difficulty and of opportunity.

Management's Response to Changing Conditions

1. Accelerative Obsolescence

One method of testing the validity of these trends is to examine the extent of activity shown by progressive management in capitalizing upon them. In the matter of accelerative obsolescence, there are at least four indications that progressive industrialists are already well under way in neutralizing the difficulty and in capitalizing on the opportunity.

Vanished Surpluses of Postwar Machine-Tool Equipment. One of the unexpected situations following the cessation of hostilities was the relatively small surplus of industrial machine-tool equipment which found its way to the open market. Relatively sparse amounts became available to industrial buyers. This was because manufacturers who had used such equipment, through leasing or other agreements with the government, were the first to purchase it outright, thus protecting themselves against the hazard of obsolescence.

Attendance at Management Meetings. A second straw in the wind has been the unusually active attendance at management meetings, conferences and congresses—an unmistakable reflection of an increasing interest in new managerial methods and procedures.

Flexibility in Operating Facilities and Policies. Again, there is clear evidence of a spirit of humility before the inability of industry to predict the exact nature of future advances, as shown by the flexibility in planning building design, erection and demolition, process layout and general operating arrangements.

Supplements to Depreciation Reserves. Most important has been the aggressive way in which far-sighted industrialists have assigned special funds, over and above normal depreciation reserves, for the purchase of new facilities to maintain their competitive parity with newly organized establishments. There is little doubt but that the inevitability of increasing obsolescence rates is widely accepted as an operating managerial principle.

2. *Waning Value of Financial Incentives*

The waning influence of financial incentives has not proceeded without hindrance. Opportunities for saving, as incorporated in pension plans, are a form of financial incentive that has been widely capitalized upon. Again, opportunity for consumer spending resulting from the increased production of consumer goods has been an indirect but effective type of financial incentive. But the bulk of administrative attention appears clearly to have been given to stimuli not in forms other than that of direct wage or salary payment.

Swing toward Indirect Economic Advantages. For top executives, the purchase of homes by the company has been cited as one form of reward for effective effort. Also, the assignment of stock interest in activities auxiliary to the business is said to have been utilized.

For middle executive groups, purchasing perquisites have been extended, facilitating the acquisition of automobiles, radios and household equipment on a more favorable price basis.

A host of new and attractive opportunities has been laid before employees. Many of these may be included under the heading of improved working conditions. But longer vacations and enlarged company facilities for organized recreation are examples of other devices which have aimed to make the total job more attractive to the workman.

Corroboration of this shift of emphasis from the financial to the non-financial incentive is reflected in British studies of industrial incentives, where it is held by such an authority as Dr. J. A. Bowie that "incentives are coming to be seen more as a matter of treatment than as a method of payment."

Growth of Non-Financial Incentives. Indeed, the effect of this lessening of appeal on the part of financial incentives has been to strengthen the stimulus of non-financial incentives. It appears that people everywhere are sensing the simple truth that the best hours of their lives are spent at their work. It is logical, therefore, for them to desire that their work-place as well as their activities should bring during working hours good living conditions as well as an adequate livelihood.

3. Decline of Arbitrary Authority

In the field of executive authority new winds are blowing. Many managers have discovered that close collaborative relationships with vendors, with carriers, and with government yield advantages greater than those previously enjoyed when managers could make decisions without fear of contradiction. More particularly, new objectives have taken form which are altering the very structure of negotiation and adjudication. It has become clear that the settlement of difficulties which leads to increased goodwill and mutual morale affords by far the best type of adjustment, irrespective of the exact gains or losses which accrue to either party.

Ultimate Goodwill as a Primary Objective. Therefore, ultimate goodwill has become the primary rather than the secondary objective of all industrial negotiations because it is obvious that in the creative world of tomorrow industry must draw upon the creativeness of all whose interests in any way relate to the business.

Perhaps this new concept is part of the ultimate answer to the problem of world peace, inasmuch as international affairs demand increasingly that we live together in a more closely coordinated and more closely interrelated world. Certainly it has become patent that victory in no sense promises subsequent isolation between the winners and losers.

4. The Challenge of Public Relations

To capitalize on the growing importance of industrial relations with the public is a challenge which has yet to be entirely perceived. In too many instances the industrial establishment has found itself initially under such strategic disadvantage that attention had first to be centered upon defensive rather than upon constructive tactics. However, some organizations already are well launched upon progressive programs which give promise of important advantage to the trade as well as to the enterprise.

The New Duality of Responsibility. One of our clearest thinkers in this field, Holgar Johnson, president of the Institute of Life Insurance, has stated that industry now faces a duality of responsibility. As an economic organization, free enterprise must justify its economic existence through the performance of economic services. Again, as a social institution, free enterprise must justify its existence through social contribution. This demarcation between enterprise as an economic organization and as a social institution is doing much to clarify both techniques and objectives.

5. *The Rising Price of National Security*

Perhaps the most fascinating response which industry has made to the rising peacetime price of national security has been that in relation to the future tax outlook. Here industry is capitalizing upon a simple and unusual opportunity. It is that the interval following upon a world war is the period offering the greatest assurance of peace, for it is in such an interim that conditions rather than attitudes or motives govern. Were there countries today eager to reopen hostilities, there are none with the necessary resources of money, men and matériel to make this possible. Therefore, it is evident that we have before us a peace of undetermined length but sufficient to permit a period in which heavy capital investments, yielding marked economies in unit costs, may be justified.

Marked Unit-Cost Economies from Large Capital Investments. These major disbursements of capital funds, when coupled with research and developmental activities, are yielding important economies. Indeed, it is only through such radical unit-cost savings that industry sees the means of meeting the inevitable tax increases which national security will require.

There is ample evidence that our progressive managers are moving actively in this direction. A short time ago the Federal Reserve Bank of Philadelphia pointed out that expenditures for new plants and equipment were being made at a rate greatly in excess of the annual average for the 20 years prior to hostilities. Naturally, these activities have not always been given the widest possible publicity, inasmuch as one of the characteristics of free enterprise is the shielding of competitive developments from view until their benefits may be capitalized upon. Yet there is no question but that many American industrialists have for some time been actively under way in the furtherance of campaigns which will take advantage of this favorable period of peacetime output which lies before us. A general policy of administration, based upon American ability under conditions of free enterprise to grow steadily in the arts of business and to continue to win those wars in which it is compelled to engage, appears to be rapidly spreading.

Conclusion

In conclusion, if we have interpreted correctly the basic trends of industry, we may say:

a. We shall have not only a continuation of an economy of plenty but an economy of better products upon which higher standards of living may be erected;

b. We are on the way to make industry and its environment a satisfying way for living no less than for a livelihood;

c. We have discovered and are discovering new techniques of associating peacefully with those with whom we shall have continuing industrial contact;

d. Our business enterprises are rapidly accepting their newly recognized responsibility as social institutions and already give evidence of competent administration of these new activities;

e. We are showing faith in the future of our country by staking corporate savings and surplus on long-term developments.

Yet greatest assurance of industrial security must continue to rest upon the ability of the business administrator first, to discover the basic trends which underlie all industrial movements; second, to neutralize the difficulties which these trends bring; and third, to capitalize upon the inevitable opportunities which these trends reveal in the future.

As Shakespeare's Cassius wisely remarked:

"There is a tide in the affairs of men which,
taken at the flood, leads on to fortune."

4 Thinking Ahead: Breakup of the Business Cycle*

By SUMNER H. SLICHTER

As a result of recent and prospective developments, one is justified in expecting that the connection between different kinds of business activity is loosening up and that the old-fashioned business cycle is slowly being replaced by a number of more or less independent cycles, each with its own timing. These independent cycles will at times reinforce each other, but in the main they will offset one another. Hence, the breakup of the old-fashioned business cycle will make for economic stability.

The most remarkable fact about the recent recession in the United States was the way in which some parts of the economy resisted the recession and other parts seem to have been unaffected by it. Thus, in the face of a considerable drop in the total production of goods from $369.9 billion a year in the second quarter of 1953 to $355.8 billion a year in the first quarter of 1954 and a rise of about 2 million in unemployment, personal incomes before taxes dropped less than ½ of 1% and the total purchases of goods by the private part of the economy changed scarcely at all. By the summer of 1954 construction was at an all-time high. The drop in employment was concentrated in manufacturing and mining; outside these two fields there were more people at work in June 1954 than there were in June 1953 at the peak of the boom.

It is apparent that what the country experienced was not a *general* decline in business but a decline in some *parts* of business accompanied by stability or near stability in other parts and by actual expansion in

* Reprinted from *Harvard Business Review,* 33 (January-February 1955), 19ff., by permission of the editor of *Harvard Business Review.*

still other parts. In other words, what we have been witnessing is, not a general recession or depression in which all parts of the economy move down more or less simultaneously with rather short lags, but the sort of diverse and nonsynchronized movements which one might expect as a result of the business cycle's being broken up into a number of more or less independent cycles.

Hence, one is bound to ask: "Has something quite fundamental been happening to the business cycle? Is the connection between various economic activities and various parts of the economy, between production and personal incomes, between consumption and investment, between employment and construction, gradually loosening up so that these various activities may have opposite trends or at least may move with considerable lags? Or are the diverse trends in various economic series during the last year to be explained in other ways—perhaps by special conditions peculiar to the current recession and not indicative of long-term changes in the business cycle?"

It would be strange, indeed, if changes in the economy, such as shrinkage in the relative importance of agriculture, the increase in the total number of industries, changes in the banking system, the increase in the size of government receipts and expenditures relative to all incomes, and many other changes did not produce effects on the business cycle itself. One could scarcely expect the business cycle to be the one unchanging thing in a changing world. In this discussion, however, I shall not attempt to trace the effects of changes that the business cycle has undergone in the course of long periods of time; my concern is with changes that are going on now.

I believe that recent changes in economic conditions and institutions are producing quite important effects on the business cycle and, unlike some earlier changes in the economy, are tending to break up the business cycle.

Before we examine the reasons for believing that fundamental changes are occurring in the business cycle, let us look at some of the reasons for being skeptical. There are two principal questions that should be raised: (1) Has the behavior of the economy during the last year been so unusual after all; and have there not been many previous recessions in which important parts of the economy did not contract or actually expanded? (2) Are there not special circumstances that explain the stability or expansion of some parts of the economy in the face of the recession—circumstances that are not likely to be repeated in future recessions?

To the extent that the behavior of the economy is not unusual or can be attributed to special, temporary conditions, there is no evidence of fundamental changes in the cycle. In some measure, the recent behavior of business can be explained along these lines.

Consider the fact that construction showed a modest rise during the contraction of total production in the last half of 1953 and the early months of 1954, and a more rapid rise while business generally remained stable in the second and the third quarters of 1954. This behavior of construction running counter to total production, which has aroused much interest and comment, is by no means new and unprecedented. The same thing has happened in previous recessions. A large part of construction has apparently been based on long-term planning or at least on conditions which are more or less independent of the immediate state of business. At any rate, construction in the past has moved through long swings and has been little influenced by small recessions or even by a few fairly severe recessions (such as the one of 1921). For example:

In 1904, when there was a minor recession and a drop of about 8% in the index of industrial production, a large rise occurred in the physical volume of construction.

In 1908, when there was a fairly sharp drop in the index of industrial production, there was only a negligible drop in the physical volume of construction—about 2%.

In 1914, when there was another small drop in the index of industrial production, the index of the physical volume of construction rose by nearly 10%.

In both 1921 and 1924, when there were substantial drops in the index of industrial production, the physical volume of construction increased substantially.

In 1938, when there was a sharp decrease in industrial production, there was only a small fall in the physical volume of construction.

The following table[1] indicates how differently the index of industrial production and the index of the physical volume of construction (1935 to 1939 = 100) sometimes move:

---

[1] *Senate Committee Print No. 4,* "Basic Facts on Employment and Production," Report of the Committee on Banking and Currency, 79th Congress, 1st session, pp. 4 and 5.

Year	Production	Construction
1903	43	95
1904	40	123
1905	49	156
1907	52	142
1908	44	139
1909	52	185
1913	64	158
1914	61	173
1915	70	184
1920	75	79
1921	58	125
1922	73	194
1923	88	156
1924	82	175
1925	90	209
1937	113	100
1938	89	95
1939	109	109

Special circumstances have also had something to do with the stability or expansion of some parts of industry during the recession. Of course, special circumstances are never absent; they are always affecting business either favorably or unfavorably. But two special circumstances have been particularly important during last year:

(1) *The enormous volume of unfilled orders in the durable-goods industries*—When the peak of business was reached about June 1953, the unfilled orders of manufacturers of durable goods were $70.1 billion, or more than 5 times the monthly sales and 2.7 times as large as the inventories. Back in June 1950, just before the outbreak of fighting in Korea, the unfilled orders of manufacturers of durable goods had been only $22.2 billion, or about 2½ times monthly sales and about half again as large as inventories. The high ratio of unfilled orders to sales and inventories during the last year was undoubtedly a powerful influence in sustaining the confidence of all manufacturers of durable goods

and in making them willing to maintain large expenditures on plant and equipment. Furthermore, the huge backlog of unfilled orders helped to sustain production and employment as new orders fell off.

Between June 1953 and June 1954 the unfilled orders of manufacturers of durable goods fell by $25 billion. Part of this drop was caused by drawing goods out of inventories, but about $23 billion of it was made possible by production in excess of new orders. It is plain that the backlog of demand represented by unfilled orders must have been a powerful influence in sustaining production and employment. Even in June 1954 unfilled orders, though well below the level of June 1953, were high relative to June 1950; they were about 4 times monthly sales and 1.8 times as high as inventories.

(2) *The tax cuts on January 1, 1954*—The ideal time for the tax cuts would have been about October 1, 1953, when the change in inventory policies brought about a considerable drop in production. But although the tax cuts were a little later than the best possible time, they helped greatly to sustain the purchasing power of both personal incomes and corporate incomes. Personal incomes before taxes (seasonally adjusted) changed very little during the decline in business in the latter half of 1953. Then between December and January the adjusted annual rate dropped from $287.0 billion to $284.9 billion. Just at this time, however, the temporary increase in personal income taxes expired and personal income tax liability dropped by over $3 billion a year. As a result, personal incomes after taxes did not drop, but rose by about $1 billion a year between the last quarter of 1953 and the first quarter of 1954.

The original expiration date of the excess profits tax had been June 30, 1953, but Congress, under considerable pressure from the Administration, was persuaded to postpone the expiration date for six months. Corporate profits before taxes had dropped sharply during the latter half of 1953. The termination of the excess profits tax was not sufficient to offset entirely the drop in corporate profits before taxes, but it went far to do so. As a result, corporate profits after taxes, which had dropped from an annual rate of $19.5 billion in the second quarter of 1953 and $19.0 billion in the third quarter to $15.1 billion in the fourth quarter, rose to a rate of $17.5 billion a year in the first two quarters of 1954.

Although the excess profits tax did not expire soon enough to prevent a short but fairly sharp drop in corporate profits after taxes, the fact that the cut was definitely scheduled to take effect at a certain date helped sustain business confidence and business spending. In fact, it is probable that the extension of the tax, combined with the establishment of a definite date for its expiration, tended to increase the total volume of business disbursements, including, of course, tax payments. A modest additional support to the economy was given by the reduction of nearly a billion a year in excise taxes on April 1, 1954—a reduction which had received no open support from the Administration.

On the whole the timing of the tax cuts was better than can be expected of tax cuts in future recessions, since it was pretty much an accident, having been provided for in 1951 when temporary tax increases were authorized to finance the Korean War and the defense program. In future recessions we can hardly dare count on such happy timing. Congress may become engaged in controversies over what taxes to cut and how much, with the result that the tax cuts will be much too late for the best results. Such a possibility underlines the *special* nature of this particular circumstance in helping to sustain the economy during the past year.

Now let us look at the other side of the picture. Although the behavior of the economy during the recent recession has not been as abnormal as might easily be assumed by persons not familiar with the history of business cycles, and although special circumstances have had something to do with the course of business in the last year, there is also impressive evidence that important and lasting changes are now occurring in the economy which are tending to break up the business cycle.

Even though the 1953-1954 rise of construction is in itself not unusual compared with the past, changes have recently been made in the financing of construction which in the future will affect the impact of the construction industry on the economy. The replacement of short-term second mortgages with long-term amortizable mortgages (some of them guaranteed or insured by the government) will prevent the accidental concentration of a considerable volume of maturities in years of depression (as in 1931 and 1932) and will prevent future recessions from producing large-scale distress selling of real estate. The low level to which real estate values were depressed by forced liquidation in the early 1930's aggravated the depression by discouraging new building. To the extent that the drop in new building is limited during future recessions, building booms will also be moderated, because building booms have partly been based on a few years of abnormally low building.

It is true that the volume of unfilled orders of manufacturers of durable goods was abnormally large at the peak of the boom in relation to both sales and inventories—or rather it looked abnormal in comparison with June 1950. But I do not believe that the ratio of unfilled orders to sales or inventories in June 1950 can henceforth be regarded as normal. An enduring change has occurred which means that from now on the durable-goods industries will at all times have a far higher ratio of unfilled orders to sales and inventories than prevailed in pre-Korean days.

One reason for this change is the defense program. As long as the cold war lasts, the defense program will be far larger in relation to the national product than it was before the Korean War. The increasingly elaborate equipment required by modern warfare lengthens the time between the receipt of orders and the making of deliveries, and thus tends to raise the volume of unfilled orders relative to sales. Even if diplomacy in the next few years succeeds in substantially mitigating the vigor of the cold war, I suspect that the volume of unfilled orders in the durable-goods industries will be kept high simply as a matter of national policy.

The United States has never had a comprehensive and carefully worked out program for developing its resources; but, in the unlikely event that a large additional drop in defense spending becomes possible, the country will probably offset the drop in defense spending by a long-term development program. At any rate, either the continuation of a high rate of defense spending or a large development program would make possible the maintenance at all times of a ratio of unfilled orders to sales in durable-goods manufacturing far higher than in 1950. In view of the obvious stabilizing influence of a high ratio of unfilled orders to sales, the maintenance of a high ratio will surely become a matter of deliberate public policy.

Even though the timing of tax cuts in the last year must be considered an extraordinarily happy accident, it is nevertheless true that federal fiscal policy as a whole during the last year has tended to aggravate rather than to mitigate the recession. Although taxes have been cut, expenditures have been cut still more, with the result that the cash deficit was reduced from more than $5 billion in the fiscal year 1952-1953 to about $500 million in the fiscal year 1953-1954. During the latter part of 1953, when the change in business inventory policy reduced gross private domestic investment by over $10 billion a year and the gross national product by over $9 billion a year, Federal Government expenditures dropped only slowly and were offset by the rise in state and local outlays. Thus, during 1953 government fiscal policy as a whole did not contribute to the recession and federal fiscal policy was only a mildly depressing influence.

Quite different was the effect of fiscal policy during 1954. Federal outlays for goods and services in the first quarter of 1954 were cut $4.8 billion a year below the last quarter of 1953 and were almost entirely responsible for the drop between the two quarters in national production from $360.5 billion a year to $355.8 billion a year. Although taxes were being cut, the drop in federal spending occurred before the partially offsetting reductions in taxes were felt. Although the existence of a large cash deficit at the peak of the boom created a difficult problem for the Treasury, federal fiscal policy in 1954 was not wisely planned. It was not prudent to allow fiscal policy to add so substantially to a recession that was already well under way.

I expect the desire of both political parties to use fiscal policy to affect the results of elections will prevent the best timing of tax cuts and will substantially limit the usefulness of fiscal policy as a device for stabilizing the economy. Nevertheless, I do not believe that fiscal policy will ordinarily be permitted to aggravate a recession as it did in the early part of 1954. It will have at least some stabilizing effect. This is one of the reasons why I believe that the business cycle is being broken up.

There are two other important changes which are tending to break up the business cycle:

(1) *Growth of influences that tend to check declines in personal incomes before taxes*—The recent recession furnishes a good example of the influences affecting the size of personal incomes before taxes. Between the second quarter of 1953 and the first quarter of 1954 wage and salary payments (seasonally adjusted) fell from an annual rate of $198.9 billion to $194.6 billion, or $4.3 billion. One might have expected other forms of personal income, particularly the income of farmers, to be pulled down by this drop in payrolls. But total personal incomes before taxes dropped less than payrolls—by only $1.3 billion a year. This meant that personal incomes other than payrolls actually rose while payrolls were dropping.

Two forms of personal income account for the rise—or nearly all of it. Farm incomes rose by an annual rate of $1.9 billion between the second quarter of 1953 and the first quarter of 1954, and transfer payments (principally pension benefits, unemployment compensation, and veterans benefits) increased by $1.6 billion. The gain in farm income was made possible by the price support operations of the Federal Government, and the growth of transfer payments was largely the result of the increase in unemployment compensation payments. Transfer payments, and particularly unemployment compensation payments, continued to rise after the first quarter of 1954. In the second quarter of 1954 unemployment compensation payments were at the annual rate of $2.2 billion—or 2½ times the rate of a year ago, an increase of $1.4 billion a year.

The future of federal supports of the prices of farm products is uncertain. The present scale of supports will undoubtedly have to be reduced, but some support scheme is likely to be retained and it will diminish the tendency for contraction to extend itself through the reduction of farm incomes.

The picture is clearer for pension and unemployment compensation benefits. Pension payments may be expected to rise every year for some years to come because most of the persons retiring from now on will be eligible for pensions. Furthermore, the coverage of the Social Security schemes will be broadened, and the benefits still further liberalized. Modest steps in this direction were taken in the last few months when Congress modified the unemployment compensation scheme to give the states an incentive to extend coverage from employers of eight or more persons to employers of four or more and when old-age retirement benefits were increased.

Unemployment compensation payments and old-age benefits are a clear case of an institutional change with a restraining effect on some kinds of economic fluctuations. They limit the tendency of drops in production and employment to produce drops in personal incomes and in the demand for goods. Likewise they limit the capacity of increases in production and employment to produce increases in personal incomes and in the demand for goods. Since the possibilities for extending the coverage and liberalizing the benefits of unemployment compensation and old-age benefits are considerable, and since the political pressures to make these changes are powerful, one may count on the social insurance schemes to have much greater influence in limiting the cyclical swings of production and employment in the future than they have had up to now.

(2) *The changing basis for investment decisions*—Changes in the

ways that investment decisions are made are tending to make these decisions less sensitive to the ups and downs of business.[2] Indeed, an important characteristic of the recent recession has been the small drop in business outlays on plant and equipment. In the third quarter of 1953 these expenditures were at the annual rate of $28.9 billion; in the third quarter of 1954, at the annual rate of $26.7 billion. While in part fluctuations in investment have been a result of fluctuations in business, in substantial measure they have also been a cause. To the extent that investment decisions become less sensitive to the ups and downs of business, they will have less tendency to aggravate these ups and downs. There are several reasons why investment decisions are becoming less responsive to business fluctuations:

(a) One reason is the great gain in the liquidity of business concerns in recent years. Enterprises with large holdings of liquid assets are under less pressure to cut postponable expenditures when their sales drop. The rise in the liquidity of business concerns is attributable fundamentally to the great expansion of short-term government debt resulting from the war and from some of the postwar deficits. It is conceivable that this improvement in liquidity will not last indefinitely; but unless business concerns are forced by an unexpectedly severe crisis to part with much of their liquid assets, most of them will probably succeed in preserving a high proportion of liquidity. (Certainly the government is likely to make available to business concerns a considerable volume of short-term federal securities.) Enterprises will be assisted in maintaining their liquidity by the two-year carry-back of losses, now provided by the corporate income tax.

(b) More important than the greater liquidity of business concerns in reducing the sensitiveness of investment decisions to business fluctuations has been the rise of technological research. The spectacular rise of technological research during the last 30 years has now become a familiar story. Research is substantially modifying the way in which investment opportunities are discovered—or perhaps one should say *created*. Behind new investment opportunities are not more-or-less accidental strokes of genius but the patient work of thousands of scientists and engineers. As a rule years are required before new research in a given area produces commercial products or commercial applications. Each year,

---

[2] I have called attention to this change in business practice from time to time; others have done so also. See, for example, M. D. deChazeau's article, "Can We Avoid Depression in a Dynamic Economy?" *Harvard Business Review*, July-August 1954, particularly pp. 39-42.

however, some of the work of the 120,000 scientists and engineers now employed in the laboratories of industry (there were only half this number in 1940) and of the additional 33,000 employed in the laboratories of the government reaches fruition in commercial products. And this means investment opportunities.

Thus, the volume of investment opportunities produced by research does not fluctuate with business conditions; it grows more or less steadily as research expands, and is just about as large in a bad year as in a good one. Enterprises may decide not to exploit an investment opportunity in a year of declining sales. But if the resources of the company permit, it is not likely to delay the introduction of a new process or a new product simply because business is contracting. Indeed, the need of the company for more sales may be a reason for not delaying the exploitation of the new process or product.

Another reason for not delaying is the fact that research is competitive. A number of concerns are usually doing research in any given area—endeavoring to develop new fibers, new plastics, for example. An enterprise which holds back the launching of a new product that has become ready for the market may give one of its competitors the advantage of first getting into the market. Hence, for this reason too the expansion of technological research tends to make investment less responsive to the ups and downs of business.

(c) Business concerns are also changing their methods of making investment plans and investment decisions. For many years there has been a gradual increase in the amount of staff work. Staff work means more careful and thorough planning of the future development of enterprises—more careful scrutiny of trends in technology and in markets and more thorough provision for adapting the plants and the operations of enterprises to new conditions, such as cannot be satisfactorily done by busy line officers responsible for day-to-day operations. The development of such long-range planning involves, among other things, the making of long-term investment plans. The McGraw-Hill survey of business' plans for new plants and equipment reports that in 1954 90% of the companies participating in the survey were able to estimate their capital spending for the next four years, compared to 81% in 1953 and 65% in 1952.[3]

This does not mean that a given amount of investment spending

---

[3] McGraw-Hill Publishing Company, Inc., *Business' Plans for New Plants and Equipment* 1954-1957, p. 9.

will be done regardless of business conditions. Thus, although manufacturing companies expect to spend $10.2 billion per year on new plant
and equipment in the period 1955-1957, they would cut their spending
to $6.5 billion per year in the event of a "substantial" drop in sales. On
the other hand, in order to take advantage of all technological developments in their industries, they might raise their expenditures to $14.4
billion per year.

Although long-range planning of the development of companies
does not preclude the adjustment of investment expenditures to business
conditions, it is nevertheless an influence for stability. When a plan and a
time schedule have been worked out, small or moderate drops in sales are
likely to have less effect on investment than when no long-range plan exists. The tendency of enterprises to adhere to long-range investment programs regardless of moderate drops in business will be fortified by two
recent changes in the tax law—the provision for flexibility in depreciation
allowances and the extension of the loss carry-back from one year to
two years.

The several influences that are tending to break up the business cycle
reinforce one another. Thus, to the extent that fiscal policy and built-in
stabilizers, such as unemployment compensation, limit any drop in the demand for goods, they also help to sustain investment spending, which
also helps to limit any drop in the demand for goods. But despite the
fact that there is a good reason to expect that each of the several influences
which tend to break up the business cycle will grow in strength with the
passage of time, one must not expect that the growth of production and
employment will ever become steady.

The placing of restraints on the expansion of credit in times of
boom is unpopular and often arouses strong political opposition.
Hence, during periods of boom, the expansion of indebtedness is likely
to go too far and to lay the foundation for a later contraction in demand.
At the present time, for example, it looks as if easy credit might push
the demand for housing up to a level at which it will not remain for
many months. Furthermore, the exigencies of politics will at times cause
fiscal policy to be administered in such a way as to aggravate booms.
More progress has been made in recent years in developing arrangements
for limiting recessions than for controlling booms, yet the complete breakup of the business cycle requires each type of arrangement.

The increase in the labor force and technological progress raise the
productive capacity of the economy by about $13 billion a year on the

average. Even if output should rise each year, in some years the growth will be less than $13 billion and in other years more. And employment will be subject to drops even after annual drops in total output have become somewhat unusual. For example, at the present time production must rise by about $9 billion a year in order to prevent a drop in employment. On the other hand, while expansion will never be at a steady rate, the day may eventually come when the growth of production and employment will not be seriously interrupted by drops in either production or employment.

5 The Atomic Revolution*

By John J. Hopkins

THE atomic age was conceived in 1939 with the splitting of the uranium atom. It was born in 1942 at Chicago when Fermi and his group demonstrated a self-sustaining nuclear reaction. The atomic revolution—now transforming our long held scientific, economic and political concepts—began at Alamagordo in 1945 as a wartime achievement triggered by a desperate wartime emergency. Yet the terrible first employment of atomic energy as the light—brighter than the sun—which destroyed Hiroshima, should not blind us to the great and enduring good for all mankind already rippling outward from these epic events.

We have learned and are learning—as we have had to do with fire—that the *uncontrolled* release of atomic energy can be the world's greatest evil. Atomic energy *controlled* can become the world's greatest material blessing—a major achievement of the spirit of man in the conquest of his material world. This is the dual destiny of the atom. Yet it must be borne in mind during this current wave of mild hysteria—and during the future recurring atmospheres of apprehension which are bound to encompass us—that the atomic fission missile has no motive, that the thermo-nuclear device has no brain, and that the theoretical bomb of cobalt would be but an inert genie unless activated by man as an instrument of complete self destruction.

The atom bomb does not decide its enemy, choose its target, detonate itself. It does what it is *directed* to do. The thermo-nuclear device is not in itself a villain—a "hell" bomb. Bombs are built with human hands. Human passions, not these infernal machines, supply the villainy and the hell.

* Reprinted by permission of the author. This material appeared in *The Commercial and Financial Chronicle*, 179 (May 6, 1954), 13, 32.

How true for today are the words of that great and wise poet, George Meredith:

> "In tragic life, God wot
> No villain need be—
> *Passions* spin the plot."

What we need to fear, and should seek to control, is not the H-bomb but rather the human spirit and thought that breed behind this bomb—and the hate, or greed, or fear that trembles on the trigger.

Greatest Potential in World of Peace

The atom has its greatest potential not in a world of war and hate and evil, but in a world of peace, and of goodwill. Not as a destroyer of cities and nations but as a builder and savior. Indeed, in its fundamentals the principles of atomic fission and fusion have given us the knowledge which now forces us to an historic choice between good and evil.

Hopefully, I believe there are indications that the world's choice will be made for atomic *creation* rather than atomic *destruction*. While atomic clouds and rains of radioactive ashes and atoms for war monopolize the news—the peaceful atomic revolution is being speeded, too, though hardly even publicized—and but little regarded by those without a scientific background.

Because creation is infinitely more difficult than destruction, the curbing of atomic energy to peacetime use has become the greatest technological challenge of our day. Indeed this is not merely a technological but a moral challenge to us all. For in order to deserve the great creative boons of atomic energy rather than the horrible consequences of its destructive power, we have no alternative, I believe, but to work vigorously and unremittingly, *and instantly,* toward the constructive benefits which it so clearly offers.

It seems fair to compare the revolutionary impact of atomic energy on our world economy with the discovery of fire, steam and electricity, and the power sources of coal, oil, wood and falling water. But the nature of the atomic revolution is infinitely more varied in scope than any mere *power* revolution. I foresee that the atomic revolution will transform not only power, travel, transport, and communication, with new portable power packs, but will revolutionize our economies, our social customs, our medicine, our finances, our politics, our agriculture, our biology!

The atom is revolt *incarnate* against the *status quo!*

To a physicist, atomic energy is a prime tool for studying the nature of the physical world, both as to its structure and the interrelation of force and matter. To the researcher in bio-physics, or chemistry, or medicine or metallurgy, atomic energy provides priceless precision tools to identify and trace chemical reactions on and within the constituents of living matter and inorganic matter. The atom offers a possibility of achieving chemical reactions—in ways not previously possible—through the use of radioactivity as a catalyst, or reaction agent. To the industrial or military man, atomic energy has provided, as we have said, instruments of unimaginable power. To electric utility management it offers a new type of fuel; one with its own peculiar problems, but also one offering competition eventually for existing fuels and reserves of energy far surpassing any of those now being employed.

As a matter of fact, more than 1,000 firms in the United States and Canada, to say nothing of the rest of the world, are already employing the atom in every-day, routine operations. The widespread industrial usage, it seems to me, more than anything else, should serve to tear from atomic energy the veil of mystery and of fear.

For example: Some 300 companies in North America alone are now using atomic energy in radiation instruments that inspect metal parts of the products they make. A further 250 firms are using atomic thickness gauges to measure and control the coating on such things as paper and galvanized iron. In a six-year period this industry has grown from a sales volume of $2,000,000 to a sales volume of over $20,000,000.

A typical radiography installation may cost a factory about $750. Its predecessor, an industrial X-ray machine, might cost $10,000 or more. The atom thus offers cheap, reliable inspection of parts—which means faster, lower-cost production. The result is that more and more industrial firms are adopting these "tools" of the atomic revolution. Automobile manufacturers use them on cylinders, pistons, connecting rods. Airplane companies, boiler manufacturers and a host of others are putting the atom to work.

Atomic tracers provide another growing source of atomic aids for industry. For an interesting example, a speck of radioactive material is dropped into a pipeline when a shipment of gasoline is pumped into the line, followed by a shipment of fuel oil. With a Geiger Counter, a workman at the other end of the line can then tell when to stop pumping the pipeline's flow into the gasoline storage tank, and switch it over to the fuel-oil tank. This workman formerly had to take samples from the pipeline in order to know when one product was being replaced by the other. Considerable inter-mixing, and delay, where the second shipment joined the first, was of course inevitable.

The Field of Preventive Maintenance

Another important application of atomic energy is in the field of preventive maintenance. At least 15 large oil and chemical concerns are already engaged in this activity. Since a radioactive pellet can be suspended from a string of wire and carried from place to place like a weight on the end of a fishing pole, it can be dropped into inaccessible places. A maintenance man can drop such a pellet down a pipe into a valve, for example, put a film on the outside of the valve, and X-ray the critical part with a minimum of difficulty.

Atomic radiation therefore is upsetting the *status quo* by faster, cheaper, more reliable ways of investigating the wear in pistons, of measuring the thickness of films of rubber, paper and metals, in the radiography of castings, in the detection of impurities in dyes, paints, crystals and chemicals. Agricultural research is making studies of great importance on plant growth and soil process through the use of radioactive stimulants and tracers.

So great is the expansion of uses of radioactivity in the field of medicine, it is estimated that already the lives of more people have been saved by the atom than were lost in the Hiroshima and Nagasaki explosions!

For example, through the use of radioactive phosphorus—which checks the over-production of red blood cells in the bone marrow—the lives of sufferers from leukemia have been prolonged. And one of our most famous ethical laboratories is offering radioactive iodine in capsule form for the treatment of thyroid disorders without the need of hospitalization or elaborate controls.

The largest single employer of isotopic materials is industry. The second largest application is in the field of medicine. Some perspective on our progress in the last few years may be gained from the figures on shipment of radioactive isotopes. In 1946 there were a total of 246 shipments; in 1953 there were 10,676. Other nations, particularly Canada, are also large producers.

Now what can we say of atomic power?

Spurred by the constantly rising cost of coal as mines become deeper and veins thinner, the British are moving swiftly to place greater and greater emphasis on power from atomic energy. The point at which atomic energy becomes competitive with conventional fuels will be reached far earlier in Britain, and elsewhere, than in the United States. Indeed, British scientists and engineers now conclude that within 15 to 20 years nuclear energy should be able to make a substantial contribution to the electricity supply of Britain at a cost comparable with the cost of coal-generated electricity. In that time it may be possible to set up a reactor system which would generate enough electricity to save 20 million tons of coal a year— the amount by which estimated production will fall short of estimated requirements in the next two decades. Not only would there be a considerable saving in cost but the partial introduction of nuclear power may also make possible a shift of manpower from marginal coal mines to more productive activities. The British are already heating buildings experimentally with atomic energy.

The atom offers great hope for the Continent of Europe which clearly faces a power shortage in the foreseeable future. World scientists find the need for energy far outstripping man's ability to produce it from hitherto conventional sources. One expert estimates that in the next 100 years the world will burn up 37 times as much energy as has been produced in the last 2,000 years. A 12-nation European pool is building the world's largest atom smasher near Geneva, Switzerland, pooling atomic research for peacetime purposes.

Here, as you know, the Atomic Energy Commission is proceeding with the development of the first nuclear power plant to produce electrical energy on a commercial scale. The engineering and cost experience in this 60,000-kilowatt project and industry's direct participation in its construction and management phases will show the way for future independent enterprise. In fact, many private concerns have already indicated readiness to build on a fixed-price basis smaller size reactors for military power plants.

Obviously it was the realization of these great portents of the atom which led the President to make his dramatic proposal to the United Nations last December. The boldness and constructive imagination of that proposal were quite in keeping with the American tradition of readiness to move ahead when our instincts tell us human welfare and conditions of life may be improved. It is obvious that implementing such a proposal involves many delicate and difficult problems, particularly in a world fraught with concerns of international security. We have, however, the assurance of Chairman Strauss of the Atomic Energy Commission that no fear for security need dissuade us from the basic purpose which lay behind the President's proposal. Rather, if we consider with care some of the potent technological factors I have reviewed for you, you may share with me the conviction that international exploitation of atomic energy is absolutely inevitable.

Atomic energy, then, as a revolutionary source for power scores its first chance on the basis of simple economics. Today experts are hesitant to say that nuclear-powered plants will soon produce power below the cost of our most efficient conventionally-fueled plants. There are few, however, that will fail to estimate even now that a nuclear-powered plant *can* be built to produce power at a cost somewhere in the upper one-third of present U. S. power costs. These estimates, bear in mind, are being made before the first, full-scale power plant has even been built. How can any one doubt that American ingenuity will bring nuclear energy into sharp competition with existing sources, *when it is already starting out at only twice the current figures?* The answer seems obvious.

Must Achieve Revolution in Energy Sources

On a second score, too, the atom *must* achieve a revolution in our energy sources. This is simply because the potential reserves of energy from fissionable materials are now estimated to be over 20 times that available from existing mineral fuels—coal, oil and gas. We must bear in mind, first, that the rate of energy used is growing more rapidly, even, than our population rate. We are therefore forced to anticipate those demands which cannot be met by our capital resources in existing fuels. Furthermore, the varied uses of coal, oil and gas, which could not be met by fissionable materials, caution us to conserve them. We cannot ignore the increasing demands of liquid fuel for mobile power, plus coal derivatives and petrochemicals. Thus, I think, fissionable materials are arriving just in time to substitute a brighter lamp for the candles we now burn at both ends.

The "Portability Factor"

Thirdly, we come to a factor which may seem like the same point I have made on economics, but actually is quite different. This I call simply the "portability factor" or the great concentration of energy contained in fissionable fuels. Given time, in our world economy, low cost energy will attract capital and seek out its own practical area of development. We can also count on atomic energy doing that in the future—extending the present range of power from coal, oil and water, with their limits of economical transmission. None of these present fuels, however, has the capacity to vault mountain barriers, jungles and desert wastelands with the unimpaired energy of the atom.

Let me describe these potentials in another set of terms. The tremendous growth in per capita use of energy in this country of ours is not merely due to the genius of our engineers in lowering the cost of energy. It goes basically to the great increase in the effective recovery of energy, in its "portable" form, from the days before the Industrial Revolution to the present Atomic Revolution. The pound of coal we use today may produce about one kilowatt-hour of energy. This is roughly 2,000 times the energy equivalent of a pound of muscle-power, our prime energy source back in the days of our colonial beginnings. Hence in the whole lifetime of our nation the "portability" or concentration of our usable energy has increased by this factor of 2,000.

In comparison with this, what does the atom offer? A pound of the pure, fissionable material, uranium 235, we are told, has the energy value of, say, two and one-half million pounds of coal. Even if we were to realize only 1% of that energy value, the portability of our energy would be increased by a factor of 25,000. Compare that factor of 25,000 and its implications on the range of energy exploitation that lies in the next generation, with the growth that has taken place from a 2,000-fold concentration of energy spread over a period of 200 years.

Progress in the field of atomic propulsion, of course, offers fantastic prospects in the years ahead. The world's first atomic-powered submarines, the revolutionary "Nautilus" and "Sea Wolf" will be able to cruise submerged at speeds in excess of 20 knots. A few pounds of uranium will give them ample fuel to travel thousands of miles under water, at top speed. They will require no breathing tubes to the surface. Thus, neither fuel nor oxygen need limit their stay under water.

Basically, it is not much of a step from atomic-powered submarines to atomic-powered combat and passenger ships and to nuclear-propelled airplanes and trains. These present different problems, but in the light of gains already made they do not look too far off—but rather well within our compass. I venture to say that we will have them—and in the not-far-distant future. Indeed, I have no hesitancy about picturing for you a world of the *near* future in which atomic energy heats and powers our factories, lights our cities, cooks our food, cures our ills and propels our ships, planes and trains.

And I have hopes that the use of atomic energy in one of its Protean forms will yet solve two of civilization's most difficult problems—the economical distillation of sea water for industrial and agricultural use, and the instantaneous disposal of human and industrial wastes. Each of these is a problem in power, or in transmutation, or in sterilization—problems which, apparently, only the atom is mighty enough and versatile enough to have hopes of solving.

A Thrilling Road

The road from the here of today to this world of the future is not so clearly marked as we would like it, but it is intriguing and challenging—*thrilling* is the word I would prefer. For we are embarrassed by our riches as well as our problems. There are literally a dozen or more promising designs of nuclear reactors for different purposes. After the tremendous stimulus our scientists have given us, the next stage ahead is to resolve our engineering choices. This will be done through the best efforts of chemists, metallurgists, thermodynamacists, mechanical engineers—plus some imaginative financiers and—I hope soon—some equally imaginative and persuasive salesmen.

But the atomic age does not provide us only with an "Open Sesame" to the treasure houses of the world's natural wealth. It has also, with classic irony, given us the key to the "Pandora's Box" of the world's ills and evils. We already have in being a rapidly growing atomic technology. We are beginning, though somewhat faintly, to foresee the *economy* of this new era. But we lack a vigorous exposition of the philosophy of the atomic age. We lack what a great and distinguished churchman has recently call a *"Pax Technica"*—a peace governed by a devoutly ethical responsibility for retaining control over this advance of science which *could* destroy the world.

Confronted with the dissolution of traditional physical forms, the pulverization of matter, and the need to understand our new world not as a world of things and events, but as a universe of infinite and fluid *relations,* the danger is that we may lose entirely any sure sense of being in touch with reality. We may, indeed, under a panic urgency to *"do something"*—do *anything,* and so precipitate disaster. I think James Joyce has well characterized our situation with his sardonic comment:

"History is a nightmare from which I am trying to awake."

And so it is—under the hideous threat of a hydrogen bomb in the hands of "trigger-happy" and frightened men. Yet one does not awaken from a nightmare by continuing to believe in its reality and thus succumbing to it—you awake from a nightmare and its influence by *knowing* it to be unreal and by *overcoming* it. Let us not, therefore, be discouraged by the complexities of the current but only *apparent* transmutation of our physical world, but rather let us be *encouraged* by the boundless opportunities, the limitless possibilities, the marvellously expanding horizons of this new and still unfolding revolutionary atomic age.

Under-Emphasis on Social Revolution

In all current talk, however, of the technical benefits and rewards of the atomic revolution, there is perhaps all too little said of the enormous demand which this atomic revolution even now is putting on our social organization, our business structure, our management men and our statesmen. It should not be difficult to foresee that we shall need to grow new kinds of executives to meet the needs of new corporations and new social structures changed, or transmuted, or born, or born again through the pervasive fertilization of this atomic revolution.

In this upset of the *status quo,* this atomic demolition not only of the "world-that-was" but of the "world-that-is," the need for new political leadership, for new management vision, for a new responsibility in *retaining control* over the advance of nuclear science is as important as, and in direct proportion to, our atomic performance capabilities.

For we have a sober necessity to deter and to defend against atomic *destruction.* We have a moral compulsion to answer the crying need of all peoples for the peace and fulfillment of atomic *creation.* Yet we have, too, a desperate need not to underestimate the power and persuasiveness and persistence of evil. With all our craft and courage, with all our physical and spiritual resources we have need to defend those things which, born of another Revolution, are, above all others, worth defending: our freedom of worship, our freedom of speech, our rights of assembly, of enterprise, of trial by jury, of "life, liberty and the pursuit of happiness," of "government of the people, by the people and for the people".

Atomic energy taunts us with ideas of new world horizons. The challenge and the opportunity for world leadership are clear—but do we have the wisdom and the initiative and the daring to rise to meet them? And if *we* do not, we may well ponder the question—who might?

I can think now of no closing comment quite so apt as William Laurence's story of an entry in "The Journal of the Goncourt Brothers" of April, 1869, just 85 years ago. The entry describes a conversation between leading scientists of the day, in which they predicted that in a 100 years "man would know of what the atom is constituted" and "would be able to create life (synthetically) in *competition with God."*

"We have the feeling," the "Goncourt Journal" states, "that when this time comes to science, God, with His white beard, will come down to earth swinging a bunch of keys, and will say to humanity, the way they say at 5 o'clock at the saloon: 'Closing time, gentlemen.' "

6 Automatic Control: Today's Industrial Revolution*

By John Diebold

From process plants to assembly lines, from metalworking job shops to insurance offices, a new industrial revolution is taking place today in America. Its concepts are rooted deep in the past, but united by recent technological advances they are emerging today as a powerful new force.

The ability to create machines that can perform the functions of *control* and of *data processing*—as well as the heavy labor of our society—lies at the heart of this revolution. The widespread application of these machines and of the principles which underlie them, is today bringing about one of the most fundamental changes our economy has ever experienced.

It is essential that business and engineering management alike understand the true nature and direction of this change. Although we are just beginning to feel its impact, it is already clear that we are experiencing nothing short of a *Second Industrial Revolution*.

The meaning of this new Industrial Revolution is as varied as it is important:

Cost Reductions, increased uniformity of product, safer working conditions, and improved operations in both plant and office, together with higher output and less waste are the most obvious results of the use of automatic control; and they are also its economic justification. In addition, automatic control equipment can now be built in such a wide variety of forms and applied so broadly to all segments of business, from assembly line and process plant to job shop and accounting office, that this primary meaning is of enormous importance to every businessman, engineer and worker in our country. But there are other, even more fundamental meanings of automatic control which are seldom made clear.

* Reprinted from *Automatic Control* (July 1954), 7-14, by permission of Reinhold Publishing Corp.

New Products and Services resulting from the use of automatic control in both production and clerical operations may be less obvious benefits, but they are very important. In addition to improving present ways of doing things, automatic control makes possible the undertaking of new tasks. Thus the production of fissionable material for either military or peacetime use would be impossible without highly developed control systems, for no human could withstand the atomic radiation of the great reactors. Similarly, it would be impossible to manufacture successfully such a new and widely used product as polyethylene, requiring exquisite timing and coordination of many variables, without the use of automatic control. In the area of the office new kinds of data processing services are already appearing that are designed to provide management with operating data on a new level of meaning through the use of electronic computers and other new data processing equipment.

Automatic Products incorporating automatic control as an integral part are opening new markets. Electronic computers—which will be a $1 billion industry by 1960 according to a recent Stanford Research Institute study—and tape-controlled machine tools are products that *depend* upon automatic control equipment for their operation and that do not merely use it in a peripheral manner to make their operation more automatic. Such machines are the vanguard of new lines of commercial equipment that are beginning to emerge as the peacetime counter-part of such military devices as guided missiles, drone planes, and radar controlled anti-aircraft guns. But it is very difficult to visualize new concepts before they come into existence, and thus automatic products have received little recognition as a field in themselves.

A New Industry engaged in the design, manufacture, installation and maintenance of automatic control equipment has already appeared. Composed of many old and well established firms as well as many new ones, the automatic control industry as such is young and incredibly vigorous. This year some 750 companies will sell about $3 billion worth of control systems, components and automatic end products to industry and government. Still in its infancy, and as yet unrecognized by the financial statisticians, its sales figures are often mixed in other aggregates.

Increased Productivity of our capital equipment, as well as of our labor force, are results of today's Industrial Revolution from which we will all benefit. One of the most significant qualities of the U. S. economy has been our characteristic ability to increase continually the output of goods and services while at the same time decreasing the human labor needed to produce these goods and services. No place has this been more striking than in the process industries—where automatic control has been used most extensively and where it has made possible continuous automatic production. Labor productivity in these industries has markedly outpaced the aggregate national gain of 2 to 3 percent per year. By employing capital equipment 168 rather than 40 hours per week, productivity of the capital investment in these industries has also gained, with benefit to us all through more efficient use of our national resources. By making possible similar strides in other areas of the economy, in metal working, fabricating and in data processing, the new technology of automatic control will permit continued increases in our productivity despite military drains and despite a decreasing percentage of our total population engaged in productive work.

American business is bringing about this new Industrial Revolution, and business—along with the rest of our economy—stands to benefit greatly from the amazing changes that are today taking place. To look upon automatic control merely as a technical device for improving existing operations would indeed be shortsighted. Actually the truly revolutionary qualities of this new movement are found in the new markets it is opening and the industries that are expanding with it.

How fantastic it must have once seemed to look beyond the use of Watt's steam engine for the performance of other than the routine tasks of the eighteenth century. For who, at the beginning of the steam age, could foresee the incredible changes, the new businesses, new products, and new jobs that would come into being as a result of Watt's invention?

To predict the future course of events accurately and reasonably is always difficult. The ability to understand and to solve day-to-day problems, while still viewing them with the perspective of the great events taking place about us (and of which they may be parts) is indeed a rare quality. Yet it is a quality that is badly needed today. We do not need to look back very many years to learn that the only certainty in life is change—remarkable change even within the short span of a human life. It is only by understanding the basis of that change that management can hope to perform its real task of leadership. To do this management needs the facts that are basic to automatic control; and management needs, as well, the perspective with which to understand these facts.

The New Technology

It was by harnessing heat energy and making it possible for power-driven machinery to replace hand labor that James Watt inaugurated the automatic control era of the First Industrial Revolution.

Today's Industrial Revolution lacks the unifying symbol that Watt's engine provided for the steam age. No single machine, no one piece of equipment, adequately represents the nature of the industrial change being wrought today by automatic control. Basic concepts and principles of operation which lead to a very wide variety of hardware, coupled with a strong conscious drive and reawakened desire on the part of American management to weld our existing know-how and experience into a new level of achievement are the true bases of today's Industrial Revolution.

In devising the flyball governor to control the speed of his engine, Watt made use of an old but rarely used principle—feedback, or self regulation. It is that simple principle, reinforced by a strong theoretical structure and a widely adaptable body of experience, that has made possible today's Industrial Revolution.

Feedback itself is neither new nor revolutionary. What is important is the new-found ability to use feedback for a wide variety of purposes. For years feedback has been familiar to many through its use in home thermostats, bathroom plumbing, windmills, and ship's steering engines. But it was not until World War II, when a vast sweep of scientific manpower was concentrated on such military problems as radar and gun control—the solutions to which depended upon the construction of reliable feedback systems—that we came to comprehend the true potential of this form of control. By the end of World War II, American scientists and engineers had learned to overcome the more important technological drawbacks to applying feedback in a general manner.

The new technology of feedback control makes possible:

Self-Regulation of Both Simple and Complex Processes. In addition to simple control problems, such as regulating the speed of an engine, it is now possible to provide for the self-regulation of systems having many variables—for example, control of a chemical plant.

Flexible Automatic Operation. Machine tools, as well as other production equipment, can be made to follow different operating sequences by alterations in control information through a punched paper tape, for example, rather than by lengthy cam changes. Feedback systems insure accurate compliance with the desired results. The job shop as well as the mass producer, assembly operations as well as manufacturing—all stand to benefit from this kind of automatic control.

Automatic Data Processing. The new approach looks upon control as information processing. This provides a common denominator on which to build automatic equipment for the performance of clerical work as well as for the control of manufacturing equipment. This time the revolution is affecting our offices as well as our plants.

Another new element today is the *systems* approach. Although many of the instruments of control have been with us for generations, it was not until the late 1940's that a true *systems* approach to our industrial control problems was at all widely adopted. Today we no longer plan control in terms of individual instruments. We think now in terms of control systems, of networks of instruments and regulators. This approach exemplifies much of what is radically new about today's Industrial Revolution.

New problems are added by the systems approach, for the qualities of systems transcend the mere sum of the connected components. Yet it is this thinking—in terms of self-regulating systems—coupled with the strong management drive to make operations more automatic, that is the principal moving force behind the Second Industrial Revolution.

Putting Control to Work

It is one thing to understand the theoretical concepts of the new technology, and quite another to put this knowledge to work. A good deal of scientific and engineering study remains to be done before we will have fully explored the potential of this complex field. But we are far enough along technically so that we can construct reliable and stable control systems for a great deal more of our industry than is actually ready for automatic control. Technological drawbacks that two or three years ago hindered the practical uses of control are today no longer critical.

The real control problems of today are the problems of *application.* An obstructive gap exists between the systems engineers and control manufacturers who have developed the principles of control, and the managers and production engineers who must make use of control. Until each recognizes the other's problems while considering his own, an obstacle will stand before a complete grasp of the application possibilities of automatic control. The main problem of our new industrial era at this stage is to bridge the gap between technology and management. In addition to learning *what can be done* with automatic control, we must also critically face the question of what it is *we wish to do with it.*

Recognizing areas which can benefit through the application of automatic control is not always simple. Efficient use of automatic control in both office and plant often hinges on a rethinking of the work and the ability to perform tasks in new ways. It is necessary to discern and realize such basic needs as:

Redesign of product, process, and equipment. Sometimes minor changes, such as a dot of ink on a web of paper (which allows automatic registration in the color printing process) is all the product redesign necessary to permit fully automatic control of an operation. On the other hand it may be necessary to redesign the entire product as was the case in the Navy-Bureau of Standards' Project Tinkertoy where the control circuit of a missile was entirely redesigned so that circuits were printed on flat ceramic plates to replace conventional hand wiring.

No better examples of complete process redesign for automatic manufacture could be found than the change from *batch* to *continuous processing* that has taken place in petroleum refining and chemical manufacturing during the past generation. It is precisely this kind of basic change in process that is often necessary to allow the full benefits of completely automatic control. But even the process industries still have much to gain through automatic control. The introduction of the systems concept, and of central control, are creating as much of a revolution here as they are in metalworking plants and in the office.

Integration of manufacturing and data processing steps into logically planned sequences. A natural step in the evolution of both the machine tool and the production line, automation is creating increased awareness of the value of careful planning. The new flexibility being introduced into automation by the more generally applicable principle of control will change the logical basis of work organization, but the need for thoroughly logical planning remains. As surprising as it many seem, the simple procedure of logical analysis is still a major obstacle to the application of automatic control in many areas to both shop and clerical work.

Systems Planning. Much of the real progress of the next twenty years will come in applying control devices such as servomechanisms and transducers to conventional production equipment, which except for such additions, will remain essentially unchanged. There will result real economic gains of considerable importance, and they should not be underestimated. But it would be self-limiting to think of the new technology of automatic control as merely providing gadgets with which to make today's machinery automatic. To say proudly, as some do, "We have added a feedback loop to our machine," indicates only a partial understanding of the true meaning of automatic control. In the ability to analyze our production processes and our data processing on an entirely *new level,* and to create far more efficient means of production, lies the real significance of automatic control. We are in some areas already reaching the point at which production processes are designed around the control system.

Marketing Problems

Selling control equipment has all the headaches of putting control to work, plus some extras. Major product or equipment changes by the end user are obviously an area in which the control manufacturer must interest himself for they severely affect his potential sales volume. Just as clearly, these problems are less subject to his influence than his best interests would demand.

Other marketing problems face him too, and some of these bear very heavily on both the rate of progress of the Second Industrial Revolution and on the rate of growth of the automatic control industry. Among the most important of these are:

Stating Requirements—knowing specifically just what the end user wants to do with control is probably the basic sales problem faced by the automatic control industry. To oversimplify the case, our technological knowledge today is such that we can build just about anything we want to build in the way of a control system, provided we can state in precise terms what we want. The problem of stating requirements presupposes understanding of both what it is that can be done with control and what we want to accomplish. This problem is common to both control equipment manufacturers and to end users. And as has been emphasized already, it is one that requires a higher level of communication between the two groups than at present exists.

Understanding User Needs in putting control to work. Many justifiable control system and computer sales are never made because the manufacturer lumps research and development expenditures onto the first few units to be produced. This is true of some of the largest manufacturers as well as of the small and financially limited ones. Few equipment manufacturers are sure enough of user requirements or of ultimate markets to allocate research and development expenditures over broad bases. The result is that any number of engineering groups can be found today who are willing to undertake development projects in all areas of automatic control. But it is those who have carefully analyzed their markets and are offering a well engineered product who are making the volume sales.

Short Payback Periods, expected by end users who consider much automatic equipment as "special purpose," mean severe market limitations for equipment manufacturers. In view of the fact that control manufacturers themselves look upon some of their equipment as special purpose, this kind of thinking by the users is hardly surprising, but it does lead to some strange purchase decisions and at the moment it is doing much to block developments that are eminently desirable according to reasonable economic standards.

Complete Control Systems are offered for sale by comparatively few companies equipped to carry out the job. Firms exclusively concerned with systems problems will undoubtedly one day become a regular part of the control picture. But today few such qualified groups exist, and it is either up to the end user to organize his own systems engineering group or to underwrite a vendor's efforts. Neither course is helpful to the extension of automatic control although end user systems engineers clearly have an important future. Some component companies such as Beckman Instruments, realizing that their component sales will skyrocket once the system sales problem is overcome, are seriously considering entering the systems field in a big way. The advantages to the end user in dealing with one vendor are obvious and the introduction of aggressive marketing practices such as the Panellit Company's plan for leasing complete systems lay the basis for considerable expansion of the entire automatic control industry.

The User Must Be Educated in the potentials of automatic control, if full market potential is to be realized; and this is an expensive process. Such education is more of a problem in end equipment sales than for component manufacturers. Educational efforts of the finished product manufacturers are one reason their profit margins were smaller than those of component manufacturers last year. Computer manufacturers as a group have gone further than any others in educating the customer. Interestingly enough, some computer manufacturers are beginning to cut back on these costly expenditures, and are planning to charge for training courses and programming manuals.

It is clearly to the best interests of automatic control manufacturers to increase end user understanding of control equipment. Business papers, trade shows, professional society meetings, and university extension programs all aid in such understanding.

Meaning to Labor

No one can long consider the fundamental nature of the Second Industrial Revolution without raising the question: What will it mean to society, and particularly to labor?

There will be many changes, just as there were following the First Industrial Revolution. On the whole, these will be favorable changes. Whatever the shortcomings of our society, we must admit that we are far better off because of technological advances than without them.

The social meaning of the Second Industrial Revolution comprises a study in itself, and an important one. A few of the most probable effects of the new industrial revolution are listed below.

More Goods and Services will be produced and many of these will be new goods and services.

The Work Week will continue to decrease and it is entirely reasonable to expect a three-day weekend within the next decade. For those of us who find our jobs interesting, there will be the opportunity to work; for those who do not, there will be increased leisure.

Service Industries, including recreation and travel, will claim an increasing share of the gross national product as our leisure increases.

Labor Will Be Upgraded. The repetitive tasks of machine operation and routine clerical work will be the areas where the advances of the Second Industrial Revolution will bring the greatest change. Operators will be free for work which requires a larger proportion of creative capabilities.

The Premium on Engineers and technical training will continue. New kinds of engineers will be needed—having the broad understanding necessary to qualify as *systems engineers.*

Increased Skill will be required by management in running tighter organizations. With decreased in-process inventory and short change-over time on the factory floor and in the office, management can react quickly to changed market conditions and the art of management will demand rapid decisions based on a higher level of judgment than ever before.

Two points should be made clear when discussing the social and labor effects of the Second Industrial Revolution: (1) the speed with which changes will take place, and (2) the extent to which our society will become automatic.

Speed of Change. Some people in talking about the field feel it necessary to explain that the Second Industrial Revolution is an "evolution," not a "revolution." To use the word *revolution* is no more to imply that these changes will occur overnight than to imply that the First Industrial Revolution took place in a week's time. In terms of the grand sweep of history, both movements will be seen as revolutionary, and it is in this sense that we use this word. The rate at which technological changes are adopted by our society has been increasing steadily for some time. There is every indication that rapid change will continue—but not necessarily at breakneck speed. We have time to plan ahead, and we certainly have reason for farsighted planning.

Extent of Change. Automatic factories will not be workerless factories —the expression is primarily a figure of speech. The worst mistake that can be made in assessing how automatic control will affect labor is to make use of "obituary accounting"—that is, to tote up the number of workers replaced by machine, multiply that sum by the number of machines, and tag the end result as "unemployment." More sophisticated economists would call this "committing the lump of labor fallacy," or assuming that only a set number of jobs exists in our economy.

Such an approach considers our economy to be static. In reality we have what is perhaps the most dynamic and productive economy the world has ever known. To sell short its marvelous capacity for growth and production has been the undoing of more than one pessimistic economist. Our needs increase continually. As we satisfy the material needs for food, clothing and shelter, we find that we have created new needs which are uniquely human—needs for books, art, travel, music, sports, and for leisure. The continual emergence of new needs is a basic cause of dynamic qualities of our economy.

We must show responsibility and humility in employing the new technology of automatic control, just as we must in using any of the powerful forces we have created. If we act as responsible human beings in using this technology, we have within our grasp a means for raising not only the material welfare of our civilization, but also its dignity.

I still believe that the following statement, made in 1951 by a nationally prominent American, has in it much truth:

"I do not know of a single, solitary instance where a great technological gain has taken place in the United States of America that it has actually thrown people out of work. I do not know of it, I am not aware of it, because the industrial revolution that has taken place in the United States in the past 25 years has brought into the employment field an additional twenty million people."

The author of that statement was the late Philip Murray, president of the CIO.

7 The Changing American Market*

By GILBERT BURCK and SANFORD PARKER

ALL HISTORY can show no more portentous economic phenomenon than today's American market. It is colossal, soaking up half the world's steel and oil, and three-fourths of its cars and appliances. The whole world fears it and is baffled by it. Let U. S. industry slip 5 per cent, and waves of apprehension sweep through foreign chancelleries. Let U. S. consumer spending lag even half as much, and the most eminent economists anxiously read the omens. The whole world also marvels at and envies this market. It is enabling Americans to raise their standard of living every year while other countries have trouble in maintaining theirs. And of course the whole world wants to get in on it. For it still can punish the incompetent and inefficient, and still reward handsomely the skillful, efficient, and daring.

The American market is all this mainly because it is a changed and always changing market. The underlying reason for the American market's growth and changeability is the nation's rising productivity, or ouput per man-hour—that cachet of efficiency without which no nation today is civilized or even modern. American productivity is of course the world's highest. For years it has been increasing unevenly but incessantly at an average rate of about 2 per cent a year, and it has done even better since 1947. And because productivity is rising so swiftly, the market is expanding much faster than the population. For rising productivity, in the long run, ends up as rising purchasing power, and the standard of living rises, palpably if not uniformly. People who could buy x amount of goods five years ago may buy x plus 8 or 10 or 15 per cent today, and x plus 16 or 20 or 30 per cent five years

---

* Reprinted from the August 1953 issue of *Fortune* by special permission of the editors; copyright 1953, Time, Inc.

from now. Such is the dynamism that gives the American Dream its economic substance.

There is another important reason for the market's changeability. The market, after all, is the people. Their energy, efficiency, taste, and capacity for change at bottom are responsible for the American market's pitfalls and prizes. Most of the basic American characteristics are well understood—the restless, enthusiastic energy, the lack of traditional impedimenta, the almost dogmatic optimism, and the special delight in the brand-new.

What is often overlooked is that all these traits are not yet fused together. The American has not yet become a type, in the sense that the Englishman or the Frenchman is a type; the American is still cooking in the national juices. It can be safely predicted that French peasants will be hoarding their liquid assets twenty years from now, and that Englishmen will not be drinking Coca-Cola at teatime thirty years from now. But only five years from now, maybe sooner, Americans may be spending billions on products that today are struggling for the merest foothold in the market. And they could stop spending billions on products that nourish great industries today.

We are concerned here with the most significant of the broad forces now influencing American consumers and their behavior in the vast and volatile American market and with the truly prodigious and little-understood changes in American income growth and distribution, population, and spending "habits."

The most important change of the past few years, by all odds, is the rise of the great mass into a new moneyed middle class—a rapidly growing market that seems bound, sooner or later, to become *the* American market. It is like no other middle class in history, either abroad or at home. When the world thinks of the American middle class, it still thinks in terms of the characters in the novels of Sinclair Lewis, who in the 1920's made literary (and financial) capital out of his ability to portray the "typical" bourgeois American.

To the extent that his characters embodied universal and enduring human traits, they are still true to life. But to the extent that they were based on economic types then prevalent, they are all but archaic. For in those days marketing men divided all consumers into two groups, the "class" and the "mass" market. The "class" market consisted of the very wealthy and somewhat less wealthy who could buy almost off-handedly all the comforts and luxuries of life, including the time of numerous menials; the "mass" market consisted of the remainder, some of whom were just beginning to buy the durables that are now commonplace.

So late as 1929, the high-water market of that gaudy but optimistic era that hoped to abolish poverty altogether, the mass-and-class pattern, was disconcertingly evident. In 1929, *Fortune* estimates, 36 million family units got a total of $118 billion in cash, in 1953 dollars, after taxes. To see just where the mass market was, let us break the $118 billion down into three groups:

At the top were a million family units[1] (3 per cent of them all) with more than $10,000, who together received $24 billion or 20 per cent of the total income. Just under them was the smaller $7,500-to-$10,000 group getting $11 billion or 9 per cent of the total.

In the middle were 5,500,000 family units (15 per cent of them all) with between $4,000 and $7,500, who together received $30 billion or 25 per cent of total income.

At the bottom were 29 million family units (80 per cent of them all) with less than $4,000, who together received a total of $53 billion or 46 per cent of total income.

The bottom group constituted the mass market of 1929. None of its members had a spendable income of more than $4,000 or about $2,500 in 1929 dollars. Few of them, manifestly, were in the market for many luxuries, or even much more than essentials. A lot of them, it is true, managed to buy cars. A new 1929 Ford sedan, without trimmings, listed for only $500. But the cost of buying and maintaining even so modest a machine put them out of the market for other and even more necessary things. It was the top and middle groups that were able to keep up with the improvements and innovations in consumer durables. And together those groups accounted for only 21 per cent of all family units.

See how all that has changed. There were in 1953 in the U. S., *Fortune* estimates, a total of 51 million family units, 42 per cent more than in 1929, who got $222 billion, or 87 per cent more than in 1929. Plainly, the nation as a whole had gained enormously. But look at how this has pushed families above the $4,000 level, where, economists agree, "discretionary" buying power becomes significant:

The $4,000-to-$7,500 group in 1953 contained 18 million family units or 35 per cent of the total. *And they got $93 billion or 42 per cent*

---

[1] Family units include (1) families consisting of related persons residing together, and (2) unrelated individuals—whether residing alone or with others.

of total income. Since 1929, in other words, this group has more than trebled in both numbers and income.

Futhermore, this new middle market has enjoyed its greatest growth since 1947. Between 1941 and 1947, *Fortune* estimates, the number of family units in it increased by only 13 per cent, and their total income by 14 per cent. But since 1947 the number of family units in it has increased by *40 per cent,* and their total income by *36 per cent.* The last few years obviously have made the new middle market.

The last few years have also expanded the hitherto narrow upper groups. In 1947 there were two million family units in the $7,500-to-$10,000 group, and they got a total of $17 billion; in 1953 there were nearly three million family units in the group, and they got a total of $24 billion. Even the $10,000-and-over group, since 1947, grew from two million to 2,200,000 family units, and its total income from $32 billion to $41 billion. But this top group is much different from the corresponding group in 1929. Although it is now slightly more than twice the size it was in 1929, it had in 1953 only 73 per cent more income than in 1929. This reflects the great decline in the top income shares detailed by Simon Kuznets in his definitive study, *Shares of Upper Income Groups in Income and Savings.* The top 1 per cent, he showed, got (after taxes) 19 per cent of the total income in 1929, but only 8 per cent in 1946. What has happened is that the extremely high incomes have been slashed by taxes, and more of the group is closer to the average than in 1929. The $10,000-and-over market, in other words, is a much more homogeneous and much less "classy" market than it was in 1929. It furnishes few if any customers for Spanish castles like those Addison Mizner built for the Palm Beach crowd in the early 1920's, but it furnishes thousands of potential customers for Cadillacs, and year-round air-conditioning systems.

Now look at the bottom group. In 1929, remember, 80 per cent of family units got less than $4,000, and together they got less than half of the total income. Today, by contrast, about half the family units get less than $4,000, and they account for a little more than a quarter of the income. The $4,000-and-under group, moreover, is now much better off, with a much smaller percentage of family units under $1,000 and $2,000:

Fewer than 10 per cent of family units got less than $1,000 in 1953—against 16 per cent in 1929.

Only 23 per cent got less than $2,000—against 43 per cent in 1929.

Only 38 per cent got less than $3,000, against nearly 66 per cent in 1929.

And now 17 per cent get $3,000 to $4,000, against 11 per cent in 1929. Many of these, of course, are farmers or live in small towns or suburbs and have their gardens and other equivalents of income. They probably enjoy a *real* standard of living equal to or better than that of many in higher income groups. And the chances are good that many will soon move to a higher level.

All in all, 58 per cent of family units today have a real income of $3,000 to $10,000, against 31 per cent in 1929.

Such has been the evolution of the "class" and "mass" market of George Babbitt's day in what might be called the new All-American market, this *growing* middle group fringed with what is left of the top "class" and old "mass" markets. Although the income range may seem fairly wide, the needs and buying power of the members of this group are remarkably homogeneous. Some spend more money on this thing, and some on the other, but essentially they buy the same things —the same staples, the same appliances, the same cars, the same fur-

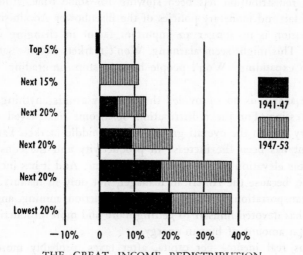

THE GREAT INCOME REDISTRIBUTION
(Per cent change in average income by groups, based on consumers' cash income after taxes in 1953 dollars)

Thanks to inflation, graduated taxes, high wages, and full employment, average income rose most sharply in the lower-income groups between 1941 and 1953. Meanwhile, the average in the top group was steady. But the trend toward equalization has slowed down since 1947.

niture, and much the same recreation. The lesson is obvious. The marketer who designs his product to appeal to the whole group has hit the new mass market.

All this adds up to one of the swiftest and most thorough-going changes in economic history—and yet a relatively easy one for almost everybody. There are two forces behind it. One is a pervasive, complex rearrangement or redistribution of incomes; the other a sharp increase in the country's real per capita income.

Progress and Prosperity

Many people would lay the redistribution of income to the graduated income tax, which indeed is a great leveler, and to the corporate profits tax. Actually, the change was brought about by many factors. Rising productivity, of course, is a background force. A direct influence was the organization of the labor movement. Another was social legislation, minimum high wage laws, etc. And finally and very important, there were two war-generated inflations with super-full employment and a sellers' market for labor.

But redistribution has been slowing for some time. And what with the tax and monetary policies of the Eisenhower Administration, redistribution is no longer an important factor in changing income patterns. This might seem alarming. Won't markets become saturated and stop expanding? Won't people have to stop "upgrading" themselves?

The answer is no—provided the economy avoids anything like a deep recession. For the redistribution of income has played only a subsidiary role in the overall growth of the middle market. Far more important has been the increase in productivity and the consequent remarkable elevation of the average real income. And it has increased, of course, because the American manager, not only in manufacturing but in transportation, communications, construction, mining, and agriculture, has devoted himself to getting more and more production out of a given amount of human energy.

Thus real income per capita, after taxes, probably more than doubled within the last fifty years. The advance, however, was not steady. It is possible that real income increased more than 50 per cent between 1900 and 1929, but very little over the next decade of depression. Output per hour of *employed* people improved in that sad decade, but the unemployed, who produced little or nothing, diluted

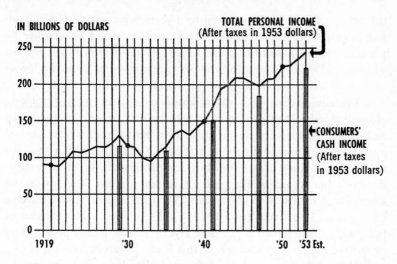

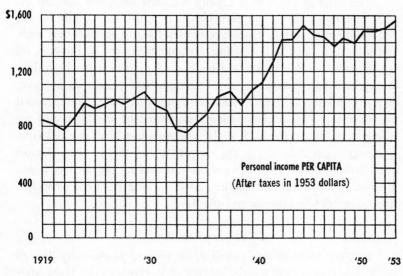

REAL INCOME HAS DOUBLED

The top chart shows how aggregate income of consumers, among other things, has risen more, both absolutely and percentage-wise, since 1947 than it rose between 1941 and 1947. (Personal income includes food or rent in kind, military subsistence, etc.; cash income is exactly what it says.) The chart below shows how per capita income, pushed by rising productivity and full employment, has almost doubled since 1932. All these figures are in terms of real 1953 dollars, after taxes.

the average. Then, in the next thirteen years, what with war and post-war boom, average real income after taxes increased by another 50 per cent—*nearly as much as it rose in the first thirty years of the century.* Thus in 1953 *real disposal* income per capita stood at about $1,566 or more than twice the estimated 1900 figure.

The rise since 1941 is so extraordinary that it is worth looking at more closely. Most of it occurred, to be sure, when the war began and eight or ten million unemployed were put to work, and so pushed up the average income figure swiftly and steeply. But that is not the extraordinary thing about the thirteen-year record. What is extraordinary is the record of the past six or seven years. There were no unemployed to absorb in these years. Yet total real disposable income since gained 27 per cent from 1947 to 1953, and per capita income 14 per cent, or better than 2 per cent a year—which means productivity must have increased even more. If this is not progress, nothing is.

This kind of progress is erasing old class lines, and altering desires, ambitions, tastes, and even ideals. Is it also responsible for the American's new urge to reproduce himself? Births are at a new high, and show little sign of decreasing. Demographers and sociologists are flabbergasted, as well they might be. For a long time it has been their theory that more prosperous and better-educated people do not have as many children as poorer and more ignorant people. Their general proposition seemed overwhelmingly supported by the facts, and nowhere more than in the U. S. itself. The American birth rate fell from thirty-seven per thousand in the early 1870's to 18.4 in 1936. Almost every layman with a point of view had a reason for the decline. It was attributed, at one time or another, to everything from the emancipation of females to Moscow and the devil.

The New Fertility

In 1937 the birth rate picked up. It spurted in the early days of the war, and again, much more sharply, as the troops came home after the war. But none of this, so far as the "experts" were concerned, did great violence to the accepted theory that the U. S. birth rate, over the long term, was descending, and that the population was approaching "stability," to be followed by slow decline. The experts predicted that Americans would stop having so many kids when things settled down.

But Americans did not stop having so many kids. The postwar

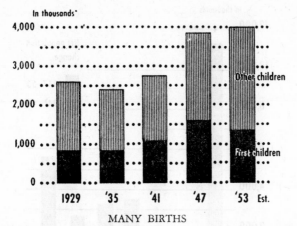

In thousands*

MANY BIRTHS

Although first births have declined in recent years—following the decline in the marriage curve—the total of births has risen to a new record, some four million in 1953. The reason is American women are bearing more second, third, fourth, and even fifth children than they've borne in years—more, indeed, than their *entire* yield in 1929.

prosperity, instead of checking their yearning for progeny, stimulated it all the more. More nubile females got themselves married than ever before, so that 67 per cent of all American females over fourteen are now married, against 60 per cent in 1940. What is more, women are not only bearing more first children than before the war. In 1953, it is estimated, they bore 1,300,000 first children, a 47 per cent increase over 1940; 1,170,000 second children, a 91 per cent increase; 620,000 third children, an 86 per cent increase; 310,000 fourth children, a 61 per cent increase. The total was about four million, the largest in history; and no fewer than two-thirds of them were other than first births. So it is that the population growth since 1947 has been the fastest since the first decade of the century. Once again the initial estimates of the Bureau of the Census, on which so many highly regarded economic studies have been based, have turned out to be much too low.

And this is not all. The number of new households ("household formation") increased, after the war, even faster than population. Between 1947 and 1953 the number of households rose by 18 per cent, from 40 million to 47 million. Aside from the fact that more people got married, more aged couples, widows and other single people had enough money to set up households. The rate of household formation, it is true, fell off from its peak in 1948. It held up better, however,

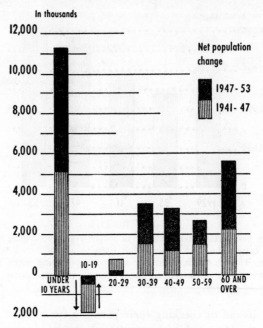

MANY YOUNG, MANY OLD

Children under ten account for nearly half the population increase in recent years. The number of grandparents is also multiplying because of rising longevity. And because of the low birth rate twenty years ago, there are relatively few young adults.

than the experts thought it would, and is still more than 50 per cent above prewar.

At all events, population changes have transformed the American market. There were in 1953, for example, 61 per cent more children under five than there were in 1941, and 45 per cent more between five and ten. Makers of children's goods have been feeling the hot wave of demand. And the increase in births is a major factor in the continuing demand for new and bigger houses.

There are more people sixty and over, and fewer ten-to-thirty-year-old people than there were in 1941, and the ten-to-nineteen age group shows a slight decline, too. This will mean a smaller market in the twenty-to-forty age group for years to come. Since this group will be supporting more young and old people, it may have to spend relatively less on personal items such as clothes and jewelry and more on housing and household goods.

As for the growing number of older people—the sixty-and-over group is more than 41 per cent bigger than it was in 1941 and 20 per cent bigger than in 1947—it means more sales not only for vitamin pills, drugs, and medical services, but also for back-saving household appliances and a whole range of products for leisure, such as garden tools, cameras, games, do-it-yourself tools, and TV sets.

How long and how fast will the U. S. continue to grow? A few amateurs see a nation of 180 million by 1960. Many demographers, adamant in their reasoning that births will decline again, believe that the most we can look forward to is about 165 million or 170 million by 1960. *Fortune* projects roundly 175 million.

And the population is not only rising, it is distributing itself and its income more evenly around the country. This growing homogeneity can be observed everywhere. What any traveler can see but may not always notice is that most towns and cities are, commercially speaking, almost exactly alike. They boast the same chain stores, liquor stores, candy stores, department stores, shoe stores, and the same prices.

During the industrial shifts of wartime, which accelerated departures from the farm, more people moved around than ever moved before. The movement has kept up. In nearly every year since 1947 some 30 million have moved—eight to ten million to different counties or states. This contributed largely to the growth of the West—to the fact that California and Arizona have grown more than 50 per cent since 1940.

At the same time—at least until 1947—regional differences in income diminished remarkably. Back in 1929, per capita disposable income of the Southwest was 50 per cent below the national average, while that of the industrialized Middle Atlantic states was 42 per cent above it. Today per capita disposable income of the Middle Atlantic states, though it has increased 75 per cent since 1929, is only 15 per cent above the national average, while per capita income in the Southwest, showing the largest regional gain (more than 270 per cent) is only 18 per cent below the national average. The Great Lakes is also 15 per cent above the national average. The New England and Far West regions are a bit above average, and the Plains states and the Southeast are below. But much less change has occurred since 1947.

Suburbia

The distinctive feature of the regional trend since 1947 is what has happened *within* regions. Today more than half the population lives in 168 metropolitan areas, which account for almost two-thirds of the retail volume and about nine-tenths of the wholesale volume of the nation. And this shift seems essentially the result of the colossal migration to the suburbs.

The suburbs, moreover, seem a major factor in today's high birth rate. Nobody knows (yet) whether people move to the suburbs because they have children, or whether they have children because they live in the suburbs. But the fact remains that rising income has enabled millions who never could live in the suburbs to live there; and suburbanites not only want children but have them.

Suburbia is becoming the most important single market in the country. No longer does the city dweller, male or female, set the styles. It is the suburbanite who starts the mass fashion—for children, hard-tops, culottes, dungarees, vodka martinis, outdoor barbecues, functional furniture, picture windows, and costume jewelry. Not all suburbs are alike, but they are more alike than different. And within themselves they are remarkably homogeneous markets. Just how much more homogeneous than the old central city, with its three or four broad income classes, is revealed in *Fortune's* series on "The Transients" and their way station, Park Forest, Illinois (May-August, 1953).

Yet homogeneity is not the whole story of the new All-American market. Thirty years ago, in one of his early editions of *The American Language,* H. L. Mencken made the point that the American speech, despite or because of its rough vigor and inventiveness, was strikingly uniform, and, compared to other languages, lacking in true regional dialects. Since then it has become even more uniform. At the same time, however, it has expanded and grown richer and more expressive, developing new variations, pungencies, subtleties. So it is with the market. It has become and is still growing more homogeneous. But the wealth of its resources is at the same time endowing it with more depth and variety—and more opportunities for the businessman who looks for them.

The $4,000-and-over consumer is one with a certain "discretionary" buying power. He is also one with more sophisticated tastes. For one thing, he is rapidly becoming better educated. Two-fifths of the adult population today has had a high-school education or better, against a fourth back in 1940. And the proportion is rising as each year's graduating class includes nearly three-fourths of today's youngsters. Moreover, the consumer is getting ideas from fashion, home, and "consumer" magazines, whose circulation has boomed.

The Mass Specialty Market

The growing wealth and improved taste of the new middle market, in other words, are creating special needs and markets within itself. They fall roughly into two groups: (1) the new mass market for the special or novel product, and (2) the market for the elabo-

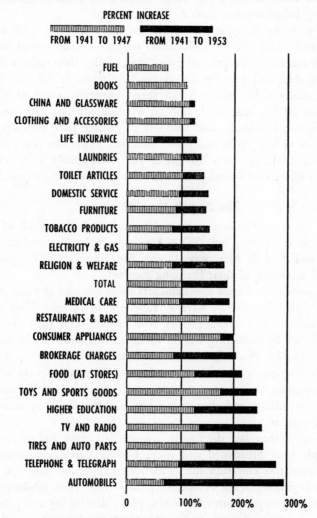

THE RISE IN CONSUMPTION EXPENDITURES

A host of important variations in consumer expenditures do not show up in broad groups because they tend to cancel one another out. This chart therefore gets down to some of the specific items that make up the broad group.

rated, frilled-up variety of what is essentially the standard, mass-produced item.

Years ago many a manufacturer couldn't afford to make specialties in quantity; the market for them was simply too small. Today,
however, the new middle-income market has created a mass demand
for them. There is now a big tall-gal market, a big little-woman market, a big baby-furniture market.

So with the frilled-up variety of the standard item. Back in the
"class" and "mass" days manufacturers tended to make several wholly
different models or varieties of everything. Today they make a standard bare shell and provide the variations afterward. All Chevrolets
are essentially alike. But you can spend anywhere from $1,500 to
$2,500 on a Chevrolet, depending on whether you buy extra chrome
work, rear-view mirrors, and bumpers to protect your bumpers. Re-
frigerators of any given make are essentially alike, but you can pay
more than twice as much for one if you want a cold wall, self-de-
froster, a fifty-pound freezing chest, butter trays, and twin crispers.

The New Buying "Habits"

So much for the new mass middle class and the wealth of new
markets it is opening up. What have people been spending their
money on? And in what way, if any, have their spending patterns
changed as a result of their changing incomes?

Economists and even merchandisers often describe the consumers'
buying "habits" as if they were a "function" of income. They relate
those "habits" to income, project that income, and then complete
the syllogism by predicting buying changes. This is becoming increasingly unreliable. Precisely because the new mass-class market has so
much "discretionary" income, it can buy so much more in the way of
frills, novelties, and variations. And so it grows more vulnerable to
competitive selling, and even pure whim, and does not buy according
to fixed pattern.

So far as they can, the figures indicate that tastes and preferences
of people have broadened and risen. Fenton Turck, consulting engineer, calls this elevation the "American Explosion," and compares
it to the beginning of the Periclean Age of Greece. He is jubilant about
the increasing expenditures for books, photo developing and printing,
higher education, flowers and seeds, phonographs and records, attendance at operas, the growing number of symphony orchestras
and local opera companies. He also notes that design of draperies and
furnishings is far better than before the war. He is, of course, right.

But what is this great explosion? At bottom, it is the rise of the great new homogeneous middle market, big and resourceful enough to support innumerable smaller markets and variations.

"A Science of Consumption"

By now, it should be clear, nothing is more important than the inclinations of the consumer. He has money, he has a big choice, he can buy as he desires, and he can stop buying many things for quite a while. What is he likely to do?

His "habits" have accordingly become a major preoccupation of American economists. The 1952 annual report of the National Bureau of Economic Research, entitled "The Instability of Consumer Spending," outlined the new approach. It was written by none other than Dr. Arthur Burns, now Eisenhower's chief economic adviser, who essayed a review of the growing concern with consumer attitudes. Dr. Burns began by giving the consumer credit (as *Fortune* had done shortly before) for checking inflation in 1951 by perversely going on a saving spree.

"The subject of primary interest concerning consumer demand has become the consumer himself—that is, his actual behavior and the kind and degree of regularity that characterize it," Dr. Burns said. "How, in what directions, and in what degree is the current spending of individual families influenced by the size of the family, the age of its members, their occupation . . . their income . . . the amount of their liquid assets, their highest past spending, their expectations concerning future incomes and prices . . . and by still other factors? How, in what directions, and in what degree is the consumer spending of a nation influenced . . . by advertising expenditures, by the rate of formation of new families, by the geographic mobility of the population? These are some of the questions now being put by economists; and while none have as yet been answered with precision and some have hardly been answered at all, the rough foundations of an empirical science of consumption are slowly beginning to take shape." The foundations are indeed rough, but much more has been accomplished than perhaps ninety-nine businessmen in a hundred are aware.

Even if the consumer's propensity to spend can ever be charted accurately, however, some smart marketer will surely come along and upset all the analyses by selling thousands or even millions of people who on paper aren't in a buying mood. Their propensity to spend, indeed, is likely to depend for a long time on those practitioners of persuasion, the sales and advertising men.

II. ADJUSTING TO CHANGING CONDITIONS

8 Insuring Company Growth Under Changing Conditions*

By Curtis H. Gager

To all astute business leaders, the insuring of company growth presents a ceaseless challenge. It is through careful and continued foresight in managing, as well as the excellence in preparation and performance of operational tactics calculated to insure growth and security, that the top management of a business justifies its usefulness to society.

"Development planning" by any management ambitious for business growth will vary with the kind and caliber of its leadership, the capacity of the people it employs, and the nature and size of the business. The process of managing which is aimed at insuring growth involves myriad considerations touching upon every aspect of an enterprise.

Bases of Successful Operation

As we all realize, there is no absolutely dependable, clearly definitive, and guaranteed formula for success in any commercial or industrial venture, but in those businesses for which growth is a practical prospect there are certain approaches to future growth and security which may be broadly applied, and there are determining influences which can be brought to bear.

Admittedly, every business has the requirement of survival. And, to survive, every business enterprise which endures has an underlying philosophy of service to the public. This philosophy may never be

---

* Reprinted from *Critical Areas in Top Management Responsibility: Guides to Strengthening the Company Position.* General Management Series No. 166 (1953), by permission of the American Management Association, copyright holder.

expressed in words. Often the products the company sells and the character and spirit of its service and its people are the only expression of its philosophy.

Out of this philosophy the management evolves the administrative principles on which it aims to do business. Out of these principles it develops basic policies as guides to the thinking and action of those who man the organization. Consistent with these policies, it develops plans—for administration, for organization, for production and sales, for service to customers, for the working efficiency and the welfare of employees, and for the growth and progress of the business. To implement these policies and plans, management defines short- and long-range objectives and develops methods and techniques for the day-to-day operation of the business.

Thus, any successful business enterprise is operated on the basis of—

An underlying philosophy, which expresses the management's faith and beliefs;

Principles, which represent its motives and convictions;

Policies, which are its operating rules and regulations;

Plans, which serve to activate the enterprise and give it both direction and purpose;

Objectives, or specific goals which need to be accomplished in performance of the plans; and

Methods and techniques with which to carry out its plans and policies.

A wise management will never tamper with the underlying philosophy of the business, nor will it change its principles except to improve their strength and soundness. But, when it comes to policies, objectives, methods, and techniques, a forward-looking management will keep itself completely alert and flexible. It *must,* if it is to survive in this world of swift and drastic changes and sharp competition. Flexibility means readiness for and willingness to meet new conditions.

Plotting a Course of Action

I feel sure we all accept the proposition that nothing in life is static. The condition we call "change" is a normal expectancy. What decisive actions may we explore in determining a progressive program to insure business growth? What action or actions should we examine in outlining a course to pursue?

Among the many elements to be considered, there are some which have an important effect on the stability and strength of the business structure. They give indication of the dimensions and characteristics of any blueprint for expansion.

If the top management of a company is determined to build for the future, it must project itself into the future by planning where, when, and by what means it will grow, and by identifying individual objectives to be reached along the way. It is within the responsibility and the power of sound leadership to clear away obstacles to constructive planning and provide the stimulants to positive thinking.

Before any fresh undertaking or attempt is made on a program for the growth and security of a business, its top management needs to satisfy itself with answers to some very serious questions. When those answers are found, it needs to communicate them to its organization and make sure they are understood. At the outset, it must be emphasized that "vague" or indefinite planning is almost worse than no planning at all, because it may create a false sense of security.

A Quiz for Management

How does a management get itself into the proper frame of mind to plan its future?

Top management may construct and answer its own quiz, which will have direct bearing on any affirmative action a business organization may take with respect to its future. This quiz should include such questions as:

1. What is your *philosophy* toward "change" itself? Is there a need for change within the business which you can bring about?
2. What do you sense to be the *social responsibility* of top management to prepare for the future, to create constructive change which will induce efficiency, protect jobs, improve productivity, and insure profit?
3. How important do you think it is for top management to project its thinking into the future and to identify *reasonable goals?*
4. What is the effect, not alone on planning for growth, but in achieving results, if top management provides, in addition to *stimulation,* the organizational *morale, climate,* and *environment* in which the spirit to grow and the will to prosper can thrive?
5. What areas need to be surveyed in developing a program for future action?

There will be many other important questions which will develop as the problem of future planning is studied.

Attitude Toward Change

In the leading businesses of this nation there are people who do not shrink from looking ahead; they count on it and anticipate change. And, as they observe the changing conditions which must be faced in the operation of a business, they value differently those conditions which are within and those which are beyond their control and influence.

1. *Those conditions operating externally:* forces, influences outside the control of management—e.g., war, the threat of war, certain technological developments, and the political and economic influences of government. These the business man can do little, if anything about, but he must gauge and act to meet the difficulties and problems which such events and conditions produce. We have all seen much evidence of this ability.

2. *Those which operate internally:* the conditions and developments—organizational, social, financial, technological, etc.—over which management does have direct influence. When viewed positively and aggressively, they become the principal opportunities for improvement and growth.

It is *within* a business that management shows whether it can produce changes which give evidence of sound and positive leadership. It is *within* the business that changes for betterment can be created by cultivating attitudes and rewards for the research viewpoint in all activities, for seeking advantages and increased efficiency by wise policy, by invention and improvement in organization, selection, and training of personnel and in the methods and techniques which people use.

Among other things, a proper attitude of top management toward "change" is what feeds the spirit to grow. It is an attitude which accepts as a fact that changing conditions are *normal*. It recognizes that nothing in life is so constant as change itself.

Importance of Flexibility

Whether we in management do anything positive to generate conditions and accelerate changes and conditions of our preference or choosing, it is entirely true that whole industries become outmoded, while others blossom and expand. Organizations change, products and processes change, people change, methods and practices change. The business climate in which we live is influenced by all the tides in the affairs of man.

A keen and farsighted management will keep a sharp eye on the economic barometer for changes which will affect its enterprise. A wise management will plan to meet all conditions it can foresee, as well as those which may be only imagined.

This necessitates deep questioning of the nature of economic conditions within which our growth must be accomplished. The hazards and obstacles to growth in any near-term economic adjustment depend on the kinds of products produced, the technological influence of research, and other factors relating to the type of industry. It is essential to consider whether a company is engaged wholly or partly in the production of defense products or material and whether it is engaged wholly or partly in making products which are being outmoded. It is utterly impractical to generalize about all situations.

Obviously, every business man—and everyone else in a position of influence—is asking this question: As we look ahead, can we have both peace and prosperity?

Answers to this may vary, but there is assurance in the record of the past. And in it we find that the two can exist together. But we have to plan for them; we have to apply ourselves, perhaps as we never have before.

Offensive and Defensive Planning

Sometimes, as a result of forces outside a company's control, there will be unprofitable periods despite the best of plans. This means that operations must be so conducted over the long term as to supply an adequate cushion for short-term reverses. In essence, a company must have defensive as well as offensive plans and programs.

The ultimate plan for developing a business will show the estimated profits to be achieved from the operation over a given period. It attempts to show where a company is to invest its money and how much—the amount to be spent for new facilities, for research projects of all kinds, as well as for marketing expenditures. It will show how much money will be needed to operate the business and how best to finance it.

In a company which is likely to survive, the approved plans are made known to all the senior supervisory personnel of the organization. There must be a full team on the field, and the players must know what kind of game they are playing.

The ever-present possibility that political forces may suddenly bring about a complete reversal of economic trends makes it clear that some companies should plan today in terms of more than one likely course. Management thinking and planning must, of necessity, protect company growth and stability *under different sets of possible circumstances.*

If an industry is subject to wide fluctuations which can produce substantially different operating results, it suggests that maximum and minimum forecasts for either products or departments, or for the business as a whole, can be an immensely valuable guide to judgments and decisions affecting growth. Subsequent to such forecasting and as actual operating figures are reported, management can decide which of the two alternatives is closer to reality and thus shape its future actions to either the optimistic or the more conservative forecast.

Looking at future prospects in terms of reasonable minimum-maximum volume levels should provide potential safeguards which are not always present in a specific forecast.

The Forward-Looking Program

Thus far we have emphasized that a business must have a philosophy toward itself, its people, and its purposes that gives adequate reason for being. Further, a business attains its potential of growth only as the management determines the direction the business should take, the principles for which it stands, and the policies which are to guide it.

But, while these offer a firm foundation for all the thinking to be done and the decisions to be made, they are of little value unless the organization making up the primary management of the business defines its goals and ultimately constructs a plan and program for reaching those goals.

In its purest application, this requires practical planning at the highest level as well as in the subordinate departments of the organization. There are many separate areas in which concrete plans should be made in preparation of an action program.

What, then, may be included in the general make-up of a forward-looking plan? Inasmuch as any plan constitutes a practical framework, it will include specific projects, whether for major capital expenditures, acquisition of new businesses, development and introduction of new products, or whatever, for ultimate examination and for evaluation. Decisions respecting the elements of a program for growth can be logically related only if *all* elements of a long-range plan are set forth.

The extent to which subjects are covered in a plan will depend, of course, upon many circumstances, including the goals and needs of the business and the judgment of the management. Nothing should be included which does not contribute to the practical purpose of telling a story which can be properly understood by the organization; nothing should be omitted which is necessary to such understanding and appraisal.

Ten Steps for Growth

Here is a suggested broad 10-step outline which may be helpful in growth planning. Perhaps it is too simplified, but my intention is to provide a skeleton on which others may build.

1. *Describe the general nature of the company.* State its potential for stability and growth and the risks inherent in its operation. Re-state those company aims and principal objectives which are conducive to growth. List trends in sales, costs, earnings, return on investment, inventory picture, capital expenditures, and so on.

2. *Determine the company's present position.* Analyze the comparative position of the business in the industry, so far as practicable. Survey the competitive standing of each product, division, or subsidiary. Inventory the human resources and organizational strengths—particularly as they may affect the filling of management positions as the company grows. Review important recent actions, whether taken to stimulate sales, increase profitability, improve product quality or the effectiveness of equipment and processes, to eliminate waste, or to utilize by-products.

3. *Predict future economic conditions as a base for projections.* Project the future of the industry, of related industries, of the nation, and of any foreign nations that may be involved as customers or suppliers.

Up to this point, the outline calls for mere reporting and—in No. 3— informed guessing. We can neither exercise any control over these facts nor have any control over the future. But, having decided that growth is both possible and desirable for the business, it is necessary to decide *how* the company should grow. This is the key decision; this constitutes setting the future course.

4. *Propose specific actions—a program.* Plan actions on quality, advertising policy, reorganization, sales strategy, or any of the other fundamentally important factors of the business which study will uncover.

5. *Propose the methods and techniques by which the company is to be made to grow.* List the objectives the methods are expected to meet.

6. *List the reasons underlying the selection of methods.* This will clarify

your management understanding of the program and make it simpler to administer.

7. *Outline the extra needs of the program:*

    a. The need for plants and equipment.

    b. The need for reassigning people, for hiring additional people, and, if necessary, for changing the organizational structure.

    c. Research and engineering needs. Here, time is very important. Research must be under way long before results may be expected.

    d. Financial needs for each forward year. There should be detailed estimates of income, cost, profit, relation of profit to investment, capital expenditures, and working capital needs of the business. Each of these needs has to be justified by a specific advantage—increased profit, lower cost, or greater efficiency.

8. *Establish means of review and control* which will provide reliable, timely facts on which to base decisions.

9. *Set standards for performance and results.* Let there be no doubt as to what is expected of every employee, group, department, unit, or division.

10. *Set a definite timetable* for the accomplishment of the agreed-upon objectives and the decided actions.

There is no No. 11. No. 11 should be assumed in the regular operation of any business. It is: *Let your people across the breadth of your organization chart know what you are about.* Give them the general objectives. Let them see whatever plans you must not keep under cover. Keep them informed as you pass the milestones of your plan. Let them know their individual roles in the plan. And give them recognition for their individual contributions.

This 10-point outline is not creative of growth itself. It is perhaps better described as a puzzle which you may solve.

Responsibilities of Management

As managers and leaders you have probably come to respect form, order, balance, and completeness in plans. Beware, then, of the temptation to make your plans and your outlines too pure, too mechanical. Allow for the unexpected, yes, and allow, too, for the genius and inventiveness of which you and your organization are capable. Perhaps you were born with these qualities, perhaps you developed them somewhere along the line. But you must be inventive, you must be creative, or you wouldn't be in your position of management responsibility. You will be shortsighted, however, if you do not stimulate creativeness among your associates and subordinates and utilize their ideas to the fullest possible extent.

The fulfillment of major management responsibilities can only be achieved—

1. By determining the direction and the goals for the enterprise as a whole;
2. By creating a competent organization, training it thoroughly and teaching it to avoid waste of every sort;
3. By communicating freely and convincing all who work in the business of the advantage which extends to them in the successful accomplishment of objectives of every kind; and
4. By inspiring the people to put forth their best efforts, increasing the will to prosper and to win.

In short, if you would insure the growth of your company, you must *instill it with life.* If your organization is a healthy, living thing, changing conditions will be, not insurmountable and unsolvable problems, but opportunities.

You who are "the management" bear heavy burdens. You carry responsibilities for actions and decisions which extend beyond tomorrow. The future is in your hands, and what you do, what plans you make, what decisions you reach, influence the lives and livelihoods of many.

The whole duty of managerial leadership requires in its performance the unrelenting application of all the talents that can be brought to the task, all the foresight, all the courage and imagination, and a sense of dedication to a trusteeship.

9 Obstacles to Business Growth*

By Keith Powlison

A COMPANY cannot stand still. If it stops growing, it starts going down hill; there is no in-between. Of course, it is the normal expectation of every company under vigorous management to keep on growing, provided it does not run up against external circumstances beyond its control. That is part and parcel of the dynamic nature of business.

But there are many obstacles to growth within the company, which are not always recognized for what they are and purposefully dealt with. See them and take action on them, and the company should continue growing. Overlook them and do nothing about them, and the company may fall so short of its due growth that it is in fact on the downgrade.

What are these obstacles to growth, and what can be done about them? Let me try to set forth some of the more typical, more important ones, as I have observed them, and suggest an approach to their removal that others may find useful.

But first of all, because no management can tackle this problem until it has a clear idea of what its present rate of growth is (or is not) and what kind of growth it wants for the future, let us look at the underlying question of measures and goals.

Measures and Goals

Nearly every management points to its company with pride as an example of *growth*. At the same time the lament of investment counselors and institutional investors is that real growth companies are so rare. This paradox indicates that there is widespread difference

---

* Reprinted from *Harvard Business Review,* 31 (March-April 1953), 48-56, by permission of the editor of *Harvard Business Review.*

of opinion as to what growth in business really is. A closer look, however, reveals some fundamental points on which we can agree.

Mere Expansion

Does business growth mean mere expansion—"progressive increase or enlargement" as the dictionary definition has it?

For 20 years the tide of business in this country has been rising. Record all-time highs have been set by every important measure of business activity. With very few exceptions the companies which have been in business throughout this 20-year span have increased in sales, number of plants, employees, and variety of commodities handled. As a matter of fact, most of those which did not share in the upward swing of business are not here today; they fell by the wayside.

Broadly speaking, the dollar volume of business in this country is today six times what it was 20 years ago. This means that if a company's sales are now six times what they were in 1932, the company has just held even; it is an average concern. Again, since it will be marketing its wares at prices which are at least twice as high (if it has done a typical job on pricing), in *physical* volume the average company will be handling now between three and four times as much business as it did 20 years ago.

A company which is no more than average is hardly a growth company. It needs something more than mere expansion—a whole lot more—to qualify as a real growth company. It seems only logical that growth should be in terms of the goal or objective of business.

The purpose or goal of a company is to make a profit by employing assets as effectively as possible to meet the needs and desires of customers. This definition, in turn, involves three factors: (a) assets or capital, (b) sales, and (c) profits—profits being the difference between sales income and all costs, including taxes. These three factors constitute the *eternal triangle* of business, and real growth depends on all three together. The measuring stick or tool used for this purpose is the "return on capital employed" or the "return on investment," as some call it.

Return on Capital

The final measure of the performance of an established company is the answer to the question: How effectively is the company employing all the capital or assets available to it? Capital or assets, as we use the term in my company and as I apply it here, means the total of all assets, principally cash, receivables, inventories, and property, plant, and equipment, regardless of where they come from or who supplies them. The total asset figure appears at the bottom of the lefthand side—the asset side—of the conventional balance sheet. The fact that it thus embraces all the basic factors of business is what makes this tool the common denominator by which companies can be measured and compared as to performance and growth.

In order to have a satisfactory return on capital employed, a company must use its assets hard. The harder assets are used, the more the sales obtained for each dollar of capital will be. This is the turnover factor.

The assets must also be used efficiently. The more efficiently assets are used, the lower costs will be and the higher the margin of profit on sales will be. This is the profit on sales factor.

Return on capital employed is *turnover times profit on sales*. Some companies, notably merchandising companies, make their return on capital employed with high turnover and low profit on sales; other companies, notably those in the extractive and heavy manufacturing industries, make theirs with low turnover and high profit on sales; and some are in between on both. No matter how they do it—and the characteristics of the business have a lot to do with it—they must have the right combination of these two factors for the kind of business they are in if the return on capital employed is to be adequate.

Now what has been the average performance as to return on capital employed? The Securities and Exchange Commission and the Federal Trade Commission, working together, have published figures representative of all *manufacturing* firms in the United States. These figures apply to the postwar period only. They show that from 1947 to 1952 the average manufacturing company (there are no comparable figures for the average merchandising firm) increased its total assets by approximately 50%, boosted its sales by 45%, but in 1952 earned 5% less in profits after all taxes than in 1947. The annual rate of turnover fell from 1.61 to less than 1.5; the profit on sales (after taxes) fell from 7% to less than 5%; and return on capital—the final measure—dropped from 11.3% to less than 7%. (The figures for 1952 have been in part estimated.)

This shows that most companies experienced mere expansion, not business growth. The real kind of growth apparently is as rare as the investment people say it is. Where there is real growth, the return on capital is also increased or held at a high level while expansion takes place. Where there is outstanding growth, all three indicators—turnover, profit on sales, and return on capital employed—are raised or maintained at a satisfactory level. Some companies have done this, but they are few indeed.

The raising of earnings to a satisfactory level and the maintenance of earnings at that point while expanding is of critical importance. A real growth company keeps its development work in balance with its established business so that earning power does not deteriorate while capital expenditures are being made. This is important to investors and management alike. In these critical times, when we seem to be tottering uncertainly on the thin line between war and peace, no company can afford to run the risk of establishing a low base for excess profits taxes, whether or not such taxes are in force at the time.

But more important than the tax consideration, in my view, is the psychological factor. Very seldom, if ever, is management on sound ground in permitting an organization to use expansion as an excuse for poor operating results. Expansion is too alluring already—for reasons which will be under discussion subsequently—without adding any further inducement or incentive such as an exemption from operating accountability.

Basic Ingredients

For the most part, so far, I have been talking simply about the figures, the accounting and financial data, which reflect growth; I have not said, in so many words, exactly what growth is. I wish I could. But I cannot, any more than the physicist can say exactly what electricity is. He tells us that electricity is an imponderable and invisible agency, capable under different circumstances of producing light, heat, chemical decomposition, and other physical phenomena. And when he has said that, he is through with definition. But more important than definition is the fact that the physicist knows how to recognize electricity, measure it, produce it, control it; and he knows a little about how to use it—just a small fraction of what will be known a few years hence.

The secrets of growth in business are just about as imponderable. We do not know precisely everything that goes into it, but we can recognize it, we can measure it, we can produce it. The approach through return on capital employed—embracing the eternal triangle of business, capital employed, sales, and profits—is fundamental. But there are other ingredients, other considerations, in the growth recipe. I should like to mention just a few of them:

(1) Attention might well be paid to the rate at which new ideas, new products, or new processes are flowing into the business, and the rate at which the old, obsolescent, or unprofitable are flowing out. Putting the new in without giving it an opportunity to grow by pruning away the old results in an enlarged, swollen, stagnant business, just as in a shrubbery garden the old, dead, and dying holds back and stifles, and the uncontrolled sucker growth saps the strength needed for sound growth.

Periodically, some companies tell us what percentage of their products were not in the company's line at some earlier time. These figures are usually net—that is, the total of additions minus the deletions. It would be helpful if additions and deletions were shown separately, thus giving a feel of the rate of flow *in* as well as flow *out*.

We all recognize, of course, that growth in business, as in all other areas of human experience, is seldom continuous and constant. Usually it is by spurts with leveling off or consolidation periods between. The chart of a typical growth company, when plotted over a long period, usually resembles the profile of a stairway.

(2) It is important, again, to know what extent the products of the business are related to the means of serving man's needs and desires—the means by which living is made safer, healthier, and more satisfying. Labor-saving machinery and appliances, electronics, pharmaceuticals, chemicals, oils, TV, air transportation, just to cite a few, come to mind in this connection.

We might even ask: What about chlorophyll? Is it a heaven-sent potion which will forever relieve all mankind from the intolerable odors of human and animal existence? If so, it is destined to be a goose that lays golden eggs. Otherwise, it may prove to be no more than a quick gimmick.

(3) We must also find out to what extent a company will participate in rising standards of living, in a war as well as a peace economy; to what extent it will be affected by long-term tendencies, such as the trend toward an ever-growing old segment in our population or the trend toward socialization of economic effort.

All of those factors plus many others well known to readers are significant. The important thing is to be aware of them.

It is good general principle that one of the best ways to find what you are looking for is to watch those who have the biggest incentive to find it. No one stands to gain more from finding growth companies than investors. For this reason, real growth is anticipated and reflected in stock values. Of course a lot of other things enter the picture too. Just the same, with skillful analysis a high degree of discrimination between growth and nongrowth companies is possible. Here is just one clue: If you have to stand in line or know somebody to get a few shares of a new offering, that is a pretty good indication that there is some real growth in the picture.

We have seen that growth is performance toward profitability—

the effective use of assets to make money—as measured by the return on capital employed; that it is not measured by mere size; and that it is constantly renewing itself by adding new vital growth products and pruning away the old and obsolescent. Now that we have an understanding of what growth is, let us see what prevents it.

But remember that in analyzing what prevents growth we are concerned only with what management *can* control. There is no use discussing what we cannot control as individual businessmen—such as war-created shortages and governmental restrictions, adverse legislation, long-term trends toward socialization, and so on—until we have done the best we can where we are free to act.

The Unprofitable Item

Every business is continuously taking risks. Profit is the incentive and reward for risk taking. Whether or not a company earns that most coveted of all reputations—that of being a real growth company—depends to a large extent upon what it does with its risks or ventures which do not pan out.

Suppose a company has a product line composed of two items. They are manufactured in one plant and distributed by the same sales force. One of the items is a good earner; the other fluctuates in a narrow range above and below the break-even point. This situation has existed for some time, but is now recognized as needing major attention. What does the company do about the weak item?

There are three alternatives: (a) to drop it—go out of that particular business; (b) to put it on a satisfactory basis; (c) to bail it out by adding something else. Let us take each of these in turn.

Drop It from the Line

Of these three alternatives, the first is the most difficult and least frequently selected course of action. The reasoning may go something like this:

(1) Progress is always the order of the day. One does not make progress by giving up—by going backwards. Going out of a business is an admission of defeat.

(2) Other companies make money on this commodity; we are at least as smart as they are; we can do it too. In other words, what anybody else can do, we can do, and we usually add "better."

(3) It is nearly always possible to cite some other product that was worse longer and then finally blossomed out into a fine profitable business,

and this one will do the same if we just give it time. After all, the product has not had a fair trial; conditions have been so abnormal.

(4) We cannot afford to drop the item until we find something to take its place. It absorbs burden that cannot be carried by the remaining commodity. If we discontinue this item, we will have an unsatisfactory return on the whole investment.

(5) An important part of the profit made on the profitable items would not be earned if we did not have the unprofitable item to attract customers.

(6) The unsatisfactory item is highly competitive. The capacity to produce is bigger than the market. If we drop out, our volume will put our competitors on easy street. We cannot afford to let that happen. This is the gin rummy game in business: we can't do anything with it, but somebody else can, so we'd better hang on to it.

Put It on a Sound Basis

If the product is continued for whatever reason, then we should put it on a sound basis. Solomon indicated the approach when he said, "Whatever thy hand findeth to do, do it with thy might." In copybook maxim style it can be stated, "If it's worth doing at all, it's worth doing well."

But it is very hard to correct a bad situation with which we have lived for a long time. If we knew how to fix it, we would have done so a long time ago. The situation is just this: since we do not know what is wrong, we cannot take for granted that anything is right. Everything has to be questioned, until the situation is corrected. This is an uncomfortable approach. Everyone who has had anything to do with the product is threatened with the possibility of having been wrong.

It is worse than that. It can even raise questions about panaceas. In business, as in medicine, panaceas are very soothing—even if they do not cure. To challenge a widely accepted and long-applied cure-all can be disturbing, even disorganizing. Incentive wages are a case in point. To some they are the answer to every ailing situation. If results do not improve or if they continue to deteriorate after the installation of incentive wages, is the soundness of incentive wages questioned? *Hardly*— or perhaps *seldom* is the word.

The more usual response is that the incentives are all right; we just need more of them. The medicine is o.k., we just did not take enough of it. The questioning of the other ingredients in the situation is potentially no less unsettling. This is true because many of them usually are of broad application—affecting other commodities beyond the one immediately under consideration. For these reasons, the correcting of the problem, as it is, frequently gives way to the third alternative—that of bailing out the item by adding to it or making it bigger.

Bail It Out

This is usually by far the most inviting of the three alternative approaches. It eliminates the pain of going out of a business—the pain of seeing sales decline, cutting back on personnel, realigning organization. In effect, it places the stamp of approval on what has been done in the past. The operation, we say, was soundly managed, but it was intrinsically untenable. Nobody is at fault because only experience could prove that.

The situation is untenable because, for example, we do not have a whole family of products. The line is too short; it needs to be rounded out by the addition of new items. Or the situation is untenable because it is a *big kind* of business. It cannot be handled profitably on a small basis. It requires bigness to do adequate advertising, research, and engineering. So, it is decided to grow out of the problem by adding products, commodities, or lines—by growing larger.

This is a very palatable solution. From the time it is decided upon, a sigh of relief goes through the organization. Everybody is off the hook. Frustration gives way to the feeling that "now we're getting somewhere."

Lure of Bigness

This is characteristic of expansion—of getting bigger—no matter what the reason. Its allure is so nearly irresistible that it constantly threatens to displace profitability as the payoff goal in business—for a number of reasons:

(1) The feeling that what is bigger is better is so widespread that it has come to be almost axiomatic.

(2) Growth occurs quickly, is easy to see, and is impressive. It is apparent that something is going on in the erection of a building from the time ground is broken. In contrast, the steps which lead to profitability are subtle; you cannot see them; they are difficult and are relatively slow in coming to fruition.

(3) It is exhilarating. It is a spending binge—like shopping (ask any woman).

(4) Personnel problems disappear like snow in the tropics. People are hired, not fired; advanced, not demoted. Every administrator knows from painful experience how great these differences are.

(5) Everybody is busy. The place literally hums with activity. The purchasing department becomes a mecca for eager salesmen. Engineers,

architects, designers, draftsmen are doing the creative work that makes them happy. The treasurer busies himself making the rounds with the commercial and investment bankers for the needed funds. The top executives are swamped with invitations to tell luncheon clubs of the policies and principles that have led to the growth of the business. In other words, the "joint is jumpin'."

(6) Everybody in a company has a warm feeling toward his associates who are expanding. It is the friendly kind of a feeling you have toward any one who helps you buy a deep freeze or an air conditioning unit at wholesale. He saves you money. In like manner, it is pleasing to hope that, with the additional business, you will have a smaller share of the president's, the controller's, and the treasurer's salary to carry. Who likes to pay a driver, a checker-upper, and a penny-pincher anyway?

The person who relieves you of these unpleasant burdens is a friend indeed. You will support whatever he wants as long as it involves expansion—and pretty soon you find that he smiles with favor upon your proposals to grow out of your commodity, factory, and personnel problems. This is working together for everyone's advantage. In a way it is a sort of automatic, unpremeditated "log-rolling" for growth—for anything that involves decreasing the overhead burden.

What is wrong with this picture?

It is spending the company's money to distribute costs over a wider area by expanding and growing—rather than decreasing costs. It is looking backwards to protect what the company already has that is weak—rather than looking forward to develop new business which holds promise for future success on its own. It is, in others words, defensive. It is playing to weakness.

Burden Absorption

The arguments about rounding out the line or adding new operations can seldom be proved right or wrong. It is all too easy for the proponents to point to somebody else who presumably is making good money on one or more of the same products or activities in question. (Actually, the other fellow may be having the same trouble.) But the clinching argument for expansion is the old, perennial *burden absorption*. By adding more volume, the argument runs, fixed charges will be made lighter for every other operation.

Of course, whenever burden absorption is claimed, it is automatically assumed that there is already excess capacity in personnel and in physical facilities to handle added business without incurring further fixed costs, and that these excesses are practically in balance—indeed that they are just what will be needed for the new operation.

Or it is assumed that the new business will be handled more efficiently than the old.

That both of these assumptions are frequently invalid is indicated by the fact that fixed costs per dollar of sales often fail to show the downward trend that was anticipated and claimed to justify the expansion move. In other words, after a reasonable consolidation period, it is not unusual to find that the ratio of fixed costs to sales tends to seek the level which has been normal for that business (provided its basic character is not completely changed), or at least fails to decline significantly.

So often the burden argument appears to be the perfect reason for expanding (or for not dropping a weak item), and so often it is accepted and then fails to materialize, that I think it should be called "the one-way street which leads to nowhere" except to the dead end of bigger volume and lower profits.

It is no accident that in some of our best managed growth companies the burden absorption argument is not accepted as valid either for going into or out of a business. Rather the assumption is that the business will be run efficiently at all times and that capacity will be balanced effectively against sales volume. This approach is far less dangerous than that of burden absorption.

Defensive growth—rear-guard expansion—does two serious things to a company's chances for real growth:

(1) It fixes profits at a low level—costs at a high level—by freezing inefficiency permanently into the company.

(2) It leads to cumbersome and unwieldy complexity. When, in the name of burden absorption, so many different kinds of products and technologies are brought together in one business family that they cannot be handled effectively within the practical limits of organizational decentralization, then diversification has gone too far. When this happens, mediocrity in earning power is almost certain to result.

Downstream Management

Another category of obstacles or hazards can be gathered under the title of "downstream management."

One example is the practice of using new job opportunities to find places for problem personnel rather than to find the right man for the job. By so doing, it is hoped to kill two birds with one stone. Unfortunately, this approach more often than not only postpones facing the personnel problem and, in addition, creates an added problem in the new job function. Availability is only one—and not the most important—criterion for selecting men for important assignments. This is taking the course of least resistance—coasting with the current—in other words, "downstream management."

Another example can be observed in the splitting up of productive operations, putting them at separate locations, even at higher costs, with the specific purpose of avoiding exposure to strike stoppages and other labor dislocations. This is "downstream management" in the sense that it tries to go around—to lighten the impact of—an inadequate labor relations program, rather than to do the job that ought to be done on labor relations in the first place. Many companies have demonstrated that sound labor relations—though not easy or cheap to achieve—really pay off. Of course the indispensable basis for sound employee relations is an efficiently run company. This is a big order. Yet without it, no matter how fancy the frills, employee relations cannot be satisfactory.

Common Characteristics

These examples of what prevents growth, and many others that might be mentioned, have a few characteristics in common about which we can generalize:

(1) They masquerade or wear the disguise of real growth; they make the company look bigger.

(2) They seem to obviate the necessity of doing a pruning or a fundamental corrective job.

(3) They make specific weakness or inefficiency less obvious by dispersing it throughout the organization—like a boil which does not come to a head but is gradually absorbed by the whole system. Instead of having isolated bad spots which can be identified, treated, and cured, the whole business area becomes mildly sick and operates at the level of mediocrity—not profitable enough to be strong, not weak enough to die.

(4) They result eventually in a company which has so many different kinds of problems that it can specialize on nothing—it is a "Jack of all trades and master of none." This means that it does an average or compromise job while being forced to compete with a number of companies, some of which are expert at what they do.

Danger Signals

We have just been looking at some of the things which prevent growth. When anything is as difficult to recognize, measure, and achieve as business growth, it is helpful to have danger signals or red lights along the way to tell us when we may be getting off the straight and narrow path to growth.

No signal, of course, is conclusive. Every one of them has to be verified and evaluated in terms of all the conditions—just as the medical diagnostician has to check and recheck symptoms and findings in order to be sure that he understands what is ailing his patient.

Let me mention, in the form of test questions, just a few of the signals that you may find it helpful to look for, since they may mean that there are serious obstacles to growth in your business:

(1) *Do you depend upon a wide diversification of old products rather than upon efficiency and dynamic product and process development to sustain your earning power throughout the cyclical swings of business?* If so, there is serious question about your having a real growth company, and you are in danger of decadence.

(2) *Has a substantial part of your expansion been achieved by adding more and more of the same thing rather than by adding new products or processes?* If so, you may be exposed to heavy obsolescence or even dry rot in a few years.

(3) *Do you hang on to, instead of obsoleting, spare equipment or parts for which you have no known use, in the hope that they may be useful some day?* If so, you are using more capital than you need, and your return on capital employed is needlessly low. It is possible also that this is a symptom indicating that it pays better to be right than it does to be profitable in your company.

(4) *Are rewards in your company based primarily upon how hard a man works, the size of his responsibility, his rank or status in the organization, or the fact that he is "in line" for bigger things, instead of being based invariably upon contribution to profitability?* If so, you are being lured off the growth beam.

(5) *Do you make some capital expenditures, because you have the money, that you would not consider worth while if you had to borrow or sell stock to finance?* If so, you are possibly placing convenience—the availability of money to spend—above profitability as a criterion for new product or process ventures.

(6) *Do your investments for cost reduction show big savings while earnings of the company are declining?* If so, possibly operating inefficiencies are increasing costs more than investment for cost reduction is decreasing them—and the stockholders are being asked to subsidize or pick up the tab for management's ineffectiveness.

(7) *Does your company evaluate technical skills in handling materials and equipment higher than it does the ability to handle people?* (The tip-off on this is revealed in the kind of appointments made to the assignments involving large segments of employees.) If so, your company may be creating costly employee relations problems.

(8) *Are capital expenditures to improve present businesses out of proportion to investments in new developments?* If so, you are losing your offensive, forward-looking pace.

(9) *When the soundest calculations you can make do not support what you want to do, do you go ahead anyway, reasoning that there are "intangible"*

values and benefits that will justify your actions? If you do, you are kidding yourself. Intangibles are unfavorable at least as often as they are advantageous.

(10) *Is "unfavorable" assortment becoming a more and more frequent reason for unsatisfactory margins—particularly since the end of the sellers' market in the early part of 1952?* If so, you are just getting volume whether it is profitable or not; you are picking up the crumbs, taking the orders that are easy to get, while the aggressive merchandisers are getting the high profit sales. In short, you are doing a "downstream" selling job.

(11) *Do you do things for a part of your business that you would not do if that part were all the business you had?* If so, you may be allowing bigness to obscure the real economics of the situation.

(12) *Do your top-management people spend most of their time working on the unsatisfactory parts of the business rather than the profitable parts?* If so, your company is playing to weakness and may be starving the golden goose.

(13) *Do you excuse low profits today on the ground that the high costs now being incurred will pay off handsomely in future profits?* If so, you may be indulging in a form of rationalization that is very popular in periods of high taxes.

(14) *Do many of your best young men leave to make more money elsewhere?* If so, maybe the cost of giving career men security regardless of performance is being paid for at the cost of superior men who have to go to other companies to find adequate reward for making a real contribution to profit.

(15) *Is your diversification so broad that, like the old woman who lived in a shoe, you have so many situations you don't know what to do, especially about long-range development work?* If so, your effort is being diluted, and obsolescence may become systemic—for lack of new ideas and opportunities.

(16) *Is the most rapid increase in such things as sales volume, number of employees, number of plants, and capital employed in the relatively low profit areas of your business?* If so, you are probably bailing out what is weak—being defensive—rather than developing and exploiting new opportunities on their merits.

(17) *Are more of your executives, principally those in so-called middle management, engaged in money-making ventures on the side?* In other words, are your executives selling their administrative services to the company and employing their creative money-making talents in their own, outside enterprises? If so, and I imply no criticism of any one, it is an indication of the extent to which some big businesses are losing the essence of free enterprise and assuming the characteristics of huge administrative units. Nothing could be more detrimental to business growth.

Significantly—not just incidentally—where are the lush expense accounts, where are the snazzy offices? In the personally owned businesses operated on the side, or in your publicly owned company? And do you ever hear it jokingly said from time to time—or is it jokingly?—"Don't mind me, I just work here."

Constructive Action

Up to this point we have found that growth is the process of employing more and more capital with increasing effectiveness—as measured by return on capital employed—in a company which is constantly being renewed by the addition of the new and the elimination of the obsolete. We have also found that every business is beset by very alluring and attractive alternatives which constantly threaten to prevent sound growth. Now, what constructive action can be taken?

Not for a long time has it been so important as it is now for businessmen to understand how to get growth. After four or five years during which the upward course of business was so strong that it was almost impossible for management to make an obvious mistake, economic forecasters tell us that we are now, for the first time in the postwar years, coming into a period in which operating results will accurately reflect the effectiveness of management and nothing else. The tide of business itself will no longer be the dominant factor eclipsing and covering up the weaknesses which have crept into management during the long years of swing-out from the depression of the 1930's.

We all know *what* to do to achieve growth. Set it as the goal, organize for it, and pursue it relentlessly. It is as simple as that—in principle. True as this is, it is not the answer we are looking for. Every management believes in its heart that it is doing this now—has been doing it for years—and yet so straight is the path and so narrow the gate that few, very few indeed, have entered into the Promised Land. The secret that has escaped us in our pellmell race for bigness is not *what* to do, but *how* to do it.

How can we get our employees to work for sound growth and to work for nothing else? Boil it down, and that is the question. Let us approach it by considering a few simple truths:

(1) A company will get what it pays for, provided the payoff is consistent. If the choice jobs always go to the expanders in the business, the company will get bigness in sales, in plants, in products, in organization—but not profitability. If the big rewards are always for technical proficiency, it will get that—but not profitability. And so on with political sagacity and other alternative goals.

(2) If the company vacillates between goals—i.e., cannot select one and adhere consistently to it—then the company will get nothing but confusion, frustration, low morale, and mediocre profits.

(3) Management has to decide what it wants to pay for. It cannot let the matter be solved by default, cannot back away from the problem.

(4) A vacuum is abhorred in business just as violently as it is in nature. If there is the slightest lapse in the rigid, continuous, and unrelenting adherence to the goal of growth, one or more of the false goals we have considered will rush in to fill the void.

Now, in the light of these considerations, how do we get a whole organization to work as effectively as it can for just one goal—namely, growth?

Rewarding Performance

The only answer that seems sound to me is to find in business the most nearly perfect example of what we want and then to discover what makes it tick. In my view, the successful, small, owner-operated enterprise has got what we are looking for. The secret of its success is the direct, positive, immediate, and proportionate reward for effort in the profits of the business, to the extent that the effort is sound— and in the certain loss through the deterioration or collapse of the business if the effort is not sound.

Most big companies do not have these rewards and consequences. Salary administration does not provide it. It is too slow and cumbersome; it is bound by the need for uniformity, for standardization, and so on. Promotions cannot do it. There just are not enough jobs into which to promote every one who makes the kind of contribution to profitability that is the essence of growth. If incentives are to be effective, the payoff must not depend upon deaths, retirements, resignations, or anything else which cannot be controlled; the reward and consequences must be as direct as in the owner-operated business.

In the typical business which does not have a well-worked-out and administered program of incentives, the consequences of unsatisfactory performance are much more direct and powerful than are the rewards for positive contributions to the goal. You can fire, demote, or cut the pay of a man in ten minutes; but you cannot give him a bonus, raise his pay, or promote him just like that. It practically takes a board meeting to reward him. The result of this is that there is much more incentive to *avoid mistakes* than there is to *venture*, to take the kind of risks that are essential to growth in business.

If we really want growth in big business, we are going to have to pay for positive action in larger measure than we penalize for mistakes. If we do not, we shall have big, safe, unprofitable administrative units called businesses.

The late Lammot du Pont told me several years ago that, in his opinion, the growth of his company throughout the many business generations of its long and successful history was attributable to the system of rewarding good performance as well as holding individuals accountable for unsatisfactory performance, more than to any other one factor. But, he went on to say, in order to do it, much more hard work is required than to do just the usual or ordinary tasks with which an executive busies himself. Nothing is so important, he emphasized, and nothing is so difficult.

Penetrating Scrutiny

From the time a company installs an incentive program, every act of management has to be consistent with the company objective in terms of which extra compensation will be paid. Everything has to stand up under the penetrating scrutiny of a smart organization to which every move means money. This is a wholesome thing for management just as audit by public accountants is good for controllers and should be welcomed in the same way.

It is not only wholesome for management, but essential to the free-enterprise system. This system is under attack from the outside; many of those who would destroy it have no understanding of how it works. We, the managers, must clearly understand it, and we must make it just as strong as we can. We can do this by gearing the rewards and penalties of performance directly to the one objective—the growth objective which we are all striving to achieve.

10 Meeting Requirements for Scientific, Engineering, and Managerial Manpower*

By J. Douglas Brown

As a pioneer in the development of mass production, the United States must also pioneer in the solution of the ever changing problems which mass production creates. Among these are problems of pricing, distribution, finance, advertising, creation of replacement demand, avoidance of saturation of markets, and the rapid obsolescence of productive equipment. The steady advancement of engineering design, of standardization of parts, and of production and assembly techniques has been assumed to be an inevitable inheritance of Yankee mechanical ingenuity rather than a problem. We have lived on that inheritance for several generations, but with the arrival of the scientific age new complexities have arisen in keeping mass production effective. These complexities have been sharply accentuated by the vast application of science to war.

The new problem is that of adjusting our manpower resources to the pattern of demand required by the mass production of a rapidly changing stream of complex goods. We have come to the painful realization that mass production of such goods places pressure upon our manpower resources not so much at the rank-and-file level of fabricators, assemblers, and distributors but, most of all, upon the far scarcer manpower which creates the ideas, designs, processes, and equipment which in turn makes thousandfold duplication desirable and possible. So long as mass-produced goods were relatively simple, like flour, cloth, washing machines,

---

* Reprinted from *Manpower in the United States: Problems and Policies* (Harper & Brothers, 1954, pages 190-197), by permission of Harper & Brothers.

or even passenger cars, the balance of creative design to plant engineering was not too demanding upon the former. However, with the urgent need for faster planes, atomic weapons, electronic controls, and high-capacity metals and fuels, the shift of demand to the creative side of the balance in mass production has been sharp and drastic.

The functions performed in modern mass production can be divided roughly into four major stages in the development of the production of a new and complex item.

1. *The creation of ideas.* This may be a new mathematical formula which explains the conversion of mass into energy, a chemical discovery of new compounds or processes, a physical principle, the further understanding of the behavior of matter, or imaginative application of new materials or structural forms to known needs.

2. *The engineering implementation of new ideas.* Such implementation selects and applies new ideas and fits them into known technology or invents new technology which can apply them. The process of implementation overlaps at one end the creative work of the scientist. At the other it reaches the borders of day-to-day understanding of plant operations. It includes the vast area of design, materials, structures, pilot-plant testing, tool design, layout, and operational standards.

3. *The initial organization of the human, financial, and technological factors for efficient production.* Here the essential idea becomes an economic reality by the combination of all the complex of complementary agents necessary to its efficient and profitable production. The creative elements at this step require a wide range of talents in human organization, motivation, control, judgment, and insight.

4. *The maintenance of efficient repetitive production at a desired volume.* It is at this point that mass production "pays out." Because of the spectacular results of American plants producing thousands and millions of standard items at relatively low cost, this stage of the mass-production cycle has received great popular acclaim. It involves a high level of administrative arts, but it is the *end* and not the *beginning* of a creative process.

In analyzing the needs in human resources required in the mass-production cycle, it is obvious but far too little emphasized in the American mind that it is steps I to III which require the highest talents available. Further, the American industrialist, as well as the American public, has assumed too easily that the talent required in steps I to III would be available whenever needed and to the amount required to meet the demands for new products forthcoming at stage IV. This misapprehension of automaticity in the supply of high talent is now giving our manpower planners a severe case of jitters.

Why has the United States been caught short in its supply of the creative type of manpower so needed in mass production? Several reasons may be suggested.

1. Whereas in more normal times demand for mass-produced items is determined by the millions of consumers of end products and, for new items, is subject to some extent to the manufacturer's desire for orderly and gradual change, in time of war or preparation for war the *government* becomes the heavy demander of new and complex items in mass production. No longer is the manufacturer able to regulate through advertising or pricing the demand for radically changed designs or to limit change to the capacity of his routine production staff. Rather the government, under the pressure of competitive armaments, demands, and can afford to demand, more rapid improvements in existing items as well as new types of items requiring sustained activity at all stages in the mass-production cycle.

2. Rapid obsolescence has become the essence of sound military technology. Rather than stocking vast supplies of aging equipment, national security now puts a premium on the constant replacement of limited quantities of one prototype in planes, tanks, ships, rockets, and electronic devices by radically improved models. This places a far greater pressure on the creative stages of the mass-production cycle, relative to stage IV, than occurs in normal times.

3. In times of peace, there has been a tendency for the pressure upon the creative stages of the mass-production cycle to vary with the general business cycle. Pressure has developed when an anticipated high potential of consumer demand and purchasing power is accompanied by a period of vigorous competition for sales. In such a period, manufacturers seek new or improved items to assure themselves their share of available markets. The United States is apparently in such a stage at present. Consumers are spending billions on new gadgets at the same time that the government seeks new types of armament. Both are putting pressure on the limited resources of American science, engineering, and management to satisfy their urge for the new and the better.

4. The human resources required in the first three stages of the mass-production cycle are the most difficult to expand. Scientists, it is almost correct to say, are born, not made. Their education must continue many years past the common high-school level. Engineers of the creative type require graduate training and thorough practical experience. De-

signers, technicians, and toolmakers must have a high level of capacity and years of experience to be trusted with creative work. The talent for executive management which can plan and organize new plants and ventures develops largely through experience. At no time can the supply be suddenly enlarged. In all these areas we are largely limited by the scarcity of native talent as well as the time required to cultivate that talent.

5. At a time of great pressure upon these scarce human resources, our most effective institutions for screening and developing such talent are seriously restricted by financial limitations. Universities and engineering schools are hard pressed to maintain their scientific and engineering faculties in the face of inflation and severe competition from industry. The cost of adequate laboratories and up-to-date equipment has risen sharply. The living cost of students has risen far faster than fellowship funds available to meet them. In many institutions a rapid expansion of the production of trained men can be attained only at the expense of quality. But it is the highly qualified graduate that is needed for the creative stages of mass production.

6. It is unfortunate but true that scarcity in any resource stimulates a tendency for hoarding. With adequate funds and a likelihood of continued prosperity, there is a temptation for the strongly established industrial firm to build reserves of talent against possible future needs. At the same time that industry has criticized the armed forces for wasting trained talent by overdemand and misassignment, some corporations have used the excuse of training requirements and necessary protection against enlarged future needs to hold graduate engineers in positions not requiring their level of education or experience.

7. It will never be possible to estimate accurately the number of creative scientists and engineers who were lost from the flow of trainees because of the interruptions and diversion of careers arising from World War II. Experience in organized military activity may contribute greatly to maturing a man's capacity in dealing with his fellows. It does not, however, offer an effective substitute for the exact, integrated, and continuous training afforded by a scientific or engineering program in a university or by intensive specialization in creative effort in industry. Interruption in the development of a scientist or research engineer, as with a medical doctor, appears to be costly in terms of quality and quantity of the end product. Too many men fail to return to their previous training programs or lose the momentum which carries them to the higher levels of attainment.

These appear to be some of the reasons for the imbalance of demand and supply of the creative types of specialized manpower needed in the support of mass-production industries at the present time. These questions are relevant: How long will this shortage continue, and, if likely to continue, what remedial steps should be taken?

It is anyone's guess as to how long the United States will be faced with the threat of sporadic local outbreaks or a world-wide atomic-age war. The plain fact is that we are now faced by such a prospect and any lulls in military preparation or activity must be considered temporary respites. If our economy must be geared to the constant improvement of a vast military technology plus the rapid proliferation of approved prototypes should large-scale war occur, it is difficult to avoid the assumption that the creative stages of the mass-production cycle will remain under unusual pressure. Any increased acceleration of technological change, such as occurred following the Korean outbreak, will sharply increase this pressure. On the other hand, a decreased acceleration, especially if reinforced by a general business recession, would reduce the pressure drastically. It will be dangerous to misinterpret such a release of pressure as indicative of a new norm. We have already made that mistake once—in the immediate postwar period.

Since the only safe course is to assume a long-continued though variable pressure on the manpower resources needed in the creative stages of the mass-production cycle, it is important that steps be taken to compensate that pressure by adequate supplies. We are, however, dealing with human resources of high talent and keen sensitivity to motivation; with long spans of education and experience; and with a growing public apathy toward any differential treatment of individuals of high potential attainment. Public policy to enhance and conserve our supply of creative talent must, therefore, be imaginative, farsighted, and understandable. Several elements of that policy may be suggested.

1. The government of the United States should assume clear-cut leadership in educating the American public concerning the vital need for a sustained flow of manpower into the creative fields. Such a flow is a brutally evident necessity in an economy of hot war or cold war. We learned in 1865 that economic strength was the essential basis of military victory. We relearned it in 1918 and 1945. We must keep that lesson before us when we are tempted to satisfy the political urge of treating all manpower alike when certain categories of manpower are far more effective in the logistical support of combat than in combat itself. We are facing an opponent which disregards sentimental considerations of "equity" and assigns men to tasks on a coldly rational basis. It is training great numbers of men in science and engineering.

2. For this reason, the degree of selectivity already attained in the assignment of men to military service as opposed to uninterrupted education or training should be sustained and enhanced. If there is discrimination according to economic status, this should be remedied by assisting qualified individuals to finance their continued education rather than by interrupting the education of all.

3. To obtain the precious cream of creative talent, a far greater volume of whole milk must be processed through our education system. Talent occurs in all groups and areas of our population. Far more is lost through lack of encouragement and resources than we can afford. Even the United States cannot support free education for all at all levels. For this reason the selective process in education must be sharpened, not to exclude individuals at the lower levels but to assure inclusion of all qualified persons at the higher levels.

4. High talent requires and warrants a superior quality of education. To a discouraging degree American education has swung toward an emphasis upon the education of the average student. The contrary emphasis in Great Britain and Continental Europe has produced results which are obvious to anyone acquainted with the progress of creative science and engineering in the last fifty years. It is not necessary for us to curtail the education of the average, but far greater support, both financial and political, must be given to the highest quality of advanced education. We have spent far more money on the education of those who enjoy the results of mass production than on the education of those who make it possible. We have failed to realize that, of all commodities, talent is the least susceptible to mass production.

5. Until the educational and research programs of the United States have become fully geared to the production of the creative talent we need, we should encourage in every way possible the transfusion of our supply with that of the best of free Europe. We have much to gain from the continued exchange of scientists and engineers between countries. The trading of production "know-how" for creative ideas is a profitable one for us, quite apart from rich cultural advantages to both parties to the exchange. The free nations can well afford to pool *all* their assets. It would be both arrogant and dangerous for us in the United States at this time to assume smugly that we can depend upon our own creative resources. If we had done so a generation ago, the atomic bomb might have first exploded over New York.

6. The problem of assuring the availability of adequate resources of creative manpower for effective military strength is too critical for cas-

ual treatment. It has already been proposed that the government establish a National Scientific Personnel Board.[1] Such a board should have the duty to watch over all steps taken to maintain our flows of those types of scientific and engineering personnel which are required for national defense and which cannot be quickly developed in time of emergency. The board should advise the government on the proper use of such manpower as between supporting industry and services, on the one hand, and the military services, on the other. It should likewise advise those agencies which are concerned with the training and placement of scientific and engineering personnel. If deemed necessary, it could cooperate in the development of a Scientific and Engineering Reserve Corps to organize more effectively that segment of specialized manpower that should be a mobile reserve in time of emergency.

The problem of assuring creative support for the accelerated improvement of military technology and logistics will be with us for a long time to come. We remain amateurs in the attack upon this problem. We must become truly professional—creative—thinkers if we are to obtain solutions before it is too late. No one, the author included, needs to apologize if early efforts appear inadequate.

---

[1] National Security Resources Board, *Report of the Scientific Manpower Advisory Committee* ("Thomas Committee"), January 12, 1951.

11 Today's Decisions for Tomorrow's Results*

By Peter F. Drucker

An objective, a goal, a target serves to determine what action to take today to obtain results tomorrow. It is based on anticipating the future. It requires action to mold the future. It always balances present means and future results, results in the immediate future and results in the more distant future.

This is of particular importance in managing a business. In the first place, practically every basic management decision is a long-range decision—with ten years a rather short time-span in these days. Whether on research or on building a new plant, on designing a new marketing organization or a new product, every major management decision takes years before it is really effective. And it takes years for it to be productive, that is, to pay off the investment of men or money.

Management has no choice but to anticipate the future, to attempt to mold it and to balance short-range and long-range goals. It is not given to mortals to do either of these well. But lacking divine guidance, business management must make sure that these difficult responsibilities are not overlooked or neglected but taken care of as well as is humanly possible.

Predictions concerning five, ten or fifteen years ahead are always "guesses." Still, there is a difference between an "educated guess" and a "hunch," between a guess that is based upon a rational appraisal of the range of possibilities and a guess that is simply a gamble.

* Reprinted from *The Practice of Management* by Peter F. Drucker (Harper & Brothers, 1954, pages 88-94), by permission of the author.

117

Getting Around the Business Cycle

Any business exists as a part of a larger economic context; a concern with "general business conditions" is mandatory to any plan for the future. However, what management needs is not the "business forecast" in the usual sense, that is, a forecast that attempts to read tomorrow's weather and to predict what business conditions will be like three, five or ten years ahead. What management needs are tools that enable it to free its thinking and planning from dependence on the business cycle.

At first sight this may look like a paradox. Certainly the business cycle is an important factor; whether a decision will be carried out in a period of boom or in a period of depression may make all the difference in its validity and success. The standard advice of the economists to make capital investments at the trough of the depression and to refrain from expansion and new investments at the peak of a boom seems to be nothing but the most elementary common sense.

Actually it is no more useful and no more valid than the advice to buy cheap and sell dear. It is good advice; but how is it to be followed? Who knows in what stage of the cycle we are? The batting average of the economists has not been impressive—and the forecasting success of businessmen has not been much more so. (Remember the all but general prediction back in 1944 or 1945 of a major postwar slump?) Even if it were sound, to play the business cycle would be unusable advice.

If people could act according to this advice, we would not have boom and depression to begin with. We have extreme fluctuations only because it is psychologically impossible to follow such advice. In a boom almost everybody is convinced that this time even the sky will not be the limit. At the bottom of a depression everybody is equally convinced that this time there will be no recovery but that we will keep on going down or stay at the bottom forever. As long as businessmen focus their thinking on the business cycle they will be dominated by the business-cycle psychology. They will therefore make the wrong decision no matter how good their intentions and how good the economists' analytical ability.

Moreover, economists doubt more and more whether there is a real "cycle." There are ups and downs, no doubt; but do they have any periodicity, any inherent predictability? The greatest of modern economists, the late Joseph A. Schumpeter, labored mightily for twenty-five years to find the "cycle." But at best, his "business cycle" is the result of so many different cyclical movements that it can only be analyzed *in retrospect*. And a business-cycle analysis that only tells where the cycle has been but not where it will go, is of little use in managing a business.

Finally, the business cycle is too short a period for a good many business decisions—and for the most important ones. A plant expansion program in heavy industry, for instance, cannot be founded on a forecast for the next four or five or six years. It is a fifteen- or twenty-year program. And the same is true of a basic change in product or marketing organization, of a decision to build a new store or to develop a new type of insurance policy.

What business needs therefore are tools which will enable it to make decisions without having to try to guess in what stage of the cycle the economy finds itself. These tools must enable business to plan and develop for more than the next three or even the next seven years, regardless of the economic fluctuations to be expected over the cyclical period.

We have today three such tools. In managing a business all three are useful.

In the first place, we can assume that there will always be fluctuations, without attempting to guess what stage of the cycle the economy is currently passing through. We can, in other words, free decisions from cyclical guesswork by testing the business decision against the worst possible and the sharpest possible setback that past experience could lead us to expect.[1]

This method does not indicate whether a decision is right or not. It indicates, however, the extremes of cyclical risk involved. It is therefore the most important forecasting tool in the determination of the minimum necessary profit.

The second tool—more difficult to handle but also more productive —consists of basing a decision on events which are likely to have heavy impact upon future economic conditions but which have already happened. Instead of forecasting the future, this method focuses on past events— events which, however, have not yet expressed themselves economically. Instead of attempting to guess economic conditions, this method tries to find the "bedrock" underlying economic conditions.

There is the case of the company which decided during World War II to turn to the production of fuse boxes and switch boxes after the war. This decision was based on such an analysis of the bedrock underlying the economy, namely, the pattern of family formation and population structure that had emerged in the United States between 1937 and 1943.

---

[1] For most American manufacturing industries this was not the "Great Depression" of 1929-32, but the much shorter "recession" of 1937-38. The rate of decline during the eight months of that depression was the sharpest ever witnessed in an industrial country other than the collapse following total defeat in war such as that of Germany or Japan.

By 1943 it had become clear that something fundamental was happening to population trends. Even if the population statisticians had turned out to be right in their forecast that the high birthrate was a wartime phenomenon and would come to an end with the conclusion of the war (one of the most groundless, if not frivolous, forecasts ever made), it would not have altered the fact that from a low point in 1937 the rate of family formation had risen to where it was significantly above the rate of the depression years. These new families would need houses, even if the rate of family formation and the birthrate were to decline again after the end of the war. In addition, there had been almost twenty years of stagnation in residential building, so that there was a tremendous pent-up demand for houses. From this it could be concluded that there would be substantial residential building activity in the postwar period. The only thing that could have prevented it would have been America's losing the war.

If the postwar period had brought a sizable depression, this housing activity would have been a government project. In fact, population trends and the housing situation indicated that housing would have to be the major depression-fighting tool of governmental policy. If the postwar period were to be a boom period, as it turned out to be, there should be substantial private housing activity. In other words, housing would be at a high level in depression as well as in boom. (In fact, building would probably have been on a higher level than the one we actually experienced in the postwar period, had the much-heralded postwar depression actually come to pass.)

It was on the basis of this analysis of a development that had already happened and that could be expected to shape the economy regardless of business conditions, that the company's management decided to move into its new business. Management could justifiably claim that, even though it planned long-range, no forecast regarding the future was actually involved.

Of course, population structure is only one of the bedrock factors. In the period immediately following World War II it was probably a dominant factor in the American economy. In other times, however, it might well be secondary, if not irrelevant.

However, the basic method used is universally applicable: to find events that have already occurred, events that lie outside of economic conditions, but in turn shape those conditions, thus basing a decision for the future on events that have already happened.

But though the best tool we have, bedrock analysis is far from perfect. Exactly the same bedrock analysis of population trends with the same conclusion for a postwar housing boom could have been made in 1944 for France. The analysis would have been right; but the French housing boom never occurred. Of course, the reasons may be totally outside of the economic system proper. Perhaps they are to be found in strangulation by rent controls and by a vicious tax system. The boom may only be delayed and may still be "just around the corner." And the lack of any appreciable postwar residential building in France may be a major cause of the French political and economic sickness, and therefore should not have been allowed to happen. This would have been cold comfort to the businessman, however. In France the decision to go into fuse boxes and switch boxes, though based on rational premises, would still have been the wrong decision.

In other words, one cannot say that anything will "inevitably" happen in the future. Even if the inevitable does happen, one does not know when. Bedrock analysis should therefore never be used alone. It should always be tested by the third and final method of limiting the risks of making prediction: Trend analysis—the most widely used of the three tools in this country today. Where bedrock analysis tries to find the "why" of future events, trend analysis asks "how likely" and "how fast."

Trend analysis rests on the assumption that economic phenomena— say, the use of electric power by a residential customer or the amount of life insurance per dollar of family income—have a long-term trend that does not change quickly or capriciously. The trend may be confused by cyclical fluctuations; but over the long run it will reassert itself. To express it in the terms of the statistician: the "trend line" will tend to be a "true curve" over a ten-, fifteen- or twenty-year period.

Trend analysis thus tries to find the specific trends that pertain to the company's business. It then projects them in such a form that decisions can be taken for the long term without too much attention to the business cycle.

As a check of the results of bedrock analysis, trend analysis is invaluable. But it, too, should never be used by itself lest it become blind reliance on the past or on a rather mythical "law of social inertia." In fact, though quite different in techniques, the two analyses are really the two jaws of the same vise with which we attempt to arrest fleeting time long enough to get a good look at it.

Despite their shortcomings, the three methods sketched here, if used consistently, skillfully and with full realization of their limitations, should go a long way toward converting management decisions from "hunch" into "educated guess." At least they will enable management to know on what expectations it founds its objectives, whether the expectations are reasonable, and when to review an objective because the expected has not happened or has happened when not expected.

Tomorrow's Managers the Only Real Safeguard

But even with these improved methods, decisions concerning the future will always remain anticipations; and the odds will always be against their being right. Any management decision must therefore contain provision for change, adaptation and salvage. Management must with every decision make provision for molding the future as far as possible toward the predicted shape of things to come. Otherwise, despite all technical brilliance in forecasting, management decisions will be merely wishful thinking —as all decisions based on long-range prediction alone inevitably are.

Concretely this means that today's managers must systematically provide for tomorrow's managers. Tomorrow's managers alone can adapt today's decision to tomorrow's conditions, can convert the "educated guess" into solid achievement. They alone can mold tomorrow's conditions to conform to the decisions made today.

In our discussions of manager development we tend to stress that provision must be made for managers capable of making the decisions of tomorrow. This is true; but systematic manager development is first needed for the sake of the decisions made today. It must, above all, provide for men who know and understand these decisions and the thinking behind them, so that they can act intelligently when the decisions of today will have become the headaches of tomorrow.

In the last analysis, therefore, managing a business always comes back to the human element—no matter how sound the business economics, how careful the analysis, how good the tools.

12 Long-Term Security for Private Industry*

By Erwin H. Schell

A PRIME duty of top-management is to so order and administer general corporate policies that the long-term security of the enterprise is reasonably assured. Such protective policies serve to anticipate the impact of unexpected happenings or to resist subversive pressures. That one of the best defenses is a strong offense is as true in business as in warfare. Protection by purely negative measures in the long run is likely to prove futile.

The nature of these aggressive measures is determined by the kind of difficulties encountered. These, too, are changing. Consequently, new trends in safeguards to American business are now appearing and already reveal new designs pecularily fitted to conserve the continuance and growth of private enterprise in the United States.

Early in our industrial history there was a common conviction that a large backlog of unfilled orders was the surest road to industrial security.

A second and somewhat later procedure was that of building heavy inventories of raw materials, stock in process, or finished parts. Prior to the First World War, banks measured industrial borrowing capacity in terms of inventory valuation no less than "character, competence, and capital."

More recently, top-management swung toward the establishment of large reserves of cash or Government securities. In addition to gracing the balance sheet, such resources brought trade prestige, enhanced buying power, and suggested that dividend payments could more certainly be maintained.

---

* Reprinted from *Dun's Review*, 57 (February 1949), 11-12, 50ff., by permission of the editor of *Dun's Review*.

These attempts to provide assurance of continuity have not been found entirely satisfying. For example, unfilled orders proved an invitation to competition. The presence of unsatisfied demand is a sure stimulant to new establishments to satisfy it.

Again, with the advent of increasing price fluctuations after the First World War and with growth in obsolescence rates, inventories suddenly became viewed as liabilities rather than assets, and the would-be borrower was frequently urged by his bank to liquidate holdings as a prerequisite to receiving financial assistance.

As for large liquid assets, the payment of dividends solely from surplus during periods of subnormal business activity was early criticised, and more recently Uncle Sam has frowned upon the financial policy of building over-large cash reserves.

Putting eggs in more than one basket has for many years been a favorite method of lessening industrial risk, yet this apparently impregnable policy has a way of developing its own peculiar pitfalls.

As an example, a line-to-lee which had considerable attractiveness after the First World War was that of foreign trade, culminating in the establishment of company-owned foreign branches. Thus risk in terms of the fluctuations of the national business cycle would be averaged over more than one country. However, limitations established by foreign governments over branch enterprises have markedly lessened the dependability of dollar income from these sources; and today investments of this nature have questionable value as safeguards for industrial continuity.

Product Diversification

Diversification of product lines has also been widely undertaken, frequently with benefit to the company. Yet the disadvantages of too great variety often more than counterbalance the gains. The fundamental weakness in diversity as a corporate protection is the fact that the most serious current hazards confronting private enterprise tend to affect all establishments alike, irrespective of diversity in the productive elements. Hence top-management is seeking elsewhere for protective measures.

The use of collaborative methods in gaining security indicates the attaining of industrial maturity and the broadening of administrative outlook beyond that characteristic of the earlier narrowly competitive viewpoint.

Increasingly, establishments are favoring active participation with trade associations, professional societies, and other national bodies of an industrial nature which are in a stronger position to exercise influence in co-operative relationships with representatives of other important segments of the American economy. It is now becoming clear that security will in the future draw heavily upon the principle that safety for one springs best out of safety for all.

For many years, top-management has sought to earn security through goodwill, for no resource serves more effectively to assure general support in times of general vicissitude. In the marketing areas where accomplishment follows upon persuasion rather than direction, the American industrialist has invested heavily in customer goodwill. For example, millions of dollars have been invested in the publicizing of trade-marks and branded merchandise, symbolizing company products that consistently give the customer more and better for his money. Resulting accumulations of consumer goodwill rarely appear as assets upon balance sheets, yet they do provide important assurances of a continuing patronage.

More recently, investments in goodwill have been directed to the employee group; for an establishment where production is constantly threatened with labor difficulties is a plant whose momentum of productivity is jeopardized. Top-management today is instituting long-range policies and programs for employee selection, training, and administration which would not have been dreamed of a scant decade ago.

Even more currently, new emphasis has been placed upon the strengthening of goodwill in the community and on the part of the general public. In no industrial area is progress so rapid as in that of public relations. In no area does success or failure more directly bear upon the continuance or discontinuance of private enterprise. It has now become clear that industry requires for its long-term security public approval of a more positive nature than mere acceptance. To gain public approval, industry, in addition to performing an economic service, is being called upon in its rôle of a social institution to make a definite social contribution.

Security in Creativeness

Early in our national life it was Yankee ingenuity that brought security to our colonial mills and factories. Indeed, the concept of patent protection sprang from the desire to reward further through long-term exclusive manufacturing rights the precious creative talents of the old-time inventor.

During the past twenty years many industrial directorates have approved the installation of research and development departments, and there are increasing numbers of administrators who look to constant advance in product and process as the surest long-term security that they can attain.

At present, organizations are favoring active and general investment in highly trained brains, inasmuch as no other resource appears better fitted to face the unique future problems. As one president put it, "The management with the most brain-power per capita will be most likely to survive in this rapidly changing world."

The vision and courage to make immediate commitments of a specific nature to the end that important general advantages in the distant future may be assured is the mark of statesmanship. This quality of mind is reflected in the words of a minister of a foreign government which, before the last war, invited an international association devoted to the furtherance of good management to meet within its borders. He said, in effect:

"Good government is long-term government.

"Long-term government is based upon a contented citizenry.

"In an industrial nation, a contented citizenry requires good management.

"This government is therefore disposed to encourage and to support the dissemination of sound management principles and techniques through the medium of this international association."

In like fashion, leadership in American industry is turning to the support of external safeguards which, over the long run, will unfailingly buttress and strengthen the position of private enterprise in the United States. Again the chain of logic supporting these industrial policies can be stated simply.

Public Approval and Support

Private enterprise requires, for its long-term security, the unfailing approval and support of the public.

Unfailing approval and support of the public can be maintained only through steady advance in the quality of industrial services.

Advance in the quality of industrial services can result only from the persistent application by industry of intrinsically new scientific and technical knowledge and skill, conceived within the framework of a free society.

Intrinsically new knowledge and skill are the primary output of institutions engaged in pure research, in applied science, in engineering, and in technical education and training, continuing in the American tradition.

Therefore, long-term support of such institutions is a direct investment in long-term security for company and for stockholder.

Opportunities for exercise of such industrial statesmanship are not lacking. Indeed, the stability and independence of the privately endowed institutions may be dependent upon industrial support. It will soon be true that individuals will be unable to make large donations as they have in the past to these institutions, and the latter must then turn to the only remaining sources of great wealth—the corporations. Unless the corporations recognize their opportunity and responbility in this field, they may well suffer from the federalization of our privately endowed institutions, with its inevitable impact upon the free-enterprise system. Fortunately, such needs are not being overlooked.

Recently, important sums have been authorized by corporate boards for the pursuance of pure research projects to be undertaken by independent institutions. Other large expenditures have been approved for technical investigations in specific areas which are to be actively fostered by trade associations, technical bodies, and other industrially-minded organizations. Finally, fresh momentum is being given to the making of corporate grants of unrestricted funds to privately endowed technical schools for the acceleration of educational and research activities.

It seems clear that industry will not again risk the hazards described in the last depression by C. F. Kettering when he said, "The trouble with us is not overproduction of goods, but underproduction of new ideas."

13 Time to Fix the Roof Is When the Sun Is Shining*

By C. CANBY BALDERSTON

BUSINESS is prosperous. Much of it is on the highest plateau in history. What can executives responsible for policy making do to keep it so? Since the collective health of business reflects the experience of a variety of individual firms, the decisions affecting their future are vital to continued stable growth in consumption, production and employment.

What are the soundest policies to follow, now that we are on high ground with all the accompanying exhilaration? One approach is to ask what government can do to prevent a descent into whatever valley may lie ahead. It is no longer necessary to argue the importance of the policy decisions made by fiscal and monetary authorities. They are among the important forces influencing the climate in which business firms grow and prosper or decline and die, but climate is only one of the conditions necessary for good crops. Plain hard work and intelligent planning and supervision are needed also. While recognizing the impact on business prospects of monetary policies, of tax provisions and a friendly governmental attitude toward constructive business developments, I prefer to discuss what business itself can do to keep in good condition. When in depression, necessity forces much head holding and soul searching to find solutions. My thesis is that the time to start hunting them is right now while business is excellent.

General Business at All-Time High

The low state of certain portions of the economy, such as coal,

---

* Reprinted by permission of the author. This material appeared in *The Commercial and Financial Chronicle* (June 23, 1955), 26.

dairying, and farms in drought stricken areas, is painful to those who suffer from lack of work and income. Though these soft spots exist and give concern to thoughtful citizens, they do not reflect the general state of industry and commerce. Business is not only good; it is at an all-time high.

To gauge how high is the path on which we are now traveling, it is instructive to look backward at the previous peak and the intervening valley. The peak occurred in the spring and summer of 1953 and the valley in the spring of 1954. At the previous peak, Gross National Product was about $370 billion and is now estimated to be over $375 billion; national income was $308 billion and is now estimated to be about $315 billion; personal income was $288 billion and is now estimated to exceed $295 billion; disposable income, $251 billion, now estimated at about $265 billion; the index of industrial production was 137 then and is now at about the same level. Looking down into the 1954 valley out of which we have climbed, industrial production was then lower by 14 points (10%); Gross National Product by about $20 billion (6%); national income by approximately $17 billion (5%); disposable income by more than $10 billion (4%). It is worth noting, however, that disposable income was maintained at its previous high in the early stages of the 1953-54 recession and moved to still higher ground during 1954.

Construction activity is also at a new peak, and steel output is 2% above the previous high of March, 1953. Likewise, as everyone knows, sales of new autos have made a new record this spring. Output of non-durable goods has reached a new maximum—slightly above that of mid-1953 and almost 25% above the average for 1947-49. Another peak has been reached in the retail sales of house furnishings; retail sales in total have also been at an all-time high, nearly 7% better than a year ago. After all, we should be making new records from time to time: our economy has grown larger as the country has grown older.

Quality of Business Decisions

Now I come to the principal point of my discussion: the quality of business decisions is important at all times, but especially so during prosperity. In short, the duration of the current expansion will be influenced by the quality of policy decisions now being made by business executives. I am talking about the heads of manufacturing, mining and commercial enterprises, about farm managers and bankers—and about union officials, too. Unless the quality of this decision-making reflects prudent judgment as well as a reasonably well-founded appraisal of present and future trends, executives will make mistakes for which they and their workers and investors will pay the penalty. What I am arguing for is that executives should risk neither too little nor too much; be willing to venture but still guard against unwarranted optimism.

The Vital Decisions

The most vital decisions are those made by businessmen themselves. Typical among these decisions are those relating to capital additions, inventories, elimination of waste by efficient controls and by mechanization, and the development of new products. No less vital are decisions to acquire other firms through purchase or merger.

Decisions to make capital additions involve many corollary decisions. How will the new plant affect the producing capacity of the company and of the industry and the relation of that capacity to the effective demand for the product? How seriously will the investment of capital in fixed form, in brick and mortar and equipment, cause the firm to be strapped for working capital? Under the spell of the current optimism, are companies becoming, in farm language, "land poor"?

Inventory accumulation does not now appear sufficiently speculative to be of immediate concern. At present there is no such rapid inventory build-up as in 1952 and early 1953. Last year inventories were reduced month by month and quarter by quarter—a salutary process. By late 1954, however, inventory decline had ceased, and some build-up of inventories is now in process. The relative stability of inventories doubtless reflects in part the unusual stability of average prices. While prices of farm products have declined sharply, industrial products have edged up and average wholesale prices (all commodities) have fluctuated relatively little over the past three years. In April, 1952 the index was 112; in the recession of 1953, 109; now, about 110 (estimate). Or, it may be that managers are keenly aware of the losses inherent in swollen inventories and keep them adjusted to the level of new orders. The fact that relative stability of prices has minimized the temptation to take long positions in raw materials and to increase stocks on hand unduly must not blind executives to the risks of speculative excesses if prices should rise sharply.

During a period of recovery such as we are enjoying, the greater volume, the economies introduced during the preceding slack period, and the installation of new equipment cause output per manhour to increase. As one would expect, therefore, last year's rate of manufacturing productivity grew faster than the postwar trend. It should be stressed, however, that as recovery is achieved, continued good times may tend to encourage wastefulness through inattention or imprudence. An attitude of "easy come, easy go" may lead to wastes of materials and manpower—wastes which would not be tolerated in times of adversity. Large volume and the extra shifts occasioned thereby may also cause machines to be run so hard as to preclude adequate maintenance.

As to product development, the period when orders are obtained easily is obviously the time to push the design of new products to the stage where they can be put into production and on the market if and when business declines. Product development is not only one of the great social benefactors of our age because of its impact on the physical basis of a good life, but to the individual firm it may be essential to remaining competitive. Inventive prowess has given American firms new products so useful and appealing to consumers as to form the basis for entirely new industries, such as the automobile and electronics industries. In the future, product development must be counted upon to provide a high and rising standard of consumption, jobs for an increasing labor force, and the competitive strength of manufacturing firms. Both industry and society at large are served by continued emphasis upon research throughout good times and bad.

Merger Questions

Mergers are once again the subject of discussion among businessmen, economists, and government officials. Whether or not mergers may lessen competition is too complex a subject for discussion here, but since we are dealing with the quality of management decisions, it may not be inappropriate to inquire as to the motives prompting the mergers now being consummated. Doubtless many result from a desire to increase efficiency and the company's competitive position. If they add to efficiency by permitting the company to offer a fuller line to dealers and other customers, or to increase the degree of vertical integration so that better coordination may be achieved over procurement, manufacturing and distribution, mergers may provide a social gain and benefit the companies that are combined. But if the consolidation of companies is prompted solely by the desire for speculative profit, or by the urge to increase company size for reasons of personal pride and power, then the merging process' is to be viewed with concern.

The central problem we are discussing is how to extend the period of prosperity and to make more gradual any future descent that the periodic undulations of business may bring about.

At the outset it is appropriate to point to certain danger spots. One source of concern—particularly if employment and incomes should decline—is the quality of mortgage and automobile credit. As terms have lengthened, there has been a tendency for quality to decrease. It should be stressed, however, that repayments have so far been excellent. Closely associated is the question as to whether the demand for automobiles and housing will be sustained sufficiently to permit maintenance of current high levels of output. And then there is the stock market, where the rate of climb of prices and credit caused eyebrows to be lifted when its speculative possibilities attracted the attention not only of businessmen but of those less sophisticated.

Offsetting Strength

To offset such potential danger spots are certain strengths for which we should be grateful. One important factor making for stability is business optimism tempered by prudence. Such optimism is evidenced by eagerness to take advantage of expanding markets by large-scale investment in fixed capital. At the same time, however, many businessmen have tended to be wary of speculative over-commitments. Those executives who were active during the thirties do not have to be reminded of depression worries, such as inventory losses, shortages of cash, inability to provide employment, inability to pay dividends, and the threat of failure. Such awareness, combined with greater economic information, adds to our business security and stability. The lessons driven deeply into the consciousness of older executives still provide an effective brake on speculative ebullience. Nevertheless, many executive jobs are now held by those who have reached posts of responsibility in recent times when orders have been obtainable with ease and profitability has been taken for granted. In general, the last decade and a half has been characterized by expanding volume in which private buying was supplemented by heavy governmental spending, and by credit that was adequate for the needs of an expanding economy. Only occasionally during this period has it been necessary for firms to stress rigorous cost reduction. It may be timely, therefore, for each company to take a fresh look at the return obtained from the

dollars of out-go. If laxity in spending has developed, the sooner such
waste is stopped, the more certain is the firm to remain competitive
without drastic retrenchment at a later time when collective retrenchment would only accelerate the forces of recession. The time to fix the
roof is when the sun is shining.

While they continue to enjoy the bounty of prosperity, company
executives may deem it wise to keep watching cash position. To maintain its strength diminishes immediate earnings perhaps, but so does
insurance of any kind. An appropriately liquid condition provides a
buffer for the shocks of bad times; protection against bad luck or mis-
calculation. It permits decisions to be based on what is best for the
company and those dependent upon it. A management short of cash
finds its decisions dictated by necessity; it cannot be as mindful as it
would like of the needs of its employees, customers, suppliers and investors.

The problem, of course, is how to balance insufficient protection
against too much; to achieve a proper balance between caution and
daring, between conserving and expanding, between the safety of a
strong cash position and the growth that borrowing makes possible.
One is reminded of the retort made by a manufacturer to a visitor who
remarked during a plant inspection that the host's plant did not appear up-to-date: "Come into the office, then, and look at the strength
of my cash account." They may have both been wrong.

Proper balance requires that we not be overly cautious when times
are bad, nor overly optimistic, to the point of imprudence, when they
are good. By and large those who are best equipped to achieve this
nice balance between too little risk and too much are those who
are intimately acquainted with the affairs of an enterprise. Knowing
the company's history as well as its secret strengths and weaknesses,
they are in a favorable position to judge what policies to adopt.

The problem is how to keep economic growth so orderly that industry and commerce can provide increased jobs, goods and services,
without the interruptions that accompany violent dips. Steady, consistent progress calls for decisions of the best quality that business
executives can make. Their decisions, if sound, will do much to
lengthen the period of prosperity that the country is now enjoying. As
Dr. Winfield Riefler has remarked: "A business situation is no better
than the quality of the decisions that businessmen make."

14 Small Business and Depression*

By ROBERT V. ROOSA

SEVERAL recent articles have offered a number of suggestions for improving small business management and for preparing businesses of larger size to face depression.[1] In view of the fact that small businesses are particularly vulnerable during periods of stormy economic weather, it seems desirable to examine the particular weaknesses revealed by their experience in the last big depression. To this end I should like to review very briefly the records of those small businesses which applied for emergency aid under the industrial loan program of the Federal Reserve Bank of New York during the 1930's.

The industrial loan program of the Federal Reserve Banks (commonly referred to as the 13b program) was instituted by an act of Congress in June 1934. Because the legislation permitted only working capital loans, the Reserve Banks discouraged applications from small businesses whose only need was for equity capital or from those requiring machinery and equipment rather than operating balances. Most of the small businesses that did come to the Reserve Banks applied for loans during the first year following the Congressional action, while the Reconstruction Finance Corporation was operating under a similar Congressional directive. As the gradual expanding of RFC powers began in 1935, and as general economic conditions began to improve, the industrial loan program of the Reserve Banks gradually passed out of the picture except for a short flurry of activity at the time of the 1937 recession.

---

* Reprinted from *Harvard Business Review*, 26 (January 1948), 58-62, by permission of the editor of *Harvard Business Review*.

[1] For example, Myles L. Mace, "Management Assistance for Small Business," *Harvard Business Review*, Autumn 1947, p. 587, and James C. Olson, "Is Your Company Prepared for Rough Weather?" *Harvard Business Review*, Autumn 1947, p. 595; and see also Richard L. Rosenthal, "R for Smaller Business," *Harvard Business Review*, Autumn 1945, p. 22.

Despite these limitations the more than 1,300 relatively small concerns whose applications were formally processed by the New York Federal Reserve Bank during this period provide a fruitful record of the depression experience of small business. Because the investigation of each concern was extended as far back as the early 1920's, wherever circumstances permitted, much of the flavor of small business operations during a whole "boom and bust" period can be recaptured by such a study.

No attempt will be made in this article to summarize the operating records of the applicant companies. What follows instead is a summary of the qualitative weaknesses revealed by these individual cases.

Uneven Quality of Management

Unevenness in the quality of management, as among the technical, the financial, the sales promotion, and the internal accounting aspects of business operation, was the outstanding common characteristic of the applicant concerns. Under the increased competition of a depression period, the specialization developed among large enterprises had burdened the small business entrepreneur with a need for highly developed skills of many kinds. The fact that most small businesses, whether in manufacturing or in trade, ordinarily relied on an individualized market was not in itself sufficient protection against the competition of mass production, mass selling, mass purchasing, and large-scale financing once depression began. The small businessman, especially during a period of declining total sales throughout the economy, had to be extremely competent in all aspects of his enterprise if he were to survive.

The typical small business born during prosperous years earned good profits by providing a limited type of service, or by serving a limited neighborhood market, which the larger concerns could not be "geared down" to furnish, or to serve, in as satisfactory a manner. Specialty lines and personalized relationships counted for much less, however, under depression conditions when every purchaser was eliminating niceties in order to satisfy only his minimum requirements. Thus the small business in depression could no longer make ends meet without introducing internal control over its costs, or without a sales promotion plan comparable in quality to the usually high quality of its technical skill, or without systematic planning of its cash requirements and disbursements. Almost universally, the applicants had succeeded as small businesses during the 1920's because they possessed one kind of management skill to a high degree, while their competence in other aspects was inferior.

None of the applicants could have survived through four years of depression, prior to their first making application under the 13b program, without having made considerable improvement at their weakest spots. The unbalance in management among the applicants was not, therefore, of the most extreme variety which had already caused the disappearance of many concerns before 1934. Except in some instances of "second or third generationism," where a son or grandson had only recently inherited a small business built up around the founder, all of the applicants demonstrated a minimum competence in most aspects of management.

Among manufacturing concerns, particularly those in the metal and metal products group, the most usual case was that of the highly skilled mechanic or engineer who had commenced his own business in order to realize on excellent technical innovations of his own, but who had little use for accounting or financial administration. Most concerns in wholesale and retail trade were similarly skilled in their knowledge of product quality, and a majority were highly competent in selling; but they, too, were impatient with systematic accounting. Many did not even hire an accountant to prepare annual statements.

There was great resistance among concerns of all types to a systematic checking of inventory turnover or analysis of receivables. To a large extent, of course, this resistance could be justified on the ground that long experience had given these businessmen a sense of the type and volume of inventory they ought to have, and a simple check of the dust on the cartons indicated whether items were moving with sufficient rapidity. Receivables, they felt, required little if any analysis because in most cases the management was personally acquainted with its customers.

But when depression came and competition increased, this lack of systematic accounting and inventory control put these small businesses at a grave disadvantage. It meant, for example, that an undue reliance was placed by management on the recollection of events from year to year. Memory often proved a poor substitute for detailed records in forward planning. An alert accounting sense among someone in management, or the advice of a trained accountant, was also needed to prevent involvement in bad receivables. Usually the business which prepared incomplete reports of its own operations did not obtain reports from its customers or, when it did, failed to understand them.

Small Business "Personality"

In large degree it was the very tradition of individual freedom which attracts men into small business that accounted for the obstinacy of managements in resisting the need for systematizing (and paying closer attention to) the "uninteresting" sides of their businesses. Frequently in all industries there was, for example, a stubborn defiance of the bank which attempted to point out needed improvements in the control of inventory, receivables, or the cash flow. There was a feeling that it was a sufficient indignity to be required to submit to the bank an annual balance sheet, with a three-item or four-item summary of operating results.

There was very little attempt to understand the purpose which banks had in mind in searching out operating details. Had there been such an awareness, many of these small businesses would have improved their borrowing potential in depression by voluntarily keeping their banks fully informed during prosperity. Instead, so long as favorable profits were being earned, the smaller business often relied on the fact that its payments on borrowings were met regularly to excuse it from permitting creditors any further insight into the nature of the business.

Another type of weakness, the correction of which called for much more self-control and insight than perhaps should be expected from anyone, was the tendency to dissipate profits as they were earned. It was a corollary of this dissipation of profits during prosperity that substantial entrepreneurial withdrawals often continued in the face of unprofitable operations during depression. While bank and trade credit continued easy, most smaller concerns were content to use it to the full. The contacts thus gained with creditors were of course useful during depression, but the advantage of such contacts could have been retained while devoting a larger share of earnings during prosperous years to the speedy retirement of debt as equity was enlarged.

With many notable exceptions, most of the applicants had not realized during properous times that their profits were much more subject to fluctuation than those of larger concerns. What their circumstances probably required was a puritanical abstinence, at the expense of curtailing the owner's personal standard of living, in order to build both liquid assets and equity for the event of depression. What happened in fact was that most of the individual owner-managers let out their belts while profits kept coming in. Many of them were ambitious in expanding their interests outside the business. In at least half of the cases considered by the New York Reserve Bank, management had succumbed to the temptation of broadening its influence and raising its prestige by "getting into real estate" during the 1920's. A substantial further number had drawn heavily on their concerns to permit stock market speculations, or investments in other businesses, which had become valueless by 1934. Liquid assets other than cash held by the concerns themselves, however, were never significant. While customarily at least half of the medium-size and large corporations set aside such reserves, fewer than one in twenty-five of the applicants had ever made such provision.

In a number of situations there had always been an intermingling of business and personal affairs; each was allowed to lean heavily on the other. Thus, the business was a source of cash and of credit standing for use in acquiring outside properties during good times, and was a source of cash to meet the resulting contractual obligations in good times and bad. On the other hand, when the business had become extremely shaky as depression continued, a surprisingly large number of managements brought back personal real estate into their business balance sheets in order to indicate a stronger net worth position to satisfy their creditors. Such increases were of course largely fictitious, since they consisted of the difference between purchase price and the outstanding mortgage on property which could usually not be disposed of for much more than the value of the mortgage itself at the time of the transfer.

Thus the typical small business was indeed in a paradoxical position. The rigors of depression required a much higher degree of competence in all aspects of management within the range of activities covered by the business itself. The principals in the business, however, often not only had failed to develop their competence in the lines along which management was weakest, but had also spread themselves even further into real estate or other businesses for which they often had less training and competence than for their own enterprises. Certainly one of the outstanding difficulties of small business management revealed by this depression experience was the failure of the principals to impose upon themselves a rigid self-discipline during prosperity, confining their interests to the growing complexities of meeting competition in their own business.

Effect of Smallness Itself

There was another side to the problems of small business which was perhaps inherently beyond the control of individual managements. No matter how difficult the forecasting of future trends might be for the larger concern, it was necessarily more difficult for the small concern to foresee probable developments in the markets for its raw materials as well as for its product. This was not merely a matter of being unable to calculate the likelihood of price changes or of major shifts in demand. Many small businessmen were simply unaware of alternative types of raw materials, or of new production methods, or of existing demands for new types of product. They frequently placed themselves in a vulnerable position by depending almost entirely on one specialized product or on one large customer. There was need for a conscious recognition at all times of the advantage in diversifying sales among various customers and of developing a versatility in manufacturing or handling other products than the one upon which a concern might currently depend for its success.

As a matter of fact the wartime procurement program, when emphasis came to be placed on the increased participation of small manufacturers, performed one of its greatest functions by counteracting the inborn myopia of smaller businesses, acquainting them as it did with the types of work there were to be done and with the many alternative materials available for turning out given products. Many of the companies applying for loans under the 13b program during the depression of the 1930's were groping about for lack of outside assistance of a similar type. It was typical, for example, among smaller manufacturers who had acquired their place in the field by producing stylized lines, that they should turn to producing lower grade standardized products when depression reduced their usual type of sales. Few of them recognized that little relief would be forthcoming from an attempt to enter fields already filled by large-scale producers. When they shifted to low-price lines, their high standards of workmanship refused to react and costs remained relatively high, so that the death of many small manufacturing companies was hastened rather than prevented by their decision to make the most obvious shift in type of product. On the other hand, those few that found new and unusual products which continued the use of their individualized skills generally fared much better even though gross sales might not have been nearly so large as those of companies which were failing.

This simple illustration relates only to adaptations in product; it was repeated in many forms among small businesses of many types but by no means exhausts the variety of forms in which the lack of knowledge inherent in smallness produced hardship during the depression. For example, the greatest difficulty lay in forecasting sales for the type of product in which the concern had long specialized. Even after four years of depression the applicants coming into the Reserve Bank were full of optimism concerning their own prospects. While the optimism itself was desirable, and greatly at variance with the traditional view of many economists that business pessimism had precipitated a contraction far greater than events themselves would have warranted, the characteristic overestimate of sales by small businesses prevented that scaling down in costs required for breakeven operations. Similarly, in a number of instances smaller businesses were unaware of the forces operating in the markets for their raw materials. Oftentimes the satisfaction at being able to arrange continued lines with trade creditors was so great that heavy purchases were made in advance of price declines, which larger concerns in the same industry were able to anticipate.

Thus a number of the characteristics of smallness in business operated with particularly destructive effect under depression conditions. Some of these characteristic weaknesses were largely the counterparts of smallness itself. Undoubtedly there was a chronic unevenness in the quality of small business management as among the various types of skill required for the fully balanced operation of a successful concern over the entire course of the business cycle. Few small businesses can, while remaining small, acquire the many-sided specialized skills found in large concerns. But that should be unnecessary. The strength of small business lies in its ability to fit local or individualized needs. Given that strength, survival through depression does not require exact imitation of large business, but rather the correction of a few outstanding weaknesses. Most of these weaknesses, if recognized in time, should be susceptible to a significant measure of self-correction.

III. MANAGEMENT ACTION IN SPECIFIC AREAS

15 Industrial Research: Geniuses Now Welcome*

By Francis Bello

Over the last several years a number of admonitory voices (including *Fortune's*) have been raised in alarm at the apparent unwillingness of industry to support a significant volume of basic and long-range scientific research. The critics usually have noted that only two business organizations—Bell Telephone Laboratories and General Electric—have distinguished themselves by a diligent pursuit of fundamental knowledge. Sometimes bows have also been made in the direction of Eastman Kodak, du Pont, and two or three of the large drug firms. Last January the critics were joined by Alfred P. Sloan, Jr., distinguished chairman of the board of General Motors, who observed: "We are not doing the basic research we ought to do in support of our applied research and our advanced engineering." Subsequently, Mr. and Mrs. Sloan gave the Alfred P. Sloan Foundation $5 million to establish the Fund for Basic Research in the Physical Sciences, which will be used primarily to aid outstanding university scientists.

Stung perhaps by the criticism, many industrial research directors are taking a fresh look at their operations. They are questioning not only their strength in basic research, but also size of budget, project-selection methods, and personnel policies. Some are even discovering that creativity of research men can be stimulated by ingenious and readily applied techniques. But perhaps the biggest news of the last nine months has been the determination of three of the nation's large business firms to give their corporate research efforts a more exploratory twist. To achieve this, General Motors, General Dynamics, and

* Reprinted by special permission of the editors from the January 1956 issue of *Fortune;* copyright 1956, by Time, Inc.

Avco Manufacturing have recently employed four high-ranking physicists. A fourth firm, Glenn L. Martin, has gone still further by establishing a new subsidiary, RIAS, Inc., "devoted exclusively to the discovery of new scientific knowledge beyond product application." One of its first objectives: to make a thorough restudy of gravity. RIAS (which stands for Research Institute for Advanced Study) will operate on the premise that fundamental research can be fostered by the same management techniques Martin has applied successfully to creative engineering of advanced aircraft.

The thinking that impelled these four great firms to seek more fundamental knowledge is reflected, on a smaller scale, in several other recent moves in industry:

Chrysler has disclosed that its new $1-billion expansion program includes substantial funds for increased research, to include "nuclear energy, electronics, and the application of solar energy."

For Ford a $150-million Engineering and Research Center is under construction at Dearborn. When finished it will house, among other activities, Ford's young Scientific Laboratory, which is also looking into atomic and solar energy.

Curtiss-Wright recently dedicated a new laboratory for advanced research and development on a secluded 52,000-acre site at Quehanna, in central Pennsylvania.

Republic Aviation has announced it is putting $12 million into expansion of research and development facilities, including a new supersonic wind tunnel. Last July, Republic named the noted scientist, Dr. Theodore Theodorsen, former chief of physical research for the National Advisory Committee for Aeronautics, as director of scientific research.

Procter & Gamble has recently expanded its basic research facilities 40 per cent to learn more about such things as skin physiology and the physical properties of human hair.

In countless other laboratories, research directors are sensing that empirical and closely applied research no longer provide an adequate foundation for a healthy business technology. "We have to work on the frontiers of science," says Augustus Kinzel, the eminent metallurgist recently elected vice president for research in Union Carbide & Carbon Corp., "if only to be able to appraise the work of others. No company can hope to make all the discoveries, but if we are up on fundamentals we can quickly evaluate work done elsewhere and take whatever steps may be necessary."

These recent developments do not mean, of course, that all research directors have altered their outlook in response to outside criticism. There are still a good many laboratories where signs might well be posted: "No geniuses wanted." One research director professes to see nothing in the G. E. Research Laboratory worth emulating. "I hear," he remarks, "that G. E.'s scientists are just a big headache. In our industry (petroleum) major advances take millions of man-hours of team work. A lone individual can do very little." Like many another research head he gives as much weight to a new applicant's extracurricular interests—to see if he can get along on a team—as to his scholastic record. Nevertheless, many big laboratories seem to be developing more flexibility in accommodating unusual personalities.

Competition Everywhere

The fresh reappraisal of research may have been inspired more by new competitive conditions than by outside criticism. In the chemical industry the traditional leaders are being challenged by such firms as: Celanese, Olin Mathieson, W. R. Grace, Food Machinery, Reichhold, Koppers, and Spencer Chemical. Several petroleum companies, alone or in joint ventures, have also pushed energetically into petrochemicals and plastics. In pharmaceuticals, the established houses have met sharp new competition from Chas. Pfizer & Co., Smith, Kline & French Laboratories, Warner-Lambert, and others. In electronics, old-line specialty firms such as I.B.M. and newly merged Sperry Rand are heavily absorbed in wide-ranging research; and newcomers such as Consolidated Electrodynamics, Ramo-Wooldridge, Beckman Instruments, General Mills, and Texas Instruments are crowding the leaders in ingenuity and technical strength. In atomic energy, the big electrical manufacturers are experiencing vigorous competition from Babcock & Wilcox, Foster Wheeler, and Combustion Engineering. One small eight-year-old firm, Nuclear Development Corp. of America, White Plains, New York—partly financed by Laurance and David Rockefeller —has assembled a group of physicists and nuclear engineers that rank with the finest anywhere. One aircraft firm, North American Aviation, has moved boldly into both nuclear energy and electronics. The catalogue of new corporate ambitions and rivalries could be extended further.

The sharpening of competition has been accompanied by a swift expansion of industrial research and development. According to the National Research Council, over 4,000 business firms now maintain research laboratories. A previous, though less extensive, survey indicated there were fewer than 3,000 industrial laboratories in 1950. Over the same period, the total industrial expenditure on R. and D. has climbed from about $1.2 billion to perhaps $2.5 billion. When government money (much of it spent in private laboratories) is included, the comparative figures show a jump from $2.2 billion in 1950 to something over $4.5 billion last year.

Still more striking figures portraying long-term trends were recently compiled by Raymond H. Ewell, a student of chemical economics who is on leave to the National Science Foundation from Stanford Research Institute. He estimates that from its earliest days through 1954 the U. S. spent a total of $39 billion on research and development. Nearly $17 billion, or 45 per cent of the total, was spent in the five years 1950-54. Ewell's figures show that R. and D. have been growing at an average rate of 10 per cent per year since 1910, compared to 3 per cent per year for gross national product. He estimates that the R. and D. outlay ten years from now will approach $7 billion a year.

With staffs limited by the shortage of trained workers, research directors are restudying their programs and looking for new tools that may increase the effectiveness of their laboratories. One trend is to "deglamorize" research. "We're really just another operating department," says E. Duer Reeves, executive vice president of Esso Research (R. and D. budget: $30 million), "except our job is to turn out a product called technology. The product is worth no more than it can be bought for on the open market. If our own laboratories can't produce technology at a lower cost than outside research organizations, our operating divisions will go outside for research. I think, however, we can make it profitable for the divisions to keep buying from us."

Like several other groups, Esso is doing "research on research," looking for systematic ways to hold creativity and performance at a high level. G. E., in doing similar "research," discovered that when it expanded one of its departments 50 per cent in size in one year, productivity dropped alarmingly as the old hands were diverted to breaking in the new. G. E. now knows about how fast it can expand and still maintain a flow of ideas.

Computers and new instruments are speeding technical advances on every front. A technique called statistical design of experiments—which can be traced to Sir Ronald A. Fisher's pioneer work in the mid-Twenties—also promises to be a big saver of time and money. By statistical design it is possible to state in advance exactly what type and volume of information will yield significant results when new processes are studied in pilot-plant scale. In the past, pilot plants—which are among the most costly research tools—have often been operated in catchall fashion with more data being collected than necessary.

What is Research Worth?

Unlike its corporate parent, the research laboratory cannot draw up an objective profit-and-loss statement to evaluate its performance. Research directors now recognize that it means little to say that x per cent of their companies' sales came from products that were unknown ten or fifteen years ago. Too many factors beyond research enter into the successful launching of a new product. Production, marketing, and advertising departments all make important contributions; and without money to finance it the new product would remain on the laboratory shelf.

Despite the difficulty of evaluating research results in detail, the gross return to the economy seems to be immense. Just how immense was recently estimated by Ewell. While disclaiming rigorous accuracy for his figures, he calculates: (a) that research may have contributed "at least 0.5 per cent and more likely 1.0 per cent or more" to the long-term U. S. productivity increase of 2.1 per cent per year; (b) that the research conducted between 1928 and 1953 probably contributed $40 billion to $80 billion to the 1953 G. N. P. of $365 billion. From the latter figure he calculates that for the economy as a whole, research expenditures have paid off at an annual rate of 100 to 200 per cent, on the average, over the twenty-five-year period. "It seems likely," concludes Ewell, "that basic research, in which we put 5 to 6 per cent of the total R. and D. investment, has the highest economic payoff in any area of research, although this is a very difficult proposition to prove."

Some top managements still speak as if stockholders had deep-seated misgivings about the money that goes into research. Why this myth persists is difficult to discern, for the Wall Street analysts, who do so much to shape stockholder attitudes, have made "research" and "growth" almost inseparable concepts. Indeed, more than one executive probably has been pressured into fudging his firm's R. and D. outlay in a luncheon speech before the powerful analysts.

Nevertheless, there are still many substantial business firms in the food, oil, metals, paper, and rubber industries that do no significant amount of research, even though they rank among the 500 largest corporations in the U. S.[1] Presumably the opportunities—and even the need—for research vary greatly among industries, and even among companies within a single industry.

For 1951 the Bureau of Labor Statistics showed the following industry research-and-development expenditures as a percentage of sales:

Aircraft and parts	12.7
Electric machinery	6.4
Instruments	6.4
Drugs	3.3
Chemicals	3.0
Motor vehicles and parts	1.2
Rubber	0.9
Fabricated metals	0.9
Petroleum	0.6
Paper	0.5
Primary metals	0.4
Food	0.3

The figures include government contributions, which finance about 85 per cent of aircraft R. and D., and roughly half of that in electric machinery and instruments. Nevertheless, in 1951 the biggest private R. and D. spender was electric machinery, which spent over $180 million of its own money. Second-biggest spender was the chemical industry with some $120 million. In a survey made for this article, twenty-nine firms (drugs, chemicals, and electronics and instruments) reported the following changes in their R. and D. expenditures, as per cent of sales, between 1946 and the present:

	1946	1955
Electronics, instruments (8 firms)	3.3	5.0
Drugs (7 firms)	3.4	4.4
Chemicals (14 firms)	3.0	3.5

The actual R. and D. outlay in dollars for the companies surveyed rose from $65 million in 1946 to some $265 million in 1955. (The firms vary greatly in size, representing a rough cross section of each industry.)

---

[1] To rank in the top 500, a company had to have sales, in 1954, in excess of $49,700,000.

When asked to indicate how their present R. and D. expenditures were divided among "oriented research" (projects aimed at fairly well-defined goals), "exploratory research" (a broad search in areas of possible interest), and "basic research" (increasing the store of fundamental knowledge), research directors answered:

	Oriented	Explor.	Basic
Electronics, instruments (8 firms) ..	80%	18%	2%
Drugs (7 firms)	75	20	5
Chemicals (14 firms)	80	16	4

They were then asked to check which types of research were "getting significantly more attention (i.e., money) than five years ago" —with this result:

	Oriented	Explor.	Basic
Electronics, instruments	1 firm	5 firms	3 firms
Drugs	1	1	0
Chemicals	2	11	5

It would probably be a mistake to press these responses too far, for most companies say it is difficult to distinguish between "exploratory" and "basic" research. Bell Telephone Laboratories distinguishes only between "research" and "development," with the difference being solely one of motive. "If the work is directed toward understanding," says Bell's Executive Vice President James B. Fisk, "it's called research. If it's directed toward making a new device, it's called development."

General Electric, after a three-year struggle with definitions, has come up with these classifications: "basic research," defined as a search for new knowledge *in advance of* specific need; "applied research," a search for new knowledge *for* specific need; and "development," application of *existing* knowledge for specific need.

Oddly, research directors are not very articulate in explaining why one industry finds it profitable to spend a lot on research and another does not. However, Esso's E. Duer Reeves, who is president of the Industrial Research Institute—an organization of about 275 research managers—sums up as follows: "What you spend for research depends largely on what business you are in, what your competitors are doing, the money available for research, and the attitudes of top management. Moreover, the ability of a company to absorb research varies all over the lot. Exploitation of research usually requires a lot of capital, plus an organization willing and able to market the new development. It is certainly possible to do too much research."

How Much Should You Spend?

Virtually all research directors agree that expressing R. and D. dollars as a per cent of sales often leads to meaningless comparisons. It would perhaps be unreasonable to expect General Motors to spend 3 per cent—or $300 million—of its $9.8 billion sales (1954) on R. and D. Actually, G. M. professes not to know exactly what it spends in all its divisions. The only figure it can readily provide is that it spent $12 million in 1954 in its Research Laboratory, which serves a central staff function. The $12 million is only a shade over 0.1 per cent of sales. Beyond that, G. M. may have spent anywhere from $50 million to $200 million on R. and D. in its divisions.

Huge outlays, however, may not be necessary for the achievement of important research advances. In 1954, Bell Telephone Laboratories spent a modest $23 million on research and fundamental development. It is with a budget of this general magnitude (representing about 0.5 per cent of the gross revenues of the Bell System) that Bell Labs has earned its great scientific reputation. To be sure, Bell Labs had a total budget of over $110 million in 1954, but most of this represented work for Western Electric and the U. S. Government.

Could Bell Labs profitably put more money into research? Executive Vice President Fisk replies: "More people have stubbed their toe on this question of how much to spend than on any question you can ask. I am afraid there just isn't any single answer. It involves a give and take of all kinds of forces. We like to feel there are many more things to work on than we can possibly get to. Selection then becomes an important part of the budget-making process."

G. E. spends an estimated $20 million in its Central Research Laboratory, and perhaps another $100 million or so in division labs. The total comes to about 4 per cent of sales ($3 billion in 1954). Says C. Guy Suits, vice president and director of research, "It's easy to justify what you are spending today in terms of what you spent yesterday. The real question is: how would you justify—objectively—what you are spending today if you had not previously been spending anything at all?" G. E. is grappling with this thorny question and believes it is making progress. G. E. lists its products, the raw materials that go into them, and the technologies behind the raw materials. Then it tries to decide how many specialists it ought to have doing research in each of the technological areas. The method is still crude, but G. E. finds it helpful.

Maurice Holland, an independent consultant and a close adviser to many companies on research policies, contends that research is the best insurance a company can buy; accordingly, he believes the R. and D. budget should be at least as large as all of a company's insurance premiums on plant and people. He finds that insurance premiums usually amount to 1 per cent or 1.5 per cent of net worth. In any case, he regards net worth as a better guide to size of research budget than sales.

Can Formulas Help?

In choosing among potential research projects many companies naturally try to estimate the potential market for an envisioned product. They also make a rough guess at development costs, to see if the game is worth the candle.

While this procedure sounds eminently sensible, it has drawbacks. Merck (R. and D. budget: $7 million plus) points out that it couldn't have justified its synthesis of cortisone on the basis of such a procedure. "Nose and judgment are the thing," says Max Tishler, scientific director of Merck's chemical division. "If there were a formula for these things, you wouldn't need a research director."

Union Carbide (R. and D. budget: $40 million) takes an equally harsh view of formulas. Says Research Vice President Kinzel: "Formulas are not only *not* helpful, they can send you off on the wrong track. They're all based on assumptions reflecting today's conditions. There's hardly a research project on our list that you couldn't knock out on the basis of present sales prospects."

How Many Labs and Where?

Granted a willingness to conduct research, the question next arises: should any research be done centrally, and if so how much? There are also questions of optimum laboratory size and location.

Du Pont (R. and D. budget: $66 million) feels strongly that each of its divisions should have a laboratory close to one or more of its manufacturing plants. Since du Pont also believes in doing central research, removed from plant pressures, it has in recent years spent $40 million expanding its Experimental Station near Wilmington. Here du Pont quarters its so-called Chemical (i.e., central research) Department as well as Engineering Research and strong research detachments from the ten operating departments. In this way du Pont believes it achieves a happy blend of business and campus atmosphere.

Like du Pont, General Electric heavily supports both divisional and central research facilities. G. E. assigns to central research, in Schenectady, chiefly those scientific inquiries that may benefit several product lines—or no immediately discernible line.

By contrast, Union Carbide, the No. 2 ranking chemical company, has strong reservations about centralized research. In the past few years, however, it has set up an annual corporate research fund, which a central committee may spend in any of thirteen divisional labs. Dr. Kinzel considers a large central laboratory undesirable because it would be inaccessible to many of his company's far-flung divisions. He also believes that when a laboratory houses many more than 500 people (of whom one-third will normally be professionals), the lab director loses intimate touch with his staff's personal problems, and performance suffers.

A third arrangement, used by Bell Labs, is essentially all central research. Bell conducts over one-third of its $110-million-plus R. and D. effort under one roof at Murray Hill, New Jersey, where it houses some 3,500 of its 9,500 people (about one-third professionals). Most of the remainder are at nearby Whippany, or in Manhattan.

The search for stimulating research environments has led several firms to establish laboratories outside the country. Union Carbide has set up a working arrangement with European Research Associates (present staff: about fifty) in Brussels. R. C. A. has a modest-sized laboratory in Zurich. And I. B. M. is just starting a Zurich lab, headed by a young Swiss who has instructions to bring in top scientists from all over Europe. Says William W. McDowell, I. B. M.'s vice president for engineering and research: "For reasons difficult to define, Europeans have an approach different from that in the U. S. We decided we wanted in on it early."

Laboratories: Loose vs. Tight

Perhaps the biggest disagreement among research directors is over how actually to conduct research: whether to follow the loose, individualistic, university tradition, or to organize things in a more closely managed fashion, which usually implies heavy emphasis on the team approach. (Teams may vary in size from a few workers to scores of men.)

Eastman Kodak (R. and D. budget: $35 million) is an outstanding example of a company that has been highly successful with an informal organization. "Frankly," says Cyril Staud, Kodak's research head, "we don't know specifically quite what we're going to accomplish in 1956. In fact, we are hoping for discoveries which will introduce new projects we cannot foresee right now. Progress depends on new ideas. When they are scarce in one field, we turn to another."

At the opposite pole from Kodak in research philosophy stands the aircraft industry. Virtually all aircraft R. and D. is on a strict project basis, complete with detailed forecasts of cost and manpower requirements. This does not mean, however, that all the technology is waiting, ready to be put together. "We have to bet a little ahead of the known technology," says George Trimble, youthful vice president in charge of engineering for Glenn L. Martin. "We gamble that certain inventions will be ready in time. If we just pasted together what we already knew, no one would buy it. One of our department rules is that we are responsible for inventing solutions to problems."

Martin feels it has learned a good deal about organizing people to make inventions to order. One trick is to refrain from settling for the first solutions proposed to any problem. Says Trimble: "It's a good idea to set the goal at least 20 per cent higher than what seems attainable at first."

The skeptic may argue that the quality of research and invention achieved by such methods must be in some sense inferior to that achieved under more leisurely circumstances. If the skeptic tries to specify quality of invention by insisting that it represent something really new in the world—he can, of course, rule out a new airplane that is merely faster than a previous airplane. But what about an artificial satellite? It will surely meet the definition. Martin can confound the skeptic by pointing out that it has the responsibility for building the device that will put the first satellite into its orbit, and that it expects to do the job—on schedule—in less time and with substantially fewer men than it takes to produce a new military aircraft.

How to Keep Them Happy

The shortage of top-flight scientists and engineers has placed a high premium on keeping them happy once hired. Good salaries alone are not enough. The best labs have dozens of scientists who presumably could step into very highly paid jobs elsewhere—and from time to time, a few do. (Example: William Shockley, famed transistor expert, who recently left Bell Labs to join Beckman Instruments.) But the great majority like to stay where they can work on challenging problems, publish freely, and enjoy the intellectual stimulation provided by outstanding colleagues.

In their large central labs, Bell and G. E. have built up intellectual communities that are extraordinarily attractive to the superior scientist. One countermeasure successfully used by I. B. M. (R. and D. budget: $14 million) has been to house a modest advanced-research group in its Watson Laboratory, strategically located near Columbia University. There I. B. M.'s scientists can associate informally with their academic peers.

Virtually all laboratories have now learned that there must be "two roads up" for the researcher, meaning that he can hope to make about as much money staying at the bench as his colleague who moves over into administration. In the large electronics and chemical firms, "bench" scientists in their early forties may expect to earn $15,000 to $25,000 per year—to which some firms add bonuses. (Drug-industry salaries seem to be confined to the low end of this range.) Even so, an administrative post carries status in the community that is not yet equaled by such contrived titles as Senior Research Associate. "What we are looking for is a non-administrative rank that will carry the prestige of Professor," says one pharmaceutical research head.

Can Creativity be Taught?

Research directors suspect that if their staffs are happy they will be creative. Meanwhile, there is widespread interest in techniques designed to increase creativity—and even to teach it to the non-creative.

The two men who have probably done the most to formulate special techniques are Alex F. Osborn, board vice chairman of the advertising firm of Batten, Barton, Durstine & Osborn, and Professor John E. Arnold, who heads M. I. T.'s Creative Engineering Laboratory. Osborn is the great exponent of "brainstorming," which he introduced to the advertising business in 1938. In brainstorming, six to twelve persons compete in trying to suggest as many solutions to a problem as possible, regardless of apparent merit. Says Osborn: "We tend to impede our fluency of ideas by applying our critical power too soon."

One way Professor Arnold tries to stimulate creativity is to have students design sundry mechanisms to fit the needs of an imaginary race of people—of unusual physiology and limitations—who dwell on a mythical planet (Arcturus IV) that has an atmosphere, gravity, and other conditions wholly unlike those of earth. Fittingly, one of the first descriptions of Arnold's course appeared in *Astounding Science Fiction*. The course has been extremely well received by industry and Arnold has been in heavy demand as a consultant.

One firm that has consulted extensively with Arnold is the AC Spark Plug division of G. M. AC was dismayed recently when it gave its engineers a battery of creativity tests and discovered that 20 to 50 per cent of them scored wretchedly. In discussing this experience last November before the American Society of Mechanical Engineers, J. A. Anderson, general manager of AC, suggested bluntly that the low scorers must have got their jobs "by accident, by friendship, by the wrong analyses of their own capabilities, and have managed to hang on through average performance, or ability to sell themselves."

With Arnold's help, AC set up a creativity training program, which has now been given to about 600 engineers. When retested after the course, the engineers have shown a striking improvement in ability to produce ideas. The least creative group seems to benefit most from the course.

One research director who finds Arnold's ideas "very stimulating and clever," believes that Osborn's brainstorming is superficial, "perhaps all right for the advertising business." Says another: "I am inclined to doubt creativity can be educated. Perhaps you can bring out what is latent, but more often creativity is squelched by organization policies."

The Persuasive New Recruiters

One of the toughest of all research-management problems in this time of acute shortages of trained manpower is to set up a new laboratory from scratch. Three large companies—Avco, General Dynamics, and Glenn L. Martin—are now absorbed in this difficult task. Here is how they are going about it:

Avco Manufacturing. An organization with sales of $375 million in 1954, Avco has four manufacturing divisions: Crosley and Bendix Home Appliances (radio, TV, and appliances), American Kitchens (cabinets and sinks), New Idea (farm implements), and Lycoming (aircraft engines and parts). To make technical sense of this heterogeneous family, Victor Emanuel—Avco chairman and president—last spring brought in Emanuel R. Piore from the Office of Naval Research. The two agreed on the importance of establishing a new research group outside the existing divisions, to be called the Advanced Development Division. The work done in this new division is, for the present, entirely government sponsored and is presumed to concern guided missiles. Much of the work, however, is sufficiently fundamental to allow Piore to attract what he calls "university types." Says Piore: "The only way you can get them is to present them with really challenging problems. They will also provide intellectual leadership for the engineers more strictly concerned with development. Our problem will be to keep feeding the scientists enough good problems to keep them happy."

General Dynamics. Guided by energetic John Jay Hopkins, G. D. now has five divisions: Electric Boat (submarines), Electro Dynamic (electric motors), Convair (aircraft), Stromberg-Carlson (electronics), and General Atomic. It is G. A. that is setting up a new organization and a new laboratory. To do this dual job, Hopkins has employed as vice president of G. D. and general manager of G. A., Frederic de Hoffmann, who worked closely with Edward Teller on the H-bomb and with Hans Bethe of Cornell on meson theory. Born in Vienna in 1924, de Hoffmann has been involved in nuclear research ever since he was assigned to Los Alamos when he was only nineteen. Says he: "In the lab we'll be as free and easy as a university. In recruiting people for research I tell them to join us and help determine the specifics of our program. Most university scientists are so suspicious of industry they think I'm kidding."

Last month, de Hoffmann named as research director of General Atomic Edward C. Creutz, forty-two, previously head of the Nuclear Research Center at Carnegie Institute of Technology. De Hoffmann has also lined up a number of top-flight senior scientists to serve as close consultants, among them Teller (University of California), Bethe, and John Wheeler, the distinguished Princeton physicist.

De Hoffmann believes his new laboratory can make a contribution by recapturing the atmosphere of a university as it used to exist, "where scientists worked on problems just because they were interesting. Today, everyone wants to work in the fashionable fields. The game is to do research fast and publish first. I think there are many good neglected problems that need solving—and the solutions would benefit our organization."

Glenn L. Martin. Concerned about its long-range future, Martin last year set up the Research Institute for Advanced Study, an organization designed to do strictly fundamental research under business auspices. RIAS was conceived by Martin's V. P. George Trimble. Its manager is

Welcome W. Bender, an aeronautical engineer who has come up through the Martin organization.

Martin intends that the great bulk of RIAS's work should be basic research sponsored by the government, though Martin will provide a laboratory building with its own funds and support the work of perhaps thirty or forty scientists. Martin has a hunch that the methods it has found effective in motivating engineers should also be effective in stimulating scientists. "Naturally," says Bender, "we aren't going to push people around. But we think we can create the type of environment which will make academic researchers want to work hard. And, of course, we'll have to limit our interests. We'll be more interested in the properties of the ionosphere than in those of the ocean bottom. Let's just say we have a yen to try this thing and not try to rationalize further." One thing of particular interest to RIAS is gravity and—if anyone has any ideas—anti-gravity schemes. Says Bender: "We don't say we're going to negate gravity, we just want to find out more about it."

Even before establishing RIAS, Martin had contracted with twenty-two outstanding German scientists for papers in their various specialties. From Eugene Saenger, famed theorist on astronautics, it is buying a dissertation called "Study of Photon Jet Power Plants for Rocket Propulsion," which will discuss the feasibility of using radiant energy to power outer-space craft. From the distinguished theoretical physicist Pascual Jordan it has bought a study entitled "Mathematical Improvement of General Relativity Theory."

How Rare is Creativity?

One way or another, all research directors are attempting to buy creativity, and even to buy it on schedule. The attempt may seem to flout the traditional concept of creativity as something that must flower spontaneously in its own good time. But is this really the way of creativity? An impressive number of the world's greatest statues, paintings, plays, and musical compositions have been produced to order, and often to meet an imperative deadline. Nor is there necessarily a preordained number of people who may be creative in any given field. In a recent article in *Scientific Monthly,* Sidney L. Pressey, professor of psychology at Ohio State University, contends that Haydn, Mozart, Chopin, Liszt, and many other prodigies were stimulated to eminence largely because serious music enjoyed a tremendous vogue in eighteenth and nineteenth-century Europe. (Also they were obliged to study hard.)

If U. S. industrial laboratories are genuinely seeking high creativity—not merely gadgeteering—they should have no great difficulty obtaining it. There is, happily, much evidence that industry is more determined than ever before to explore the challenging—and profitable —unknown.

16 Product Planning*

By CHARLES H. KLINE

PRODUCT planning, as a specialized function of management, is a relatively new concept in industry. While some planning of products has always been carried on in industry, the function has generally been scattered throughout sales and research management. In order to ensure that product decisions are reached only after careful consideration of all business factors, progressive companies today are beginning to center responsibility for the overall analysis of product problems in specific individuals. In large companies where there are a number of different product lines, each with its own sales manager and separate sales force, the product planner is generally on the central marketing staff and usually reports directly to the chief sales or marketing executive. In smaller companies the line sales manager himself may carry out the product planning program, alone or with a staff assistant.

The basic objective in any product planning program, regardless of size of company or type of organization, is to provide continual analysis and advance planning of the product line. Among the important elements of the program are the following:

1. Establishing profit standards as a guide to product decisions.

2. Establishing and maintaining a sound product policy.

3. Analyzing existing products to determine which should be dropped and which expanded.

4. Simplifying product lines by reducing the number of grades, sizes, models, colors or other varieties.

5. Controlling the volume of small orders by establishing suitable pricing and packaging practices.

* Reprinted from *Advanced Management*, 13 (March 1953), 10-14, by permission of the editor of *Advanced Management*.

6. Establishing methods to improve the development and introduction of new products.

7. Analyzing new areas of product development.

Standards of Profitability

In many companies insufficient emphasis is placed on profit standards as a means of guiding product decisions. Most businesses appraise profitability simply on the basis of margins on sales. Gross margins in particular are very deceptive, since comparisons based on them assume a uniform selling and administrative expense for all products—a situation often very far from the facts. Net margins are somewhat better measures, since they do take into account sales and general expenses. Neither gross nor net margins, however, consider turnover, the ratio of sales to invested capital.

The most appropriate measure of profitability is the percentage net return on investment. This is the ratio of net profit to total investment—the value of the land, buildings and equipment (preferably at first cost) and the inventories, receivables and cash required to produce a given product. The return on investment is a measure of the efficiency of use of facilities. Oftentimes it gives a much different picture than the margins on sales. In one company, for example, there were ten products, and most effort and attention were given to Product A because its net margin (before taxes) of 27% was the highest in the company. Actually, there were five other products which, although their net margins ranged only from 23% to 11%, still showed a more satisfactory net return on investment. Net return (before taxes) on total investment for these products ranged from 54% to 25%, while the favored Product A returned only 23%. In this case misdirected effort arising from the use of a faulty profit standard undoubtedly cost the company a considerable loss in total profit.

The principal use of profit standards, of course, is in allocating funds to various projects. Here one company requires that the following minimum standards be met:

	Net return (after taxes) on investment
Labor-saving devices	10%
New products	18%
Process improvements on old products	25%

This company is interested, first, in reducing the direct labor content of its present products; second, in developing new products; and third, in improving its existing manufacturing processes. Different emphasis could, of course, be given to these activities simply by changing the required return.

Product Policy

A product policy expresses the long-range strategy of a business. It answers the question, "What general type of product can this company make and sell most efficiently?" In other words, a product policy is a statement of a company's reason for existence in the economy.

A good product policy capitalizes on the special strengths and resources of a company and avoids its weaknesses. For example, if a company is large, has strong financial backing and extensive research facilities, it is admirably suited to the development of highly technical products requiring large research and engineering staffs and heavy expenditures. On the other hand, such a company is generally much too slow in decision-making and too cumbersome in action to engage successfully in the manufacture of fashion goods. Here financial requirements are lower, large size is not desirable and extensive research facilities are unnecessary. The real needs in this latter type of business are anticipation of styles, quick decision-making and fast action, and for these a small tightly-knit organization is generally best.

Every company must develop its own product policy on an individual basis. The number of different, but equally successful strategies is fairly large. All policies, however, must consider the following points:

1. Desirable level of investment.
2. Desirable level of sales.
3. Area in which the company is technically most competent.
4. Types of product the company is best equipped to manufacture.
5. Types of product the company is best equipped to distribute.
6. Desirability of patent protection.
7. Preferred types and sources of raw materials.
8. Desirability of mass production or small-volume specialty production.

The product policy should be stated in writing and widely circulated so that it can be used to direct the efforts of all personnel towards the same business objectives. A sound policy, well expressed and well taught to all members of management, makes for a more decisive, more alert and faster-acting organization. It is especially important to explain the policy carefully to the product research and development department. Here the product policy serves as a guide both to the individual researcher in the conception of new research projects and to the research management in the initial screening of proposed projects.

The product policy also provides a set of objective criteria to assess the relative desirability of alternate products or research projects. Such assessments are often necessary when a limited amount of manpower or capital must be allocated to several different products, and when there are too many uncertainties or not enough data to make a comparison strictly on the basis of profitability. To simplify comparisons, some companies express their statement of policy in terms of a numerical scoring procedure, so that an approximate measure of the product desirability can be expressed as a single number.

Similarly the product policy is often useful in the analysis of products with an unsatisfactory record of sales and profit. It is frequently difficult at first glance to determine whether such products are basically unsuited to a company's operations or whether they are merely suffering from faulty organization, insufficient effort or poor management. A statement of policy provides a framework for the business analysis of each product and a set of criteria for judging its suitability. This use is discussed in the following section.

Existing Product Line

In many companies the development of product lines has been very haphazard. New products have been introduced as the opportunity arose or the needs of the moment required. The successful ones have generally received close attention from management, but the less successful have often survived from year to year through sheer inertia. Sometimes too many unrelated products have been introduced, or obsolescent products have been continued too long. In all these cases there is usually a natural reluctance in the sales force to drop any item that contributes to total sales volume.

An important phase of any product planning program is a thorough analysis of all suspect items in the line. Products definitely unsuited to the company's operation should be dropped or sold as going businesses. One company with annual dollar sales in the middle eight figures eliminated in three years 16 different products with total sales of several million dollars—nearly ten per cent of its total volume. Nevertheless, over this three-year period the company's total sales increased by roughly half and its net profits by some 20 times. Of course, these spectacular results were due to a number of factors, principally an improvement in general business conditions in this period. The company management has stated, however, that it believes an important part of the improvement arose from the elimination of the discarded products, several of which had been unprofitable and all of which had diverted the efforts of management and workers alike from the company's main products.

A number of the products eliminated in this case were sold or transferred to other companies better suited to handle them. Investment in inventories and equipment was thus recovered, and, in addition, moderate royalties were received. In one case royalty income over the five years after sale was considerably greater than the estimated net profit that would have been realized if the company had retained the product.

Although this product review made a sizeable reduction in the company's product line, its basic aim was not to eliminate products but to improve overall operations. In several other products analyzed in this same program, the company assigned additional personnel to technical or market development, installed new production equipment or adopted new policies to increase sales. The net result of the whole program was the concentration of more effort on all products with any real promise.

Simplification

In most companies each product is offered in a number of different grades, sizes, colors or other varieties. The number of individual items handled is often very large. One manufacturer of semi-finished industrial materials recently found to his horror that it was possible to order from his catalog some 43,000 different standard varieties of his products. A concerted drive to concentrate effort on fewer items led to some startling reductions, as shown in the following figures:

Percentage reduction	Product	Number of grades, sizes and colors	
		Old	New
96	Fabricated specialty	734	28
76	Maintenance and service items	51	12
67	Processed material	3	1
39	Semiprocessed material	75	46

In this company most of the eliminations or consolidations of grades were readily agreed to by engineering, manufacturing and sales as soon as the facts were developed. This company, however, had been using an outmoded system of manual accounting that made no record of sales by item so that there had been no way of knowing at any one time just how many items were actually being sold. The introduction of automatic accounting machines made possible regular monthly reports of sales by item. These were analyzed periodically by the sales manager, production manager, technical director and accountant for each line, and the sales manager was authorized to make the necessary deletions. The reports of sales by item also served as a basis for compiling for the first time an accurate master list of authorized products and grades. This list was revised every six months and analyzed periodically for trends in the expansion or reduction of the overall line.

Control of Order Size

The problem of small orders, often filled at a loss, is always a difficult one. On a typical small order the clerical, accounting and handling charges often run higher than the gross margin realized. Where a company does its entire business in small orders, it can organize all its distribution and clerical procedures specifically to handle such items. The simplified methods required often involve some risk of loss, but since the orders are small, the actual cash loss is slight. A more serious case arises when a company basically organized to handle a relatively small number of large orders also attempts to process a large number of small orders. The careful procedures and safeguards necessary for the large orders are far too costly for the small.

An example of this problem is shown in Figure 1, which analyzes

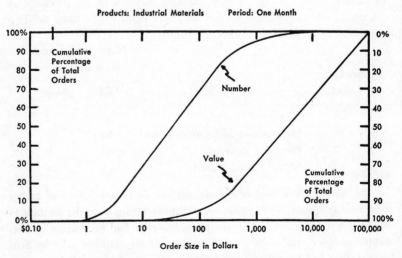

FIGURE 1—ANALYSIS OF ORDER SIZE

sales by order size for an actual group of products for one month. Total sales of the product group in this month were approximately $500,000, and there were in all about 600 orders. Only 5% of the total number of orders received exceeded $1,000, but these orders accounted for 69% of total sales. Similarly the 31% of all orders over $100 in value accounted for 95% of all sales. On the other end of the scale, 29% of all orders were for amounts of ten dollars or less, but these contributed much less than 1% of total sales. Even the 69% of all orders of $100 or less in value amounted to only 5% of all sales.

The manufacturer here was attempting to be a mass producer, a specialty producer and a retail distributor all under the same roof. Profits, however, came only from the mass production and sale of a few large-volume items. The solution in this particular case was the institution of standard packages, the contents of which had minimum values of 20 to 40 dollars. This one step reduced the volume of incoming orders by nearly half. In other situations minimum order limits and, in custom-made lines, service charges on orders below a certain value are used to control the size and volume of orders.

The policy on small orders will obviously vary from product to product. In new products in particular small orders are necessary to develop the business. Limitations imposed on older products must not be allowed to impair the success of development programs by restricting the sale or gift of sample quantities.

Control of Product Line

The three preceding sections have dealt chiefly with means of improving existing product lines. Although analytical reviews of existing products and programs to reduce the number of grades, sizes and colors in a line are periodically necessary, these steps are essentially repair work to rectify mistakes of the past. The creative aspect of product planning lies in shaping the future. One of the most important steps in preparing a company for the future is to ensure a continuing flow of new products for the future.

The history of product development in many companies has not been entirely satisfactory. Sometimes laboratory groups have scattered their efforts by attempting to carry on too many unrelated developments at once. In small companies where technical service work in support of sales and the development of basically new products are carried on in the same group, there has occasionally been an unwise distribution of laboratory effort between the two functions. Most serious of all, there has often been poor coordination between laboratory and engineering groups on the one hand and sales and manufacturing on the other, so that many promising developments have failed through lack of a complete, well directed and properly timed program of commercial development.

The improvement of these conditions is partly a matter of training and partly a matter of formal control procedures. As to training, the product planner should make sure that all sales and development personnel understand the company's product policy, its profit standards and its strategic aims as a business. Where research scientists and development engineers are encouraged to think of their work in terms of general business requirements and overall company policy, there will often be a surprising increase in enthusiasm and morale and an amazing outpouring of new ideas and new product developments. Ivory towers are not particularly fertile; the laboratory must be an integral part of the *business* organization it serves.

As to procedure, a product planning program must provide a workable system for the control and coordination of development activity. This requires listing and defining the various phases of a complete development program and assigning specific responsibility for each phase to a particular individual in the company. The scheme employed by one manufacturer of industrial goods is shown in simplified form in Figure 2. Control was achieved through the use of two forms, the first authorizing development work and the second authorizing the introduction of the new product. Each of these control forms provided space for a marketing analysis, a technical analysis and a manufacturing analysis of the proposed product. In this particular business the sales manager had primary responsibility for the overall development program, but the specific approval of the technical director and production manager were also required on both forms. This company had but one laboratory to work both on research and development and on trouble-shooting, product improvement and technical service to sales. Provision was made for proper distribution of effort between long-range development and short-range laboratory services by a system of budgetary control.

At first there was considerable fear in this company that the control procedure would stifle development work. In practice, however, these fears proved unfounded, and it was later generally agreed that the procedure was a real aid to the development program. Differences of opinion were brought out early on any project, and decisions were made more quickly by management. Fewer projects were started, but a higher percentage were carried on to the successful introduction of new products.

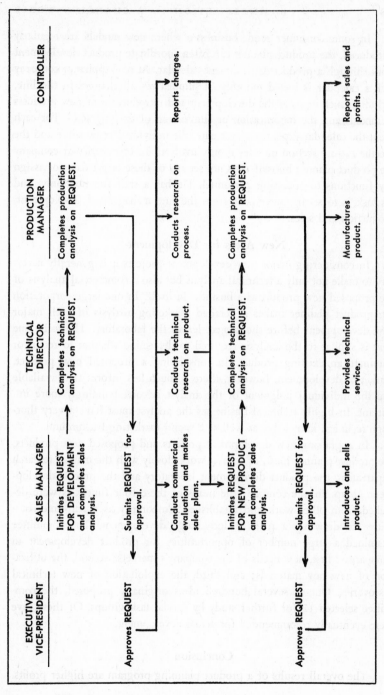

FIGURE 2—PRODUCT DEVELOPMENT PROCEDURE

In some consumer-goods businesses where new models are regularly introduced, the product planner can often coordinate product development work through a product development calendar. At one appliance company such a calendar is issued monthly. It summarizes all changes in the line, including such items as the development and introduction of new products or models and the modification or elimination of existing ones. For each event the calendar gives the target date, the individual responsible and the specific factory section or sales group involved. In this particular company the product planner himself does not set any of these target dates or assign any functions to operating personnel. He has a staff function only, and his task is to secure agreement from the line managers of development, production and sales.

New Areas for Development

In considering major new development projects it is generally necessary to make not only a technical analysis but also a commercial analysis of the proposed new product as a business in itself. In one large corporation the product planner makes a detailed marketing analysis of each major new development before the project leaves the laboratory. The technique here is similar to the analysis required to determine whether to retain or eliminate an existing product. In considering a proposed new product, market or development, however, there is much less information available and the individual judgment of the analyst is correspondingly more important. In highly technical businesses the analyst must have a very thorough technical knowledge as well as a sound marketing background.

In appraising new development projects and proposed new products, the product planner must, of course, work closely with the market research department, the product development laboratory and the process development group. In one company the heads of these four functions were detached from other work and established temporarily as a full-time committee to draw up a plan of long-range development. The committee examined a large number of opportunities for product development in three areas: first, new needs of the company's markets; second, the utilization of new raw materials; and third, the exploitation of new technical discoveries. Out of several hundred ideas originally proposed, the committee selected 12 for further study by special task groups. Of these, five were eventually recommended for actual development.

Conclusion

The overall results of a product planning program are higher profits.

Companies with such programs believe that they make an immediate contribution to profits in clearing away marginal products, small orders and excessive product varieties. The major contribution of product planning, however, is the guidance of product development through the establishment of profit standards and product policy and through careful control of the development program. Sound planning over the years results in the more rapid and more successful introduction of new products and builds a more profitable product structure for the future.

17 Conditions of Marketing Leadership*

By ARTHUR P. FELTON

A TREMENDOUS number of companies are experiencing marketing difficulties these days. Businessmen know this. Consultants are made keenly aware of it because so many of the problems management gives them are marketing problems. Many consumers do not need to be told that companies have troubles in this area, for they have been on the "receiving end" of them—service difficulties, for instance.

But as we look ahead, the prospect is that business will have even more marketing difficulties next year, more still five or ten years from now. For technological progress is still outstripping marketing progress, and the peculiar nature of technological progress today is making the marketing job harder.

Take automation, for example. As James R. Bright recently pointed out in discussing its impact on management: "The marketing man is going to have to be *very* right or else he may have nothing to eat but a stream of unsalable products."[1] Indeed, in the years ahead we will probably see marketing become a more challenging problem than it has ever been in our industrial history, even though over-all sales volume continues to increase. It will be easier to make things but not to sell them.

It is quite true, of course, that marketing is not standing still. We have come out of the doldrums of the 1940's. Companies are experimenting with new methods and techniques—motivation research, better sales training, various kinds of market audits, and so forth. However, none of them offers anything in the way of a *basic* solution to the marketing prob-

* Reprinted from *Harvard Business Review*, 34 (March-April 1956), 117-127, by permission of the editor of *Harvard Business Review*.
[1] James R. Bright, "Thinking Ahead (Some Effects of Automation)," *Harvard Business Review*, November-December 1955, p. 27.

lem. None of them would relieve the real difficulties which so many companies are getting themselves into today, although they might prove very useful once other steps are taken.

Three Essentials

Judging by the experience of a wide range of companies with all sorts of marketing problems, there are three essential conditions of marketing leadership—and they are becoming increasingly important:

(1) Top management must recognize that the nature of the marketing problem is fundamentally different from the nature of the production problem. This fact has vital implications for (a) executive selection, (b) marketing strategy, and (c) sales organization. Failure to take the differences into account has got countless companies into serious trouble.

(2) Management must recognize the dynamic quality of the marketing problem—the constant change which is continually taking place not only in the market but also in channels to the market. The change is so continuous and so widespread that it makes every sales plan in the country out of date to some extent. Failure to grasp this point, perhaps more than anything else, has kept companies from getting *out* of sales trouble when they might otherwise have succeeded.

(3) The crying need in marketing management today is for greater conceptual skill—the ability to see the enterprise as a whole and to understand how the various functions of the company and its sales organization depend on one another.[2] The specialists who devise techniques and conduct studies have been "going to town," but the general managers have not.

The tendency has been to think in terms of formulas such as "working back from the market" or in terms of a particular group such as the distributors, rather than to consider all parts of the marketing problem in relation to each other *and to the rest of the company*—for example, executive resources, productive capacity, and procurement.

The aim of this article is to describe the nature of these conditions in more detail and show how they can be met.

Marketing vs. Production

How do companies get into marketing difficulties? In all the cases with which my associates and I are familiar, ranging from small companies in the paper industry to large companies in the steel industry, certain causes keep recurring with almost demoniacal frequency.

One such cause is the failure to recognize that marketing calls for a different executive temperament than does production. A factory-trained

---

[2] See Robert L. Katz, "Skills of an Effective Administrator," *Harvard Business Review,* January-February 1955, p. 33.

executive usually follows a logical line of reasoning that works best in factual situations. By contrast, sales executives must often think with only intangibles as a guide. In general, they are not accustomed to a clinical or analytical approach. Although successful sales executives are practical men, with push and drive to get things done, they typically count more on an intuitive feel for situations than do executives in other departments.

The rules that work in selling are just not the same, in letter or in spirit, as the rules that work in other business areas. It is in companies where this fact is not appreciated that we often find production and financial influence to be greater than marketing influence. Sooner or later that situation usually leads to poor or unprofitable sales, large pile-ups of obsolete inventories, and high administrative overhead.

In addition, the physical aspects of a marketing problem are different in many respects from the physical aspects of a production problem. The four walls of the plant may bound a problem in manufacturing but scarcely ever do they confine a problem in marketing. Machines, materials, and skilled men are the usual elements of a production problem; but the uncertain attitudes of distant consumers or industrial buyers may dominate the marketing problem. There are not as many facts and figures in marketing as in production.

Moreover, the data that do exist are not so easily controllable, nor can they be checked so easily. Perhaps more important, it has not been customary for marketing men to make the best use of their data; the sales executive works in the midst of quite different currents of thinking than does the factory superintendent or industrial engineer who works in a tradition of scientific management and careful methodology.

Red Flags

When management fails to recognize the important differences between marketing and production, and particularly when the production influence becomes stronger than the marketing influence, telltale symptoms of "production-mindedness" soon become evident. Here are a few of them:

1. *Designing in isolation*—There may be a tendency to believe that a couple of smart people can design products and packages in a sheltered laboratory, run as a wing of the production facilities—without regard to the often-learned lesson that the artists and designers can and should be supplied with market facts. For all their ability, the creative geniuses cannot insure acceptance by consumers or industrial buyers unless they take into account people's habits, motives, and feelings.

2. *Avoidance of consumer research*—Attitudes about consumer research are an especially sensitive indicator in industries which are several steps away

from the consumer, and in which it might seem plausible for manufacturers to leave it up to retailers, wholesalers, and jobbers to learn what their customers want and to pass this information back. In fact, this attitude was once prevalent in virtually all industries producing primary goods, but some of them—notably steel, asphalt, and chemicals—have now come to the conclusion that distributors either will not or cannot do the job for them, and so they have gone into basic market research themselves. They reason that if their customers down the line do not sell end products, they will not buy raw materials.

However, not all such industries have come around to this point of view. The textile industry is a well-known example. There is some well-informed opinion to the effect that textiles would not have run into so much trouble in the postwar years if they had not taken a "let-George-do-it" policy about consumer research.[3]

3. *Misdirected advertising*—Too much production influence in the company's marketing effort usually shows up in advertising copy. Is it aimed at the industrial buyer or consumer, whichever the case may be, or does it glorify the company's research and engineering effort? Compare automobile advertising, generally a good example, with textile advertising, all too often a bad one. The automobile ads aim to make last year's model obsolete in the consumer's eye; by contrast, during the recent "battle of the fibers" the manufacturers of wool, cotton, and man-made fibers, instead of trying to make wardrobes seem obsolete, vied with claims of longevity and durability.

4. *Inadequate market investment*—Another symptom is insignificant expenditures for developing consumer markets in comparison with tremendous sums spent on research, cost reduction, and new plant and equipment. Thus, when the can makers first attempted to get the public to use beer in cans rather than bottles, they spent huge sums developing the can but left it up to the brewers to do the selling job—and no progress was made. It was only when a leading beer-can manufacturer stepped heavily into consumer promotion based on preference studies that buying habits were revolutionized.

Perhaps what all this adds up to is a plea for taking a fresh look at the complexities of marketing. One who goes from company to company and from industry to industry working on marketing problems is continually impressed—or, more accurately, appalled—by the tendency among executives everywhere to simplify, to reduce to rules, or (using one of their favorite terms) to try to "engineer" a sales program. This is nearly always fatal. Systematic thinking—yes. Efforts to analyze a problem—yes. But the attempt to apply to marketing what has worked in production (or, for that matter, in finance)—no.

Why should management underrate and belittle its job? Marketing is an area for awe and wonder. It is full of questions, unsolved problems, and baffling inconsistencies. It is dominated by the whims of consumers and the fancies of buyers. When management recognizes marketing for

---

[3] See the editorial in *America's Textile Reporter,* June 24, 1954.

what it is and then proceeds to try to master it, the credit for a job well done is the greater because the job is more difficult.

Change & Counterchange

There is probably no marketing plan in industry today that is not out-of-date. This may seem like a startling statement, but we actually have not been able to find any exception to it. The reason is that there are so many constantly changing factors in any company's marketing situation that it is practically impossible to keep revising a plan so rapidly and so accurately that there is no lag in it. The factors that keep a plan dated are not only those of the "changing American market" which *Fortune* and other publications have discussed—suburbia, the new middle class, the Negro market, etc.[4] The dating factors have also to do with changing selling problems growing out of the major upheavals—shifts in consumer psychology that necessitate different kinds of advertising and packaging, trends in distribution that affect the company's relations with wholesalers and jobbers, changes in the "customer mix" that affect the efficiency of the sales organization, and so on.

The practical significance of the foregoing is that if management does not have a carefully thought-out marketing plan, or has a program based on insufficient facts, or—worse yet—has no real plan at all, the company's selling effort may fall dangerously out of phase with the times and may precipitate a company crisis. What are the most important steps management can take so that this will not happen?

Long-Range Objectives

The keystone of a strong marketing plan—the part of the program on which all the others depend—is a long-range objective. It is difficult to overemphasize the importance of this cardinal principle. Many companies find themselves in the position of not knowing where they are going and of having only vague ideas as to how to get anywhere. These companies rock along from month to month taking expedient action for each problem. The sales department consequently rides from one crisis to another—and nothing is done to determine the underlying reasons for the crises.

Why does all this happen in the absence of objectives? The reason

---

[4] The Editors of Fortune, *The Changing American Market* (Garden City, N. Y., Hanover House, 1955); see also Pierre Martineau, "It's Time to Research the Consumer," *Harvard Business Review*, July-August 1955, p. 45.

is largely human nature, and especially "executive nature." Managers are opportunistic, and unless counteracted their opportunism tends to dominate decision making. Sales managers and salesmen seek to capitalize on short-run deals and on tempting but (as it so often turns out) only transient markets. Before long the sales organization is confused and unwieldy; the company is committed to too many projects, many of them fast becoming abortive; and production costs are rising because production is spread too thin or becomes out of balance. In effect, there is wasted effort in sales, which causes wasted effort in other departments of the company. The sales managers call louder, "Let's get out and make calls, men," and the men spin their wheels doing it. To illustrate:

A manufacturing company that had specialized for 45 years in the production of certain kinds of engine parts began losing business when its jobbers began turning to competitors offering wider lines. (Also, a competitor had found a way to make one of the parts automatically.)

Without formulating a long-range sales plan, management began a vigorous search for business in other lines. Orders were approved for many items which the company had not made before; if the new business looked profitable, and if production could find some way to get it out, the customer's order was solicited. In effect, the company tried to be all things to all people. However, it turned out that the plant was not equipped to make many of the new lines well or cheaply enough. Both production and sales costs rose to dangerous levels.

In reorganizing the strategy of this company, the emphasis was put on concentration. What sections of the market was the company best equipped to sell to? What specific objectives in certain areas could the sales force best be set up to reach? Only when a marketing plan with long-range objectives was developed in such a manner could the company move back into a strong profit position.

Here it is important to stress that objectives can be stated in more ways than in terms of sales volume. For example, management's No. 1 objective may be to become the *quality* leader in its field—and advertising copy, public relations, and the selection of new business may be governed by that criterion. (A management pursuing this kind of an objective knows full well, of course, that sales will eventually follow a reputation for quality; at the same time, the marketing history of such a company will develop quite differently from that of the company which sets as its objective becoming the leader in *sales volume*.) Objectives can also be translated into specific tactics. To illustrate:

Last year it was announced that Indian Head Mills would spend $300,000 to advertise a tablecloth-making project, urging people to go to their neighborhood stores and request two yards of Indian Head's fabric. While management expected to sell enough fabric to justify the cost of the campaign, and accordingly set quotas high enough to do so, the objective was not just to sell tablecloth fabric. Management's main purpose was to solidify Indian Head's leadership in textile merchandising, in this case by initiating the largest single promotional campaign in piece-goods history.

In addition, management knew that the campaign would sharpen up the "pitch" of company salesmen; they could refer to the numbers of people going into stores to request Indian Head and capitalize on the story to sell industrial buyers. In short, part of the objective was to gain dealer cooperation by a tie-in promotional campaign rather than to promote the company name through an institutional approach. This is the kind of shrewd tactic that only a management with its longer-range objectives clearly in mind is likely to seize upon.

Whatever its objectives, a management will probably want to set dollar-volume goals—for purposes of control, if nothing else. Progressive companies today are setting goals at least five years in advance and then programing sales objectives for each year. These objectives not only should be stated in total dollar sales and total unit sales but also should be subdivided by specific products and product groups—and even by number and type of distributors needed to achieve the objectives.

Why all this detail? One of the most important reasons has to do with changing market trends. Specific objectives make it possible to check the sales performance of each product (and distributor). A product's failure to live up to expectations may be a danger signal—the first sign that there are new consumer trends affecting design or general suitability, or the first sign that there are new selling problems with implications, say, for the sales or service organization. Maybe product B increased only 10% instead of 20%, but product C increased 30% against an expected 20%. In both cases, it is important to know why; "management by exception" should work both ways.

"Central Intelligence"

All of us are familiar with the hackneyed phrase, "Know your market." But we sometimes tend to think of the market only in the static terms of the dictionary sense of the word. "Market" should mean to us not only today's customers but tomorrow's and those we will have in 1960; not only today's price but also the likely price (and quality) four years from now; not only present methods of reaching customers but also the methods we will be using when current living and working *trends* become established *habits*.

It is because there are so many constantly changing factors in sales that market information is the problem that it is. Often management gets into trouble—or cannot get out of trouble—simply because of its data. The data are not accurate enough, timely enough, or well enough organized to allow executives to realize the full significance of changes which have occurred or are in the making. To illustrate:

The managers of a company making an automotive product received many reports each month on *total* sales of their own products and of automobiles. No direct action was ever taken on the basis of the reports, however, although they were read "with interest." Then management got the idea of making the reports specific and, more important, of showing the figures "in motion." New reports began going out revealing that within total car sales of all makes, sales of model X were holding their own, sales of model Y were decreasing, but sales of model Z were rising.

When the managers saw these consumer preference trends, they really sat up; Z was what their company was best equipped to manufacture parts for! Moreover, when price trends were portrayed, it appeared that the company could realistically shoot for a larger share of the market if the selling price could be reduced about 10%. Management cut its price on the basis of increased volume expectations and a determined cost-reduction program—and this turned out to be a very successful move.

Judging from industrial records and actual company case histories, it is hard to escape the conclusion that most firms do not know their market very well. Granted the data may not be hanging out in bunches ready to be plucked, but good market data can always be obtained. Often a rich source is government and trade association reports, and it is unfortunate that more managements do not take advantage of them.

For instance, a manufacturer of woolen goods who wants to size up the market for his fabric lines can use information compiled by the Department of Commerce, National Association of Wool Manufacturers, National Outerwear Association, Dun & Bradstreet, National Credit Office's Market Planning Service, Fairchild Publications, and several confidential trade sources. All of this material, except for the last, of course, is published.

Forecasts are another good example of market data relatively easy to get—in almost any industry. According to a recent Federal Reserve Board study, 437 trade associations provide some sort of economic or statistical information for their members; over 250 of these associations regularly assemble and disseminate information on the future prospects of the economy, the industry, or both.

More often the trouble is not so much lack of sources as lack of imagination and skill in the *use* of sources, including tests of the representativeness of samples and checkbacks of results against predictions. For example;

In the case of a firm making a product for interior decoration, an important factor in the market naturally was the number of interior decorators. In a market study, management turned to the Census, which indicated that there were some 1,300 interior decorators. According to this figure there was not a great deal of room for increasing sales of the present line, so the management, being aggressive, decided tentatively to branch into new product lines.

As subsequent events showed, this would have been a sad mistake. But, fortunately, the management did what few managements do: it had a more professional survey made. By just taking the further steps of checking the circulation data of an interior decorators' magazine, talking with an informed credit service, interviewing company salesmen, and making a spot mail survey, it was learned that there were actually *9,700* interior decorators and that they spent some $75 million a year for this product alone. The company's biggest and best market for expansion was the one it was already selling!

Distribution Trends

Nowhere is constant change a more important factor to watch than in a company's channels of distribution. These will be periodically reviewed by alert managements, and modern techniques of distribution cost analysis will be used to aid in making policy decisions. Sometimes new trends will operate in the company's favor, sometimes not; but always there are in the making trends which do affect sales and profits, and because it is impossible to keep any plan completely in pace with them, it is never correct to say that "our marketing effort is more than 90% efficient." To mention just a few of the possibilities for change:

(1) The company's market may be changing from a few relatively large customers in a concentrated area to several thousand smaller customers all over the country, with the result that the existing distributor setup is becoming less efficient. In one well-known company where this recently happened, the trend was so pronounced that it led to hundreds of thousands of dollars' worth of obsolete inventory, heavy markdowns, and a sharp increase in administrative overhead.

(2) Distributors' lack of merchandising ability may emerge as a decisive factor in the market. Television is a case in point. Last year over 7 million television sets were sold (7½ to 8 million according to one source); yet many manufacturers, notably medium-size firms, were forced out of business. The larger companies were able to spend a good deal on advertising and promotion, and some ten heavily advertised makes became well known to the public.

The key is the fact that the distributors were able to sell the well-known sets, but lacked the merchandising ability to push the lesser-known sets. With the "squeeze" on to sell, distributors concentrated on the big ten and left many other makers stranded. Significantly, some of the medium-size manufacturers did do well in certain localities where there happened to be a larger number of good distributors.

(3) Many progressive distributors, wholesalers, and retailers are tending to concentrate purchases with a few suppliers. For manufacturers dealing with

these outlets, the trend means that management must either offer a complete and well-promoted line or else risk having to turn to other—and probably less progressive—distributors.

Some sales executives have become so deeply involved with one method of distribution that they overlook the possibilities of other methods which, though once inappropriate, are now more closely attuned to the company's needs. Often the answer is not a single method but a combination of methods. Thus, one large manufacturing company that recently found it could no longer afford to service a large percentage of its retail accounts has turned away from tradition and carefully selected several distributors to handle a large volume of small repetitive orders at an attractive discount—and at lower cost to the manufacturer.

In fact many companies today are in a position to undertake what they might consider "radical" approaches to distribution. For some firms, such approaches might be house-to-house selling or direct selling by mail; for others, merchandising nonfood products through supermarkets, rack jobbing, or allowing supplementary sales organizations to sell the company's regular products under different brand names (a policy which, new studies show, may be more practical than many businessmen are inclined to think[5]).

Retailers, too, are looking for better selling techniques. One large chain of building-supply outlets has found that a self-service retail lumberyard offering a complete line of home-building and repair products direct to home owners can be quite successful under certain market conditions—another reflection of the do-it-yourself trend. It is too soon to pass judgment on many of the specific new approaches in marketing, but let us look at some of the *possibilities* which an imaginative executive group might consider:

(1) In most states of the South, school buying practices have forced publishers to centralize their warehousing operations in "book depositories." All public schools and other educational institutions order and receive from this one control point. The book depository performs all the functions of a wholesaler or a branch operation *except* owning and actually selling the merchandise; it receives and stores merchandise, controls the inventory, receives and processes orders, packs, ships, invoices, and collects.

Some alert manufacturers are considering an adaptation of the book-depository idea to their own needs, particularly where individual volume is not sufficient to warrant a branch warehousing operation. The obvious economies in paper work are supplemented greatly by economies in warehousing and

[5] See Ross M. Cunningham, "Brand Loyalty—What, Where, How Much?" *Harvard Business Review*, Jan.-Feb. 1956, p. 116.

handling. Much special-purpose equipment (lift trucks with special clamps, for instance) can be justified because of the greater volume. The manufacturer can reserve for himself any functions that he wishes (invoicing, for example, to keep prices confidential).

Small or medium-size manufacturers of appliances, automotive parts, and home furnishings might well look into this idea of specialized warehousing. Its main limitation is that it is not always easy to get together manufacturers of similar enough merchandise.

(2) There is, in many industries, an increasing trend toward the use of specialty jobbers. These jobbers, who are sometimes set up with the backing of a single manufacturer in the early stages, handle a narrow range of products —in some cases, the products of only one manufacturer. In one case, a midwestern manufacturer got, as a captive specialty jobber distributing its products exclusively, a man who had formerly distributed 4,500 items of 110 manufacturers.

More and more companies are becoming dissatisfied with the mediocre sales effort of distributors who are spread too thin. These companies are selecting the outstanding men with the important contacts and setting them up as specialists in their own territories. Granted, the specialty jobber will make a good living on perhaps just one account; but the manufacturer will benefit from the increased profits that will come from the intensified sales effort of a topnotch representative.

In some cases, management might find the answer it is looking for in specialized warehousing *and* specialized jobbing.

(3) Another interesting approach tried recently is the automobile supermarket. A large dealer in the Midwest is offering—for drive-away delivery— any model of any make of car, at bargain prices and with a full guarantee. With the increasing practice of preselling merchandise through national advertising and sales promotion, at least one school of thought believes that there is very little need for specialized sales training of retail personnel. It is felt that a large percentage of prospective customers have been sufficiently presold so that much "shopping" comes down principally to a comparison of quality and prices.

The automobile supermarket offers the buyer a chance to compare, at one location, all his alternative choices without visiting a myriad of showrooms. This is, in essence, an open-air discount house. The supermarket owner claims that his high turnover and low overhead justify his low prices, and his volume is so great that no manufacturer can afford not to sell to him.

Merchants experienced in selling reasonably high-price merchandise with a high gross margin might well consider applying the automobile supermarket principle to those of their own products which are presold at the national level.

Sales Organization

To a certain extent, every sales organization is created on the basis of the past experiences and prejudices of top officials. It has to be. But when these influences completely displace *analytical* judgments based on present-day market facts and anticipated future trends, the firm's marketing effort is almost certain to suffer. As selling conditions become more fluid in these years of a growing population, greater consumer spending power, and other "accelerators" of change, and as production tends to become more inflexible (at least on a short-term basis) because of automation, the importance of analytical judgments in organizing the sales effort will increase.

The unsound sales organization is commonly found in companies where it is headed by a sales manager who was hired from another industry in which he was successful. He tends to impose a similar plan of organization in his new surroundings, overlooking the fact that the former plan was for a different industry, different products, or different marketing conditions. Transplanting set ideas is not the answer to the problem of building a good sales organization.

Where the nature of the marketing problem is such that, say, quick decisions and specialized knowledge are needed, it would not be good to have a functional type of organization, however satisfactory for the company in times past or for other companies at present. On the other hand, it might be profitable, as a stimulus to constructive thinking, to look around at different ways of decentralizing sales responsibility. Here is an example of what can happen if sales management is not on its toes, and of what can be done when the danger is recognized before it is too late:

A New England manufacturer of a household product marketed through a variety of outlets—department, furniture, chain, and general stores, mail-order houses, club plans, and house-to-house agents. The product, slightly modified, was also sold to institutions, hotels, and motels. Over the years, the sales organization had grown here and there, this way and that, as expediency directed. There was one salesman who specialized in wholesalers, another who concentrated on all outlets in New York City, others who sold any and all accounts in stipulated territories. All salesmen reported directly to the sales manager, who also handled all "important" accounts personally.

One day, after 21 years on the job, the sales manager died. The department found itself in a crisis as it tried to carry on. However, its troubles were only symptomatic of a much deeper crisis which had been building up under the era of sloppy control of the deceased manager. For many years, unrecognized by the company, distribution methods and market conditions had been changing. Inevitably, creeping inefficiency had advanced to the point where there seemed to be nothing that the new sales manager could do *within the existing framework* to save the corporate neck. Sales were slipping, selling costs were mounting, and the sales manager himself had no time for policy thinking and forward planning.

When this situation became clear, the sales department was reorganized completely. The new setup provided for an office manager, a field sales manager, several staff directors, and a manager for advertising and merchandising, all with clear-cut responsibilities and authority; this relieved congestion at the top. As for the salesmen, their jobs were set on the basis of (a) territory and

(b) type of outlet. For instance, where in the same territory one salesman had been selling to retailers and another to wholesalers (with the result that in effect they had been fighting each other), now the salesman for a given territory sold to both types of customers. But where the outlet was a unique one requiring specialized merchandising methods, as in the case of institutional sales, the business wherever located was put in the charge of one salesman.

The results showed up almost immediately, with a rise in sales and a reversal of the selling cost trend.

Conceptual Approach

Whenever top management begins to get worried about the marketing outlook, it is only natural that slogans like "Think retail" and "No sale, no profit" gain appeal—especially if the company suddenly realizes that production, finance, and research have been playing too dominant a role. This is all very well. But suppose management carries its sales consciousness a good deal further; suppose it buys the view which holds, as one expert stated in a national magazine, that "today you start with the market—not the factory—as the base for your organization and then work back."[6] Is this bolder, more extreme position desirable in a competitive industry with a dynamic market?

At first glance, the answer might seem yes. And probably it *is* yes in certain cases—for example, a detergent soap or a ball-point pen may be purely a merchandising proposition. But in the great majority of cases the extreme point of view just described is a troublemaker. *Marketing cannot be effective if considered from a marketing point of view alone.*

For the marketing officer, this means continual compromise and negotiation with other departments of the company. These compromises—or, better, adjustments—will be less hard to take as he develops a company viewpoint and understands why they must be made. For the president or executive vice president, the proposition just described means that "coaching" all department heads in conceptual skill—the ability, as Robert L. Katz described it, to see the enterprise as a working whole—is one of the most effective ways of helping *any* department to be effective. The less the managers of any department, marketing included, have to battle narrow, specialist viewpoints, and can count instead on a *meeting of the minds* in top-level conferences (not necessarily agreement), the better off they will be.

Here are two examples of the conceptual approach applied at the interdepartmental level:

1. *Marketing and production*—From a market survey the sales manager

---

[6] *Business Week,* December 11, 1954, p. 67.

of a large midwestern company in the electrical industry learned that there was a substantial market for a new line of consumer products. The survey showed that the line should be offered in eight sizes, with a wide range between the two extremes. The sales department drew up tight and definite specifications for the manufacturing department. The engineers went over these specifications and determined that the products could be made as detailed—but at an extremely high cost.

At this critical point a serious impasse might easily have developed, as often happens. An impasse of sorts was in fact beginning to develop in this situation. It was broken in the only possible way—by informal talks between the persons at odds. The sales manager hinted that more automatic machinery might be the solution; the plant manager at first reacted negatively because he feared loss of flexibility, then thought it over and came back with the proposition that maybe it would be feasible if specifications were relaxed a little; the sales manager indicated he was willing to contemplate this possibility; and together they went to the engineers and found that by changing the design of some of the internal components and applying some automatic controls, costs could be cut 20%.

As a result, the company launched an entirely new line of products on the market. The price was competitive, and a good profit was earned.

2. *Marketing and top management*—Toward the end of World War II, an old, established New England manufacturer of fabricated metal parts looked ahead to postwar conditions and decided to market a line of consumer products to retail outlets. As plans for the new venture were developed, it became apparent that a large amount of imaginative promotion would be necessary through a wholly new type of sales organization.

One fact loomed ominously when a realistic appraisal of executive resources was made: the president was vigorous and healthy, but any abilities which the other managers (either relatives or stockholders) had in relation to their jobs were purely a matter of coincidence. Tests and interviews conducted by psychological experts showed that the managers had neither the experience nor the aptitude for manufacturing and selling high-volume, low-cost consumer products.

The upshot of all this was that the president reversed his earlier decision. The postwar marketing plans had to be tailored more to the management resources that were available.

Marketing Activities

Having looked at marketing's relationship to other parts of the company, let us now look at the relationships of different activities within the marketing effort itself. Here the contribution of conceptual thinking is as important as it is anywhere else.

Take motivation research, for example. It is one of the most interesting new ideas in the field. It has great possibilities. But its values must all be realized through the agencies that design, distribute, sell, and influence opinion. The buying decisions which a motivation study seeks to analyze are affected by the number and type of outlets; by the merchandising abilities of the dealers; by the freshness of the advertising copy, salesmanship, and public relations of the company (what consumers may read about it in the newspapers and see on television, etc.) ; and by other factors.

If marketing executives really want to capitalize on new findings about purchasing behavior, they will not merely revise product design *or* advertising *or* packaging in the light of what the researchers tell them—they will revise *all* of these activities to reinforce each other and have a total impact on sales greater than the sum of the individual contributions. Here is an illustration of the way conceptual thinking works at the intradepartmental level:

An appliance manufacturing company with a tough sales problem to lick made a survey of its dealers. The dealers were part of the problem because they were more interested in competitors' lines than in this manufacturer's. The survey showed that three product features would appeal to dealers: (a) superior quality, which would reduce service costs, typically borne by the dealer in this particular industry, (b) highly salable design, and (c) high price and high gross margin consistent with the quality features, giving dealers more flexibility on trade-ins.

In revamping its line of appliances, management naturally worked hard to please the consumer, but it also tried to please the dealer. Why design for consumers if dealers lacked an incentive to handle the line? This way of looking at the problem made quite a difference. For instance, the company had been manufacturing appliances in the low-price range; now it withdrew these models but extended its line in the medium-price and high-price ranges. In addition, one luxury model was added as a prestige item.

As a result of the new strategy, dealers began giving much more support to the company's products, and sales rose. Significantly, the most popular model in the line now sells for nearly twice as much as the lowest-price competitive model.

Summary Case

Now let us look at a case which ties together many of the ideas discussed in the preceding pages. It points up the "chain reaction" of questions that occur when conceptual thinking is used, the kinds of conflicts between points of view that arise, and, in short, what happens that is different when executives go at a marketing problem this way rather than some other way.

The Facts

The case involves an eastern manufacturer of a well-known staple product. (As far as the basic problems are concerned, the company might just as well have been a midwestern furniture manufacturer, a west coast lumber producer, or a southern plastics firm.) For our purposes, the story began several years ago when the management realized that its market was changing. Several important trends were seen to be in the making:

(1) The industrial market was becoming more important than the consumer market. Whereas two-thirds of the company's output had been going through wholesalers to retailers, and one-third to industrial users, it now looked as if the situation would completely reverse itself within another ten years.

(2) On the retail scene, independents were playing a less important role in the distribution of the product, and chains a more important role.

(3) Geographically the market was changing too. The consumer market, which bade to become less important, was growing faster in the plant's home territory. But the more important industrial market was expanding faster in an area 1,500 miles west (with an average annual growth trend projected at 3%).

(4) Transportation costs—in particular, freight rates—had been increasing, and it looked as if they would continue to increase.

Within Marketing

These trends posed a series of important questions for marketing executives:

First of all, *what about the company salesmen?* They had been selected and trained to sell to wholesalers; it appeared now that, if they were going to go after a bigger share of the growing industrial market, they would need to be well instructed in materials and materials handling, the problems of commercial users. Obviously, selection and training procedures would need revision.

But *would not the sales organization need to be changed too?* The existing system emphasized clearcut sales territories and strict "territorial protection" for the individual salesmen who called on jobbers and commercial dealers. Perhaps it would be better to organize a task force of industrial salesmen who would freewheel across the country showing prospects how to use and handle the company's product; or to reorganize sales into commercial and domestic divisions, with managers of each reporting to a senior manager who would not be bothered by individual salesmen's problems.

Then the question of supporting the direct sales effort with other efforts was raised. For example, *what about packaging?* As for retail sales, the important fact was that in chain supermarkets there was less personal selling in the stores and more impulse buying. Therefore, the traditional black and white package should take on a little color and eye appeal; and maybe the routine labels could be supplemented with some attractively printed information for consumers about uses of the product. As for commercial sales, it seemed desirable to explore new, improved means of bulk shipping.

But just what package designs and colors would be best? And what kinds of advertising appeals would add to the impression? These questions pointed to another, more basic one: *Was more market research needed?* Little had been done in the way of pretesting, motivation research, or "bird-dogging" market statistics.

And if greater efforts were made along this line, as well as in the areas of packaging, sales training, and organization, could they be managed efficiently? *Were existing controls adequate?* In particular, there seemed to be a need for getting the control data in such form that it would lend itself to better distribution cost analysis.

Beyond Marketing

So much for the "chain reaction" within the marketing department. Now let us look at some of the questions which were raised and disputed outside or beyond marketing.

Was plant expansion needed? The general manager, who had come up through engineering and manufacturing, presented a plan to the board of directors calling for a 50% increase in capacity at the eastern site—the maximum possible within the land and technological limitations. His plan was based on the fact that the company was currently operating at 105% of capacity, and that a 45% increase in the market was projected for the next ten years.

But another plan presented to the board took a more "marketing-minded" viewpoint. *Should a new factory of equal capacity be built in the area 1,500 miles west, where the booming industrial markets were centered?* The supporters of this plan pointed to the usual advantages of proximity to the market, and also to the savings in transportation of the finished product. They estimated that a $1,800,000 freight bill would have to be absorbed in five years if the proposed plant was not built (this figure would have been offset somewhat by the fact that new material freight costs would have been less at the eastern site).

When this plan was presented, some of the production men immediately pointed to problems. In the area of the proposed site, there was comparatively little skilled labor available, and it looked as if there would be "one hell of a training job." In addition, the area was heavily unionized. These were difficulties that had not been serious at the eastern plant. *Would new management skills in industrial engineering and industrial relations be needed—and just who was going to manage all this work?*

Still another viewpoint had to be considered. A good percentage of owners and board members were financial men. *Was the proposed second plant a sound enough investment?* Projected earnings showed that it would take nine or ten years for the new plant to equal the return on investment that could be achieved immediately if the eastern plant were expanded. Moreover, there was always the risk of a depression or of revolutionary new methods being developed in the industry.

So, *would it be better to expand on a more limited basis in the more mature, slow-growing eastern sector and capture larger short-range profits?* The younger executives in the firm took issue with this conservative view. They were more inclined to "grow with the economy." Their views were held in great importance by the board because both the first-line and second-line managers were older men nearing retirement age.

Further, the balance in capabilities of the present management was an issue if any kind of expansion was undertaken. The present managers were generally men who had been "pushers" in production (the firm was operating on a seven-day week, with three shifts a day) but with something of a laissez-faire attitude toward other areas of management—research and development, for example, and public relations. They had matured in an era when competition, while very much present, had never been dangerous. If the company bid for a greater share of the market, it seemed bound to run into much more vigorous competition than it had ever experienced before. *Did executives need to be brought in from outside who could complement the talents of the present management—and what about the need for executive training?*

These and many other questions were considered. What might have seemed to some at first as a fairly straightforward problem of marketing strategy became, with further thought, a problem with company-wide repercussions.

The Outcome

When all the different viewpoints were carefully considered, the board decided on the general manager's plan to expand the present plant. However, when it appeared that many of the younger executives might leave the company as a result, the board hit upon another solution: merger with a larger corporation in a related but noncompeting field. That firm was willing to supply the risk capital needed for the new second plant venture; it could also supply some of the management reinforcements needed in industrial relations and marketing. The price for these advantages, of course, was that management control would now have to be shared with another group, but that did not seem as serious as the risk of going ahead with either of the two plans proposed.

Concluding Note

The moral of this case is not that merger is a good solution, but that conceptual thinking is a good approach. Applied within the marketing department, it produced a broad, well-balanced attack that, whatever tactical errors might be made, was strategically sound. Applied to the company as a whole, it produced a solution which combined the marketing virtues of the original two-plant plan with the features demanded by the financial and production interests in the company.

Of course the conceptual approach is difficult. In the long run, it tends to build understanding and agreement among managers, but in the short run it may tend to create friction simply because of the multitude of questions raised. More conferences are needed; and so are more legwork and more painstaking planning. Discouragement may be encountered as once simple problems magnify in scope and difficulty. But if marketing is to be recognized as the very complex management problem that it really is—different from production, beset with change—then conceptual thinking is a necessity. And there is always this to be said in its favor: *it pays.*

18 The Principles of Production*

By Peter F. Drucker

Manufacturing management, as the term is commonly understood, is not the concern here any more than the management of selling, finance, engineering or insurance-company investments. But the principles of production must be a serious concern of top management in any business that produces or distributes physical goods. For in every such business the ability to attain performance goals depends on the ability of production to supply the goods in the required volume, at the required price, at the required quality, at the required time or with the required flexibility. In any manufacturing enterprise, ability to produce physically has to be taken into account when setting business objectives. Management's job is always to push back the limitations set by the hard reality of physical production facts. It must so manage its business as to convert these physical limitations into opportunities.

There is, of course, nothing new in this. But traditionally management reacts to the physical limitations of production by putting pressure on its manufacturing function: there are few areas in which "management by drives" is as common. And production people themselves see the answer in a number of techniques and tools, ranging from machine design to industrial engineering.

Neither, however, is the key. To push back the physical limitations or to convert them into opportunities requires first that management understand what system of production its operations require and what the principles of that system are; and second that it apply these principles consistently and thoroughly. Production is not the application of tools to materials. *It is the application of logic to work.* The more clearly,

* Reprinted from *The Practice of Management* by Peter F. Drucker (Harper & Brothers, 1954, pages 95-108), by permission of the author.

the more consistently, the more rationally the right logic is applied, the less of a limitation and the more of an opportunity production becomes.

Each system of production makes its own demands on the management of the business—in all areas and on all levels. Each requires different competence, skill and performance. One set of demands is not necessarily "higher" than another, any more than non-Euclidian geometry is higher than Euclidian geometry. But each is different. And unless management understands the demands of its system of production, it will not manage well.

This is particularly important today when many businesses are moving from one system of production into another. If this move is considered a mere matter of machines, techniques and gadgets, the business will inevitably reap only the difficulties of the new system. To reap its benefits management must realize that the new system involves new principles, and must understand what these are.

The Three Systems of Production

There are three basic systems of industrial production known to us so far: unique-product production, mass production and process production. We may perhaps count four systems; for mass production "old style," that is, the production of uniform products, is different from mass production "new style," which manufactures uniform parts but assembles them into diversified products.

Each of these systems has its own basic principles; and each makes specific demands on management.

There are two general rules for advancing production performance and pushing back limitations: (1) The limitations of production are pushed back further and faster, the more consistently and thoroughly the principles pertaining to the system in use are applied.

(2) The systems themselves represent a distinct order of advance, with unique-product production the least advanced, process production the most advanced. They represent different stages of control over physical limitations. This does not mean that opportunities for advance lie everywhere in moving from the unique-product system to the process-production system. Each system has its specific applications, requirements and limitations. But it does mean that we advance to the extent to which we can organize parts of production on the principles of a more advanced system and learn, at the same time, how to harmonize the two systems within the business.

There are also two general rules concerning the demands on management competence made by each system.

(1) The systems differ not just in the difficulty of their demands, but in the variety of competence and the order of performance. Management, in moving from one system to another, has to learn how to do new things rather than learn to do the old things better.

(2) The more we succeed in applying consistently the principles of each system, the easier it becomes for management to satisfy its demands.

Each management has to meet the demands of the system it ought to have according to the nature of its product and production, rather than those of the system it actually has. Being unable or unwilling to apply what would be the most appropriate system only results in lack of performance; it does not result in lower demands on management. Indeed, it inevitably increases the difficulties of managing the business.

One case in point is basic steel making, which has—in the "batch process"—primarily a unique-product system. There is probably no industry that has worked harder or more successfully on perfecting a unique-product system. Yet, the problems the managements of basic-steel companies face are all process-production problems: high-fixed capital requirements and the need for continuous production resulting together in high break-even points, the need for a high and constant level of business, the need to make basic investment decisions for a long time ahead, etc. At the same time the basic-steel industry enjoys few of the benefits of process production.

It is, in summary, of major importance in managing a business to know which system applies; to carry its principles through as far as possible; to find out which parts of production can be organized in a more advanced system and to organize them accordingly; to know what demands each system makes on management.

And where, as in the basic-steel industry, historical and technological obstacles have barred the organization of production in the appropriate system, it is a major challenge to management to work systematically on overcoming these obstacles. Indeed, emphasis in such a situation should not be given to working a little more effectively what is basically the wrong system. I am convinced that a great deal of the tremendous technological effort in the steel industry has been misdirected. Focused on improving the traditional process, it will turn out to have been wasted when steel making will finally become process production—which is in all probability not too far off any more. A business using the wrong system has to satisfy all the demands that the appropriate and more advanced system would make on management. Yet, it does not have the wherewithal to pay for them, for this can come only out of the increased ability to produce which the more advanced system provides.

Unique-Product Production

What, then, concretely are these three systems of production and their principles?

In the first, the production of a unique product, each product is self-contained. Of course, strictly speaking, there is no such thing as manufacturing unique products—they are produced only by the artist. But building a battleship, a big turbine or a skyscraper comes close to turning out a unique product. So does the building of a house, and in most cases "batch production" in a job shop.

Under this system the basic principle is organization into homogeneous stages. In the building of the traditional one-family house—one of the simplest examples of unique-product production—we can distinguish four such stages. First, digging the foundation and pouring concrete for the foundation walls and the basement floor. Second, putting up the frame and the roof. Third, installing plumbing and wiring equipment in the inside walls. Finally, interior finishing. What makes each of these a distinct stage is that work on the house can stop after each is completed, without any damage—even for a fairly long time. On the other hand, within each stage, work has to be carried right through; or else what has been done already will be damaged and may even have to be done again. Each stage can be varied from house to house without too much trouble or adjustment and without delaying the next stage. Each of these stages by the inner logic of the product, that is, of the house, is an entity in itself.

Unique-product production, with its organization of the work by homogeneous stages, is radically different from craft organization, in which a carpenter does all the carpentry, a plumber all the plumbing, etc. Properly organized, unique-product production does not go by craft skills but by stage skills. The model is the telephone installation man who, without being a skilled electrician, carpenter, plumber or roofer, installs electric wiring, saws through boards, makes a ground connection and can take up a roof shingle and replace it. In other words, either every man engaged in the work of a particular stage must be able to do everything needed within that stage; or, as in the building of a big turbine, there must be an integrated team for each stage which contains within itself all the stage skills needed. No skill is needed by individual or team that goes beyond the requirement of the particular stage.

This is largely how we succeeded in building ships at such a tremendous rate during the war. It was not mass production that resulted in the unprecedented output of ships. It was the division of the work into homogeneous stages; the systematic organization of the work group for the specific requirements of each stage; and the systematic training of a large number of people to do all the work required within one stage. This in turn made possible the progressive scheduling of the work flow which was the greatest time saver.

Mass Production "Old Style" and "New Style"

Mass production is the assembly of varied products—in large numbers or small—out of uniform and standardized parts.

In the manufacturing industry mass production is today the prevailing system. It is, and with good reason, considered to be the typical system of an industrial society—though process production may soon become a strong contender.

So universal is mass production today that it might be assumed that we know all about it, certainly that we know all about its basic principles. This is far from true. After forty years we are only now beginning to understand what we should be doing. The reason for this is that the man who ushered in mass production as a universal system misunderstood and misapplied it—so often the fate of the pioneer.

When Henry Ford said that "the customer can have any color car as long as it's black," he was not joking. He meant to express the essence of mass production as the manufacture of uniform products in large quantity. Of course, he knew that it would have been easy to give his customer a choice of colors; all that was needed was to give the painter at the end of the assembly line three or four spray guns instead of one. But Ford also realized, rightly, that the uniformity of the product would soon be gone altogether once he made any concession to diversity. And to him the uniformity of the product was the key to mass production.

This old-style mass production is, however, based on a misunderstanding. It is the essence of genuine mass production that it can create a greater diversity of products than any method ever designed by man.

It does not rest on uniform products. It rests on *uniform parts* which can then be mass-assembled into a large variety of different products.

The model of mass production is therefore not the old Ford assembly line. It is rather the farm equipment manufacturer in Southern California who designs and makes specialized cultivating machines for large-scale farming on irrigated land. Every one of his designs is unique. He makes, for instance, a machine that performs, with various attachments, all operations needed in large-scale cucumber growing—from preparing the hills in the spring, to harvesting cucumbers at the right stage of their growth, to pickling them. He rarely makes more than one of each machine at a time. Yet every one of his more than seven hundred different machines is made up entirely of mass-produced, uniform, standardized parts, which someone in the American economy turns out by the thousands. His biggest job is not to solve the problem of designing a machine that will identify cucumbers of the right ripeness for pickling, but to find a mass producer of a part that, though originally designed for an entirely different purpose, will, when put on the cucumber cultivator, do whatever is needed.

The specific technique for applying this principle is the systematic analysis of products to find the pattern that underlies their multiplicity. Then this pattern can be organized so that the minimum number of manufactured parts will make possible the assembly of the maximum number of products. The burden of diversity, in other words, is taken out of manufacturing and shifted to assembly.

One large manufacturer of electric implements produced, ten years ago, 3,400 different models, each composed of 40 to 60 parts. The analysis of this line of products first made it possible to reduce the number by about one third; 1,200 models were found to be duplications. The analysis still left 2,200 products—and to make them the company was making or buying well over 100,000 different parts.

After the products had been analyzed, their pattern established and the parts determined, it was found that almost all of the 2,200 models fell into 4 categories, according to the voltage they were supposed to carry. Only 40 products did not fit into this pattern. This made it possible to reduce the number of parts for all the other products. Then the number of variations for each part could be cut down to the minimum. Only one part now requires as many as 11 variations; the average today is 5 variations per part.

Production in this company is production of parts—even though the final products are widely different. The burden of variety is thrown on assembly. The parts themselves can be produced continuously against a schedule determined by the size of the inventory rather than by customer orders. And the size of the inventory is again determined by the time needed for assembly and delivery.

This new-style mass production is the most immediately useful production concept that we have in our possession today. It is still understood only by a minority of production people, and applied only in a fairly small number of companies. Also the techniques and methods to take full advantage of the concept have only now become available. It is above all the logical methods of "Operations Research" that allow us to make the complicated analyses of products and parts that are necessary to put the correct mass-production principle into effect.

Wherever this new principle has actually been applied cost reductions have been spectacular—sometimes reaching 50 or 60 per cent. Nor is its application confined to the production process itself. By making it possible to keep an inventory in parts instead of in finished products, it often enables a company to cut its cost and yet give the customer better service.

This new principle does achieve, in other words, what Henry Ford was after; the continuous production of uniform things without interruption because of an irregular flow of customer orders, or the need to change tools, styles or models. But it does this not by producing uniform products but by producing standardized parts. Uniformity in manufacturing is coupled with diversity in assembly.

Obviously the application of the mass-production principle is not simple. It goes well beyond manufacturing and requires hard and extensive work on the part of the marketing people, engineers, financial people, personnel people, purchasing agents and so forth. It carries risks, as it must be based on a fairly long production cycle at a constant rate of machine utilization—three, six, in some cases, eighteen months. It requires new accounting tools.

New-style mass production can also not be put in overnight—the development in the electrical implement company took all of three years. But so great are the savings that the company recovered the expense of a virtually complete redesign of its products and manufacturing facilities in less than two years.

Process Production

The third system is process production. Here process and product become one.

The oldest example of a process industry is the oil refinery. The end products that a refinery will obtain out of crude oil are determined by the process it uses. It can produce only the oil distillates for which it is built and only in definite proportions. If new distillates have to be added, or if the proportion between the various distillates is to be changed significantly, the refinery has to be rebuilt. Process production is the rule in the chemical industries. It is, with minor variations, the basic system of a milk-processing or a plate-glass plant.

And both mass production "new style" and process production are ready for Automation.

What Management Should Demand of Its Production People

Management must demand that those responsible for production know what system of production is appropriate, and apply the principles of that system consistently and to the limit. These are the first and decisive steps in pushing back the limitations of production on business performance.

Only when these steps have been taken can the next one be made: the organization of parts of production on the basis of a more advanced system.

The result of doing this without first analyzing the production process and organizing it properly is shown by the failure of the prefabricated house. It would seem the most obvious thing in the world to build a house from prefabricated, standardized parts. Yet the attempt, when made after World War II, proved abortive.

The reason was that uniform, standardized parts—mass production, in other words—were superimposed on a badly disorganized unique-product system. Instead of homogeneous stages, the organizing principle was craft organization. The use of prefabricated parts in a craft system proved more expensive and slower than the old methods. When, however, the Levitts in Long Island organized home building by homogeneous stages, they could immediately use uniform standardized prefabricated parts with conspicuous savings in time and money.

Similarly, standardized parts brought no savings in a locomotive repair shop as long as it was craft-organized. When the work was organized in teams, each containing all the skills needed in a particular stage of the work, when, in other words, craft organization was replaced by stage organization, standardized parts brought tremendous savings.

This is of particular importance in a mass-production industry, which produces diversified products. For there the great opportunity lies in the application of Automation; and this can only be achieved if production is properly understood and organized as the manufacture of uniform parts and their assembly into diversified products.

The electrical instrument maker mentioned above could fairly easily put his production of parts on an automatic basis, approaching closely the continuous flow and automatic self-control of an oil refinery or a plate-glass plant. There are other illustrations.

The U. S. Bureau of Standards has recently worked out, for the U. S. Navy, a method of automatic production of electronic circuits. This process does away with the soldering of individual circuits; it eliminates, in other words, the traditional "production by assembly" of the electronics industry. At the same time it makes possible the use of a large number of different circuits and their combinations without redesign of the process and without change in production. It does this by replacing the wiring in a radio or television set with a fairly small number of predesigned parts that can be plugged together in assembly to give many circuits or combinations of circuits.

My favorite example is a shirt manufacturer who faced the problem of an almost infinite variety of sizes, styles and colors, seemingly making impossible any production planning. He found, however, that three quarters of his production were in white shirts; and that there were only three basic qualities of fabric used in making white shirts, and in fairly predictable proportions. He then found that all shirts were made of seven parts: front, back, shoulder yoke, collar, right sleeve, left sleeve, cuffs. Size adjustments could all be made in assembly where the finished shirt is sewn together by cutting off excess length or width; for it is cheaper to sacrifice a few inches of material than to turn out parts of different size. Style adjustments could be made by using different collars and cuffs and different buttons. As a result all parts except collars and cuffs could be produced in the three grades of cloth without variation; cuffs required three variations; collars six. Only collars, which are simple to produce, are therefore made according to customer's orders today. And a job that, twenty years ago, was still almost entirely run by hand on individual sewing machines, is now done as a continuous automatic process, controlled by inventory standards. The result has been a sharp cut in cost, a tremendous increase in the variety of final products—sizes and styles—and greater customer satisfaction.

What Production Systems Demand of Management

But management must also know what the various systems of production demand of its own competence and performance.

In unique-product production, management's first job, it might be said, is to get an order. In mass production, the job is to build an effective distributive organization and to educate the customer to adapt his wants to the range of product variety. In process production, the first task is to create, maintain and expand a market and to find new markets. To distribute kerosene lamps free to the Chinese peasants to create a market for kerosene—the famous Standard Oil story of fifty years ago—is a good example of what this means.

Unique-product production has high costs for the individual product but great flexibility in the plant. Mass production "new style" has the ability to supply wants cheaply and within a wide and flexible range of products. But it requires much higher capital investment than unique-product production and a much higher level of continuous activity; it involves inventory risks; and it needs a distributive organization that can sell continuously rather than one that goes after a specialized, individual order. Process production requires the highest capital investment—in absolute dollars—and the most nearly continuous operation. Also, since products and process have, so to speak, become one, new products will be created by changes in the process even if there is no demand for them in the existing market—a common occurrence in the chemical industry. Management must therefore develop new markets for any new products as well as maintain a steady market for the old. Indeed, under Automation it is a major responsibility of management both in mass production and in process production to maintain a steadier level of economic activity and to prevent extreme economic fluctuations, whether of boom or of depression.

Under the unique-product system the time-span of decision is short. Under mass production it becomes longer: a distributive organization, for instance, may take ten years to build, as the Kaiser-Frazer Automobile Company found out after World War II. But under a process system decisions are made for an even longer future. Once built, the production facilities are relatively inflexible and can be changed only at major expense; the total investment may be large; and the development of a market is long-range. The marketing systems of the big oil companies are good examples. The more advanced the production organization, the more important are decisions for the future.

Each system requires different management skills and organization. Unique-product production requires people good at a technical function.

Mass production—"old style" and "new"—requires management trained in analytical thinking, in scheduling and in planning. New-style mass production as well as process production requires management trained in seeing a business as a whole in conceptual synthesis and in decision-making.

Under unique-product production management can be centralized at the top. Co-ordination between the various functions is needed primarily at the top. Selling, design, engineering and production can all be distinct and need only come together where company policy is being determined. It is this pattern of unique-product production that is still largely assumed in our organization theory—even though unique-product production may well be the exception rather than the rule in the majority of American industry today.

Mass production "old style" can still maintain this pattern, though with considerable difficulty and at a high price in efficiency. It does better with a pattern that establishes centers of decision and integration much further down. For it requires close co-ordination between the engineers who design the product, the production people who make it, the sales people who market it, and so forth.

In both mass production "new style" and process production, functional centralization is impossible. They require the closest co-operation of people from all functions at every stage. They require that design, production, marketing and the organization of the work be tackled simultaneously by a team representing all functions. They require that every member of the team both know his own functional work and see the impact on the whole business all the time. And decisions affecting the business as a whole have to be taken at a decentralized level—sometimes at a level not even considered "management" today.

There are significant differences with respect to the work force and its management. Unique-product production can usually adjust its work force to economic fluctuations, keeping in bad times only foremen and a nucleus of the most highly skilled. It can, as a rule, find what other skills it needs on the labor market. Precisely because they have limited skill, the workers in old-style mass production must increasingly demand employment stability from the enterprise. And in any business that uses Automation—whether new-style mass production or process production—the enterprise itself must make efforts to stabilize employment. For the work force needed for Automation consists largely of people trained both in skill and in theoretical understanding. It not only represents too great an investment to be disbanded; it can normally only be created within the company and with years of effort. It is neither accident nor philanthropy that the oil companies—typical process businesses—have tried so hard to keep employment steady even in bad depression years.

Under Automation there are few "workers." As said before, Automation will not (in the traditional sense of the word) cut down the total number of people employed—just as mass production did not do so. What we can see so far in the process industries shows clearly that the total work force does not shrink. On the contrary, it tends to expand. But Automation requires totally different workers who are actually much closer to the professional and technical specialist than to today's production worker. This creates a problem of managing people that is quite different from any "personal management problem" businessmen are normally familiar with.

Automation—Revolution or Gradual Change?

I have learned to be extremely skeptical of any prediction of imminent revolution or of sweeping changes in technology or business organization. After all, today, two hundred years since the first Industrial Revolution, there still flourishes in our midst the New York garment industry, a large industry organized on the "putting-out" system which, the textbooks tell us, had become obsolete by 1750. It would not be difficult to find other examples of such living ancestors who are blissfully (indeed profitably) unaware that they died a long time ago.

Certainly the obstacles to the Automation revolution are great—above all, the lack of men properly trained in the new concepts and skills. Also it has been estimated that only one tenth of America's industries could readily benefit from Automation at the present state of its technology. Even a real "Automation revolution" would be a gradual and highly uneven process.

Still revolutions do happen. And in the American economy there will be one powerful force pushing toward an Automation revolution in the next decade: the shortage of workers. As a result mainly of the lean birth years of the thirties, our labor force will increase only 11 per cent until 1965. Yet, our total population will go up much faster, even if present record birth rates should not be maintained. To reach minimum growth objectives indicated by population figures, technological progress and economic trends would require, in many companies, a doubling of the labor force were production to continue on the present system.

Even without a revolution, the most significant, the most promising and the most continuous opportunity to improve the performance of business enterprise will not lie, for decades to come, in new machines or new processes. *It will lie first in the consistent application of the new mass-*

production principle and secondly in the *application of the principles of Automation.* The techniques and tools of production management will continue to be a specialized subject with which only production people need to be familiar. But every manager will have to acquire an understanding of the principles of production—above all, an understanding that efficient production is a matter of principles rather than of machines or gadgets. For without it he will not, in the decades ahead, adequately discharge his job.

19 How Flexible Shall We Make Our Plant and Facilities?*

By Robert P. Neuschel

ACHIEVING the right balance between specialization and flexibility is one of the most perplexing problems management faces in facilities planning—i.e., in the planning of new plant construction or changes in process layout. Should it build a specialized plant around the process flow? Should it build a multipurpose plant? Or should it build a plant that strikes a happy medium between the two?

Today, the incidence and importance of the facilities planning problem have increased because of two developments: Marshall Plan spending and our own defense needs have stimulated the building and conversion of industrial facilities. To encourage voluntary expansion, the Government now gives the businessman a five-year period to write off facilities created for defense purposes. This development has caught many companies off guard. Since they had no immediate expansion plans of their own, they had not bothered to figure out how they would tackle the facilities planning problem when it did arise.

The second development, by no means so recent as the first, is the increasing tempo of technological progress. Constant changes in product make-up, new developments in processing equipment, and shifts in market demand all conspire to make it harder for the facilities planner to resolve his basic problem. Shall our plant be specialized? All purpose? Or a judicious blending of the two?

Many companies are at a serious competitive disadvantage today merely because their facilities are so highly specialized. To keep pace with technological progress, which has substantially improved competitive

---

* Reprinted from *Advanced Management*, 16 (January 1951), 16-18, by permission of the editor of *Advanced Management*.

products, they find that they must spend unusually large sums of money for building and layout changes. More astute facilities planning in the past would have saved them much of that expense.

Admittedly there are some industries in which companies can operate successfully only with the use of highly specialized facilities. Petroleum refining and cement manufacturing are typical examples. There the possibility of designing truly flexible facilities is limited and is accepted as a characteristic of the industry.

The important thing to recognize is that the problem of facilities planning has no black and white solutions. The degree of flexibility that is ideal for one product situation may be totally ineffectual for another. Each problem must be individually studied to determine the effects of flexibility and specialization on the current and long-term profit position. The manufacturing and *marketing* aspects must be carefully weighed to arrive at a sound conclusion.

Factors for Balance

Recognizing that facilities planning must be based on a broad appraisal of the whole problem—ranging from the general economic outlook to a very detailed analysis of equipment data—nevertheless our attention here is directed to what steps a company may take to secure a better balance between flexibility and specialization.

1. Determine the basic cost-selling price (gross margin) relationship in the industry. If the sale of a product depends on its price, which leaves a very small profit margin, it may be imperative to plan highly specialized facilities so that manufacturing costs can be kept to the absolute minimum. Here the need for the lowest possible current operating costs may be so vital that designing flexible facilities is out of the question.

Often, however, the spread between manufacturing costs and selling price will permit some loss of current efficiency in expectation of greater long-term gains from flexibility. If the higher manufacturing costs do not seriously affect the current competitive position of the company, long-term profits may be greatly enhanced by designing highly flexible facilities.

But, before any decision is reached, the facilities planner should look into the effects of flexibility and specialization on capital costs and unit operating costs. *Elements of flexibility can often be incorporated into facilities which have little or no effect on either operating or capital costs.* Many companies have been well rewarded by searching for this "free" flexibility. A chemical company, for example, recently planned to build several large drying ovens. As was customary in the industry, the ovens were initially designed as an integral part of the building. This, of course, would have committed a substantial portion of the plant floor area to just one use. The company then found that it could use movable ovens for the same operations with no increase in operating costs or any other disadvantage. The ovens were simply placed on the floor. With those units, the plant achieved flexibility in the use of floor space at no extra capital cost.

2. *Assess the future characteristics of the present product and its process.* Only when management executives consciously try to visualize the future of *the product* and *the processing equipment,* and the effect of those two on *plant building or equipment layout,* can they hope to foresee and offset the effects of product obsolescence on plant facilities. Listed below are some of the questions they should consider in planning new facilities. Although they can seldom find complete answers, they can at least get partial answers that will help them avoid costly and time-consuming errors in facilities planning.

(a)   How often have the raw materials, make-up, etc., of the product changed?

(b)   What were the nature and extent of those changes?

(c)   What effect have they had on equipment layout and building structure? On unit cost to manufacture?

(d)   Have past changes kept the product competitive?

(e)   What has been the pattern of product changes in the industry? How frequent? How severe?

(f)   What share of the total market has the product enjoyed during the past years?

(g)   Are the manufacturing costs of the product currently competitive?

(h)   What is the current status of product research? What developments are likely to be completed within the next few years?

(i)   How does the scope and intensity of product research compare with that being done by competitors?

(j)   How does the present position of the product in the present market compare with its historical position?

(k)   Is the industry currently increasing or declining in importance?

(l)   Why do people buy the product? What is the probable strength of that desire? How effectively does the product satisfy it?

(m)   What strong and "comer" substitute products are appearing in other related industries?

Today, many companies are making important facilities planning decisions without adequately considering what might happen to the product or its process in the future. In one recent instance, a medium-sized consumer goods manufacturer decided to spend a considerable sum of money to enlarge plant floor space and facilities so that production volume could be substantially increased. He took that step even though the company's product research group had successfully tested a new process method in the laboratory. If the method were equally successful in passing actual production floor tests the desired production increase could be attained with existing floor space. Even though it would have taken several months for the production tests to prove out the economics of the new process, the possibility of its success should have deterred expansion plans. There was too much risk that the floor area added at a substantial cost would have been made idle in the very near future.

3. Appraise the possibilities of complete product obsolescence. Whether to provide flexibility in plant and layout design depends not only on the likelihood of changes in the present product but also on the possibility of complete obsolescence. In this connection, management executives should ask themselves two basic questions:

(a) Is the product apt to become obsolete before the plant investment has been written off?

(b) What product might be made as a replacement?

Analysis of the product's history and its current market position (as outlined in the preceding section) should enable management to answer the first question.

As to the second question, it is obviously difficult to foresee future substitute products. If, however, a company has an extensive research and development program that is closely coordinated with manufacturing and sales, it may be possible to predict the product with some assurance.

Almost as important as trying to make the actual prediction, however, is constant awareness that changing technology and changing markets may some day force the company to make a new and different product. One of the major manufacturers of fine chemicals and pharmaceuticals has reflected such awareness in his basic approach to plant construction. In an industry that is plagued with constant changes in products and processes, this company has minimized the possibilities of plant obsolescence by designing only standard, multipurpose buildings whenever construction is needed for new products. No matter how specialized the product is, the company plans a standard type multipurpose building which appears to be two stories in height but actually does not have the second floor completed. This permits the use of unusually tall processing equipment which is common in this industry. Cantilevered mezzanines are generally built in to make better use of part of the head room. By such building planning this company has been able to adjust its operations when technological progress has forced a change in its products or processes.

4. Appraise the difficulty of plant disposal. Another point to consider is whether the plant buildings can be easily disposed of should the necessity arise. How much weight to give to this consideration will depend, of course, on individual circumstances. Even discounting complete business failure, a company will find it advantageous to have a readily salable plant for any one of the following reasons:

(a)　Should the company outgrow present plant facilities, the best course of action may be to construct a new plant.

(b)　Should the company have to use new raw materials, it may be desirable to relocate a plant nearer the source of supply.

(c)　Should there be a major shift in market geographically, the company may find it advisable to move the plant closer to the market.

Many other reasons might be added, but one point stands out: management executives will want to be sure that a real need for changing factory location in the future will not go unsatisfied merely because existing plant facilities cannot be sold without great sacrifice.

One medium-sized manufacturer of consumer goods operates at a loss today because he has too many over-specialized, single-purpose buildings that cannot be sold for even a fraction of their original cost. This current operating loss could be readily changed to a profit if the Company relocated and consolidated present facilities into one plant. But inability to dispose of present plants has made this management reluctant to relocate.

5. Recheck points of view that affect facilities planning. Certain prevailing attitudes and concepts about process flow and technological progress make it difficult to achieve an effective balance between plant specialization and flexibility. One of these points of view—namely, that low current operating costs are the primary objective—has led some building planners to overemphasize the benefits of molding the plant around the present process flow. Another misconception is that technological progress is a revolutionary change.

Because of the first point of view, many engineers and industrial executives start plant designing by determining the one best process flow for the operation. The building is then constructed around this predetermined flow.

This concept, of course, is essential to low operating costs, but it is only part of the facilities planning problem. Because it stresses the details of process flow, it naturally stresses also the characteristics and the processing methods of the product as it is today. This absorption in the present product and its process may and sometimes does preclude consideration of the product's future. As a result the solution does not incorporate the elements of flexibility, i.e., the multipurpose facilities, needed to stay abreast of future technological progress.

Technological Evolution

Many people erroneously consider technological progress as something gigantic or revolutionary in its impact—something that affects our whole economy. This point of view fails to recognize that technological progress is, in most instances, the accumulation of rather insignificant, day-by-day changes. To handle successfully the plant and equipment layout problems that follow in the wake of technological progress, it is necessary to realize that these slight changes are taking place constantly in one phase or another of the product. Because they are usually so small and frequent, many companies fail to plan for them. The results of that oversight are often, unfortunately, not recognized until an accumulation of small changes brings about a crisis in company affairs. This is nowhere more clearly apparent than in the failure of many companies to provide flexibility in plant design which will permit technological changes to be made at minimum cost.

To summarize briefly, management executives should make sure that their facilities planning incorporates the flexibility necessary to cope with the problems of technological progress. To do so, they should realistically answer the following questions:

1. *Do product manufacturing cost requirements demand facilities specialization, or will they permit designing to ensure flexibility?*

2. *What characteristics of flexibility can be included in facilities without adversely affecting current operating costs?*

3. *Has planning made due allowance for changes in the future characteristics of the products and processes?*

4. *Have we considered and evaluated the possibilities of the products becoming completely obsolete in the foreseeable future?*

5. *What new products might be made in the future to replace present products?*

6. *How much premium, if any, should be placed on ability to dispose of the plant at some unknown time in the future?*

7. *Are we overemphasizing the importance of "tailor-making" the plant to the process flow because of the lure of low current operating costs?*

8. *Do we recognize clearly that technological progress is not something revolutionary or far away but the accumulation of small changes in product and process which take place each day? Do our plans look ahead to place us in a position to keep pace with such changes at minimum cost?*

20 Measuring the Productivity of Capital*

By Joel Dean

THE president of one of our largest oil companies, who was pushing through a program of drastic decentralization of management, stated recently that the last thing he would delegate would be decisions about capital expenditures. This is understandable because capital-expenditure decisions form the framework for a company's future development and are a major determinant of efficiency and competitive power. The wisdom of these corporate investment decisions, therefore, has a profound effect upon a company's future earnings and growth.

From the standpoint of the stockholder and of the consumer, capital expenditures are the principal bulwark against the seemingly endless progression of wage increases. From the standpoint of labor, capital expenditures are the basic economic source of future wage advances since they embody the creative forward strides of advancing technology. Finally, capital expenditures, both by their aggregate size and by their cyclical timing, have a great deal to do with the character of the economy as a whole, and thus with the government's role in maintaining stability.

Management Program

Farsighted judgment is an essential requisite for wise decisions about capital expenditures. But such judgment, to be sound, must be based on analysis of all the facts, many of them extremely technical and complex. In particular, top management needs an objective means of measuring the economic worth of individual investment proposals in order to have a realistic basis for choosing among them and selecting those which will

* Reprinted from *Harvard Business Review,* 32 (January-February 1954), 120-130, by permission of the editor of *Harvard Business Review.*

mean the most to the company's long-run prosperity. The basic measure of economic worth is the productivity of capital, which means its power to produce profits. The purpose of this article is to suggest better ways of making that measurement.

Need for Specialized Skills

Unfortunately, the problem of managing capital expenditure has not generally been attacked with the kind of thorough and objective analysis that has paid such big dividends in other management areas. I have made a study of the capital-expenditure methods of some 50 large companies. These are all well-managed companies so far as production, engineering, and marketing methods are concerned, and I have a great deal of admiration for their executives. But on capital expenditures they show widespread failure to measure the investment worth of individual proposals directly, lack of defensible objective standards of an acceptable investment, and distorted dedication to procedures and paper work, with inadequate understanding of the economic content of the concepts used. In other words, when it comes to capital expenditures, they are still forced to play by ear to a distressing extent.

The development of an effective system for managing capital expenditures requires a complex combination of disciplines: (a) application of economic theory at several vital points; (b) knowledge of financial mathematics, which most of us acquired in our apprenticeship days but have inevitably forgotten long since; (c) economic forecasting; (d) techniques for projecting the amount and timing of outlays and receipts; and (e) techniques of control through comparison of actualities with projections. Top management clearly needs technical help. No executive, even if he had the time to analyze each capital proposal personally, could be expected to have all the necessary disciplines at his command; they can only be gathered together in a team of specialists.

Ten Elements

This article concentrates on the measurement of the economic worth of individual investment proposals. But we must remember that, though this is likely to be the critical element, it is only one of many components in a well-rounded program of capital management. Exhibit I, describing the ten components of a complete management program for capital expenditures, may serve to put this particular element (No. 4 in the exhibit) in its operational setting.

EXHIBIT I. TEN COMPONENTS OF A CAPITAL-EXPENDITURE MANAGEMENT PROGRAM

A realistic way to see how these elements tie together is to trace the biography of a single project, such as a proposal to invest $10,000 in a fork-lift truck and pallets for mechanizing materials handling in a warehouse.

1. *Creative Search for Profitable Opportunities.* The first stage is conception of the underlying profit-making idea which is to be embodied in the capital facility, in this case the fork-lift truck. Turning up profitable opportunities for investing the company's capital is in part a by-product of good management. But this cannot be depended on to provide the plethora of enticing capital proposals that constitute the raw material for good management of capital expenditures. Inadvertent opportunities should be supplemented by an active program of seeking out and investigating such opportunities.

Competition is a great creator of investment opportunities, as when equipment manufacturers vie with one another to make facilities obsolete. Comparisons of costs, earnings, and facilities with those of rivals often suggest productive avenues for investment. One company has for several years been going over its entire product line with a comprehensive survey of product design and product components pointed at reducing costs by changing design, substituting materials and processes, and reconsidering past buy-or-make decisions.

2. *Long-Range Capital Plans.* The second stage in the life cycle of our fork-lift truck proposal is to see whether it conforms with long-range dreams of company development as embodied in future facilities plans.

Because today's capital expenditures make the bed that the company must lie in tomorrow, today's decisions must be based on definite assumptions as to what tomorrow will be like. For example, decisions on warehouse facilities need to be made in the light of an over-all long-range plan for the number and general location of distribution facilities needed for the future. Based on projections of future economic conditions, some companies have prepared detailed plant and equipment targets, toward which their entire capital-expenditure program is oriented. Others have been content to draw up their future facilities plans in broad brush strokes, leaving the details to be worked out and adapted as the program is implemented.

To provide consistent bench marks for proposals originating in all parts of the organization, it is necessary to have *some kind of plan* sketched out for the future, no matter how tentative.

3. *Short-Range Capital Budget.* The next hurdle our fork-lift truck project must take is that of getting onto the one-year capital budget. Listing a project in this budget should not mean that the expenditure is authorized but only that it is approved—such *approval* indicating that the project is considered sufficiently timely and promising to warrant careful study for the coming year.

The short-run budget has several purposes. One is to force operating management to submit the bulk of its capital proposals early enough to give top management an indication of the company's aggregate demand for funds. A comparison of the capital requested with the available supply of funds will help management in weighing the desirability of outside financing or the need for cutbacks. Another purpose is to stimulate creative thinking about the capital-facilities program early in the game, so that there will be a reasonable amount of time for analysis.

4. *Measurement of Project Worth.* The next stage is *justification* of the fork-lift project on the basis of a financial and economic analysis of its investment worth to the company. In order to permit an objective ranking of projects, this analysis needs to be summarized in a single measure of the productivity of the proposed outlay.

This is the critical component of capital management and, as our central concern, will be discussed fully below.

5. *Screening and Selection.* Next, our project must pass the screening tests set up by the company to compare this fork-lift truck proposal with rival projects. Screening standards should be set in the light of the supply of cash available for capital expenditures, the cost of money to the company, and the attractiveness of alternative investment opportunities. If our project survives these rejection tests, the capital expenditure is *authorized*.

6. *Control of Authorized Outlays.* The next stage is *control* of the outlays authorized for acquisition (or construction). Controls are needed by top management at this life stage in order to assure that the facility conforms to specifications and that the outlay does not exceed the amount authorized. A system for the prevention of overages will keep estimates of investment amount "honest."

7. *Post-Mortems.* Capital-expenditure management cannot stop when our facility goes into operation. In order to preserve the integrity of the estimates of projected earnings and to provide an experience base for improving such estimates in the future, a post-completion audit of the earnings performance of our fork-lift truck is needed.

One company recently instituted a profit audit of all major projects that had been put into service in the preceding year. On a third of these projects it was found that the earnings had been overestimated by an average of 25%, including one new product investment aggregating several hundred thousands of dollars which was rendered obsolete by a competitive development two weeks after it went into production. On another one-third of the audited projects, the available data were found to be inadequate to the task of checking on the original estimates. This points up the need for a system of record keeping which will permit competent post-completion audits.

A sound program of post-mortems can do much to make earnings estimates more conscientious and realistic. Without some comparison of projections with actual performance, estimates might be inflated to the point of making a joke of the entire capital-rationing system.

8. *Retirement and Disposal.* Management's responsibility for an investment project ceases only when the facilities have been disposed of. The usual expectation is that the asset will be retained throughout its economic life so that it will be virtually worthless at the time of disposal. In a dynamic economy, however, economic life projections are necessarily imprecise. One impact of change is that the specialized assets may come to have more value to others than to the company itself. To find out and take proper action when the future earnings' value falls below the asset's market value requires an investment analysis focused on the desirability of disposal.

9. *Forms and Procedures.* At many stages in our project's life it will have to tangle with forms and procedures. An effective system of capital-expenditure control must in any large company be implemented by specialized forms, written project analyses, and routines of approval, which are tailored to the company's needs. This paper work, though a nuisance, is essential to smooth operation.

10. *Economics of Capital Budgeting.* Good estimates of the rate of return on capital-expenditure projects require an understanding of the economic concepts that underlie sound investment decisions, as well as ability in estimating techniques. Such understanding can be achieved only through special training. To assure a good job and to underscore the importance of education for capital expenditures, the financial vice president of one company personally conducted a training course for head-office executives and then took the show on the road to all plants.

Are Profits Controlling?

As we turn, now, to the phase of capital-expenditure management that is our main concern here—measurement of capital productivity— we must face an underlying question: To what degree are investment decisions actually controlled by profit considerations?

Concern with capital productivity of course implies that the company's goal is profits. But actually in many cases money making is a secondary objective. Often the primary goal is strategic—to maintain or increase the company's share of the market, to achieve growth in sales volume or number of employees, or simply to build reputation and status. Often capital expenditures capture and embody this kind of motivation in the form of corporate monuments made "just to become the kind of company we want to be." I am thinking of welfare and prestige investments like gymnasiums, country clubs, and palatial offices.

A corporation is not single-minded. It is composed of groups and individuals whose interests conflict. The concept of management as arbiter among employees, customers, and stockholders can lead to capital-expenditure policies and commitments that stray from the directional beam of capital productivity. Not that this is necessarily wrong. But, at least, when a company does let such goals as welfare or prestige govern, it ought to know the cost of such a policy. The only way to find out this cost is to determine the profitability of capital projects and see how much profit is being passed up in order to build such corporate monuments. The cost of prestige, then, is the amount of earnings foregone by departing from a pattern of investment ruthlessly directed at profit maximization.

Even where money making does dominate, the theory that a company tries to maximize its profits needs some qualification. Much more prevalent is what can be described as the doctrine of *adequate profits.* Of course, when profits performance or outlook is inadequate, the stockholder's power does come into play and capital expenditures are likely to be oriented toward profit maximization. But so long as the company is making adequate profits, the drive to have all capital expenditures selected on the basis of profit maximization is blunted.

Thus, I am well aware that making maximum profits is often not the sole or even the dominant goal in managing capital expenditures. But that does not lessen the importance of being able to measure the productivity of capital (i.e., its power to produce profits). Moreover, my viewpoint here remains that of the missionary rather than the anthropologist. As in other applications of managerial economics, the objective is to help executives improve policies, not simply to report practice (or malpractice).

Yardsticks of Investment Worth

The heart of good capital-expenditure management, then, is the measurement of the investment worth of individual proposals. But in order to measure how good a project is, we must have the right kind of yardstick. Just what should a good yardstick do?

The productivity of capital can be indicated in several ways, but the central requirement of a good yardstick is that it should measure what the proposed outlay will do to net earnings, and do this in a way that permits realistic comparison of one investment proposal with another. What we seek is a measuring rod which will help decide, for example, whether a $5,000 project that will earn $2,000 a year for three years is more attractive than a $60,000 project that will earn $10,000 a year for ten years.

A good yardstick of investment worth should summarize in a single figure all the information that is relevant to the decision whether or not to make the particular investment, and none that is irrelevant. It should be applicable to all types of proposals and should permit appraisal in terms of a single set of standards. Also, it should provide an index that is relatively simple to compute; once the basic data on the proposal have been assembled, the operating people should be able to measure the project's worth easily and without any need to explain how they do it. Finally, the yardstick should permit simple adjustments to allow for ranges of uncertainty in the earnings estimates, since one of the facts to be taken into account is man's inability to see very far into the future with any great precision.

How do the three most commonly used yardsticks—(a) degree of necessity, (b) payback period, and (c) rate of return—stack up against those criteria?

Degree of Necessity

The degree of urgency of the proposed project—that is, the extent to which it cannot be postponed to later years—is one kind of yardstick for assigning priority to investment proposals. For example, a railroad might put a power crane replacement proposal ahead of a repair shop modernization request because the old crane had broken down and something had to be done about it immediately, whereas the repair shop project could wait.

Degree of necessity has a place in the capital budgeting scheme. Some investments must be made to meet requirements imposed by a government agency. Grade-crossing eliminations for railroads, sanitary facilities in food-processing plants, and mandatory smoke-control installations are examples. Other investments clearly must be made if the company is to remain in business, e.g., replacement of a washed-out section of a railroad's main line. In these cases the alternative is such that its adoption would have a catastrophic effect on the firm's profits. Projects of this nature seldom bulk large in a company's over-all capital-expenditure program.

A serious defect of degree of urgency is that it fails to measure the capital productivity of a proposal—that is, the effect it will have on the company's earnings. A plant-modernization project may be highly postponable; but if it can produce annual savings which will yield 30% on the added capital tied up, it is to be preferred to a less postponable but less profitable project. Or, replacement of a shop destroyed by fire may seem completely unpostponable, whereas actually the company might find its over-all profits enhanced by subcontracting the operations formerly performed in the destroyed facilities.

Moreover, the degree of urgency is not a measurable quantity. Proposed projects cannot be assembled and arranged in a single priority ladder; acceptance standards cannot be set up to choose wisely among projects submitted on a necessity basis.

The most serious result of accepting or rejecting proposals primarily on the basis of how urgent they seem to be is that the capital budgeting program is likely to degenerate into a contest of personalities. The biggest share of the capital-expenditure money will go to the division heads who are the most eloquent or most persistent in presenting their requests, rather than to those who have taken the time and effort necessary to make an objective appraisal of the project's economic worth. The result is that all projects come up for review in an atmosphere of haste and emergency, with full scope allowed for the arts of persuasion and exhortation. Not only will projects whose economic desirability is dubious be pushed through to acceptance, but also a large proportion of investments that would yield big savings and high profits may be put off almost indefinitely.

Payback Period

The yardstick of payback period—that is, the number of years required for the earnings on the project to pay back the original outlay with no allowance for capital wastage—is unquestionably the most widely used measure of investment worth. Payback is superior to postponability since it takes into consideration the projected gross earnings, and it does have certain uses in capital-expenditure management:

> Payback can serve as a coarse screen to pick out high-profit projects that are so clearly desirable as to require no refined rate-of-return estimates and to reject quickly those projects which show such poor promise that they do not merit thorough economic analysis. In addition, it may be adequate as a measure of investment worth for companies with a high outside cost of capital and severely limited internal cash-generating ability in comparison with the volume of highly profitable internal investment opportunities. If a shortage of funds forces the company to accept only proposals which promise a payback period after taxes of two years or less, the use of a more refined measure might not affect the list of accepted projects.
>
> It also can be useful for appraising risky investments where the rate of capital wastage is particularly hard to predict. Since payback weights near-year earnings heavily and distant earnings not at all, it contains a sort of built-in hedge against the possibility of a short economic life.

For most corporations, however, payback is an inadequate measure of investment worth. It is a cash concept, designed to answer the single question of how soon the cash outlay can be returned to the company's treasury. As such it fails in three important respects to provide a satisfactory yardstick for appraising all the profit-producing investments of a firm:

(1) Payback tends to overweight the importance of liquidity as a goal of the capital-expenditure program. No firm can ignore needed liquidity. But most can achieve it by means that are more direct and less costly than sacrificing profits by allowing payback to govern the selection of capital projects.

(2) It ignores capital wastage. By confining analysis to the project's gross earnings (before depreciation) it takes no cognizance of its probable economic life.

(3) It fails to consider the earnings of a project after the initial outlay has been paid back. By concentrating on liquidity, it ignores the vital matter of what the life pattern of the earnings will be. Up to the end of the payback period the company has just got its bait back. How much longer the earnings will last is what determines the profitability of the investment. A three-year payback project may yield a 30% return on average investment if it has a long life, but only 12% if its life is four years, and no return at all if just three years.

In short, because payback does not measure or reflect all the dimensions of profitability which are relevant to capital expenditure decisions, it is neither inclusive enough nor sensitive enough to be used as the company's over-all measure of investment worth.

Rate of Return

Measurement of the economic worth of an investment proposal by means of rate of return relates the project's anticipated earnings to the amount of funds which will be tied up during the investment life of the facility. Rate of return embodies the concept of *net* earnings after allowing for capital wastage. Neither degree of necessity nor payback period uses this concept, since payback is measured in terms of gross earnings, and urgency does not consider earnings at all.

Rate of return has its shortcomings. A sound rate-of-return system is more complex than most of the methods of rationing a corporation's capital that are in current use. It costs more to install and put into operation. Also it may run into obstacles because it is unfamiliar and possibly because it will block privileged channels from access to capital funds.

But such limitations should not be decisive. Good management of capital expenditures is too vital to be blocked by ignorance, caution, or smugness. Overcoming the old organization's natural resistance to learning new tricks and training it in a new pattern of thought about capital expenditures is a one-shot affair. Once the system is installed, very little effort and cost are needed to keep it going.

Superiorities of This Yardstick. The positive superiorities of a rate-of-return measure of investment worth are imposing. It takes account of the full lifetime of a capital-expenditure proposal. Two projects, each of which shows a three-year payback, may differ greatly in the length of time for which they will produce earnings for the company. Take this experience which one company had:

Certain refinery equipment that showed a three-year payback actually became obsolete and was replaced in less than three years. This project's rate of return, therefore, was less than zero, despite what appeared to be a very satisfactory payback. In contrast, a pipeline that had the same three-year payback kept on earning (and promises to continue for twenty years more). Clearly its rate of return was much higher.

Capital wastage—that is, the gradual loss of the economic value of the facility over a period of time—is of vital importance in the appraisal of an investment proposal. Capital productivity should be measured by earnings over the whole life of the investment, even though estimates of the distant future may be subject to wide margins of error.

Because rate of return considers the full life of an investment proposal, correct comparisons of the degree of value of projects can be made.

Proposals can therefore be arranged in a ladder of priority even where they seem to be of the same degree of urgency or to have the same payback period. Moreover, the fact that the projects themselves may differ widely in their characteristics does not impede the comparison. New-product investments can thus be compared with cost-reducing projects; or a proposal this year can be compared with one which will not be ready until next year.

Better standards of rejection are made possible by rate of return. A company's combined cost of capital—say, 15%—can be used to determine the proper rate of cutoff on the capital-demand ladder just discussed; i.e., the minimum acceptable profitability of a proposal. This not only provides an objective, defensible basis for acceptance or rejection; it also aids top management in delegating authority by providing sound bench marks for personnel down the line to use in killing off the worst propositions before they have gone far up the chain of command.

Finally, rate-of-return rationing is likely to produce more earnings for stockholders, since it directs the flow of funds to their most profitable use by measuring the productivity of capital correctly and comparing it with a relevant standard of acceptable profitability.

Making the Estimates

We have seen that for most companies rate of return is the best yardstick of economic worth. Two problems arise in the practical application of this yardstick. The first concerns the concept for making the empirical projections that are needed to get the three basic determinants of project worth: (a) earnings, (b) economic life, and (c) amount of capital tied up. The second problem (discussed later) is how to combine these determinants in an index of profitability.

Ten Fallacies

The part of this measurement problem which is most often muffed is the job of getting a clear idea of just what needs to be estimated. Why should there be any problem in clarifying the concepts for rate-of-return measurement? The nature of the difficulties and their importance for good measurement can be seen by looking at ten common fallacies:

1. *"No Alternatives."* Perhaps the most common mistake in analyzing a capital proposal is the failure to consider any alternatives. There are always alternatives to an investment proposal, and a systematic analysis of the alternatives is the bench mark for estimating both the investment and the earnings of a capital project. What will happen if the requested investment is not made measures what the company will get out of it if the investment is made. If, as

usual, there are several alternatives differing in the amount of investment required, earnings estimates should logically be built upon the smallest investment alternative which is acceptably profitable. Alternatives which require greater investment are preferable to this one only if the *added* investment over this amount produces enough *added* earnings to yield a satisfactory rate of return.

2. *" 'Must' Investment."* Closely related is the "must" investment fallacy. The common conviction that certain equipment replacements are indispensable for continuing operations implies that top management has no alternatives. True, the alternative is sometimes so catastrophic that it is academic. But even in such a case the reason for making the investment should not be that it is urgent or indispensable, but that its profitability is terrific measured against the catastrophic alternative. Thus the rate of return from replacing a burnt-out pump in an oil pipeline may be astronomical; the investment is small and its earnings are the profits from the whole line, since the only alternative is a complete shutdown.

High-profit investments of this special nature are rarer than realized. Skeptical study of supposed "must" investments will reveal alternatives to many of them and will show that some of them are neither necessary nor even acceptably profitable.

3. *"High Strategy."* Another fallacy is the notion that some projects are so pivotal for the long-run welfare of the enterprise that they possess high strategic value which overrides mere economic considerations and lifts their evaluation into a mystic realm beyond the ken of economic and financial analysis. For example, the dogma that an integrated oil company should own 75% of its crude oil sometimes precludes economic analysis of integration investments.

It is true that some capital expenditures do have benefits which are hard to measure because they are diffused over a wide area of company activity or because they stretch over a protracted time period. And there are some investments which must be made on almost pure faith (e.g., a new research center). Nevertheless, the idea that there is such a thing as strategic value not ultimately rooted in economic worth is demonstrably wrong. If a contemplated investment produces results that do not have any economic value, then directors and stockholders should question its wisdom.

4. *"Routine Replacement."* This fallacy maintains that scheduled periodic replacement of capital facilities is a practical and inexpensive substitute for an investment analysis of the economic desirability of individual replacements. For example, many fleet owners replace motor trucks on a routine basis (i.e., after a certain number of years or a certain number of miles), without determining whether the added net earnings from replacing this or that old truck with a new one will produce an adequate return on the specific added investment. Routine replacement has the virtues of simplicity, orderliness, and predictability. But vintage retirement will not produce as profitable a pattern of investment as will a capital-earnings plan.

5. *"Prediction is Impossible."* Scoffers maintain that since the future cannot be predicted with accuracy, it is futile to try to guess the useful life of a proposed facility or to project its earnings beyond the first year. The consequence of this fallacy is an unwillingness to define concepts in a way that will force

explicit projection. People try to duck out by proclaiming that "with a four-year payback, it doesn't matter" or by embracing "unfair" Bureau of Internal Revenue depreciation rates.

The basic mistake is refusing to recognize that forecasting, though difficult and subject to error, is nevertheless necessary in appraising the worth of capital projects. Prediction, whether or not it is done consciously, lies at the heart of any executive judgment about a proposed investment. Usually it is better to *know* what is being done.

6. *"Fair Share of Overhead."* A common error in project analysis is to use allocations of current overhead instead of estimating the added costs that will be caused by the project. This cost-proration fallacy confuses problems of equity with problems of economic consequences. This is illustrated by a question frequently raised: Should a new product line, acquisition of which is being contemplated, carry its full share of the overhead now borne by mature products, or should it get a free ride? Neither of these suggested solutions is correct, at least for estimating project earnings. Old overheads do not matter—only new overheads. What is needed is not a reallocation of past overheads but a forecast of how future overheads will increase by acceptance as opposed to rejection of the project. This cost increment is wholly unaffected by the conventions of apportionment of common costs.

7. *"Free Ride."* A related fallacy that frequently misguides analysis of capital proposals errs in the opposite direction. It holds that new products or added volume are "plus business" in the sense of incurring negligible additional costs. This "free ride" fallacy leads to the conclusion that earnings from expansion investments are almost equivalent to their revenue. There is something to this notion; long-run incremental costs are often smaller than fully allocated average costs. But they are larger than short-run marginal costs and never negligible.

While short-run marginal costs are relevant for operating decisions, long-run added costs must be used for investment decisions. Herein lies the peril of the "free ride" fallacy. What, for instance, are the earnings from an added gasoline service station when pipeline and bulk plant capacities will just take that added volume? If only the marginal cost of using this bulk-movement capacity is included, rate of return is high. But continued normal growth will soon force expansion of the bulk-movement capacity; the new service station brings this time that much closer. If the full cost of this expansion is included in estimating lifetime earnings, the return of course shows up as much lower.

8. *"Carrying Charge."* The practice of charging the earnings of all projects with an interest cost might be called the "carrying charge" fallacy. Usually this charge is computed by applying the company's short-term borrowing rate to the capitalized portion of the original investment. This approach has the virtue of recognizing that money is not costless, even though no entry is made in the accounts. It has, however, two defects: (a) it uses the wrong cost of money, since high-cost equity capital is left out, and (b) it introduces cost of money into the capital-management program in the wrong way. Instead of subtracting carrying costs from individual projects, it is better to use cost of capital as a cutoff rate to select acceptably profitable projects.

9. *"Book Value."* Determination of the investment amount looks so easy that it is often done wrong. Bookkeeping is the root of error here. Accounting

conventions that are indispensable for financial reporting give the wrong steer for estimating a project's investment base. The test of what should be included in the investment amount is not how it is handled on the books, which bears only on the tax effects of the proposal, an important but quite separate issue. The test is whether or not the outlay is necessary to produce the stream of earnings contemplated in the proposal.

The "book value" concept would exclude outlays that are expensed (rather than capitalized) from the amount of investment serving as the base for the rate-of-return estimate. Take a proposal to convert an unused portion of a building into a sausage factory requiring $100,000 of capitalizable machinery plus $150,000 of expensed repairs. The pretax investment amount is the whole $250,000; after deflating the expensed portion for 50% income tax rates ($150,000 minus $75,000), the after-tax investment amount is seen to be $175,000. But the book value is only $100,000.

Book value also gives bad investment guidance in propping up, transferring, or abandoning existing assets. The book value of an existing asset is based on recorded historical cost less accumulated depreciation. For investment decisions, its value should be determined by what the company can get for the asset or what the company can do with it in its next best internal use, rather than by the figures that happen to be on the books.

10. *"Taxes Don't Matter."* There is a surprisingly widespread conviction that adjustment for corporate income taxes is academic. This "taxes don't matter" fallacy assumes that the underlying worth of a project is obscured (rather than revealed) by allowing for tax effects, and that the ranking of capital products will be the same whether or not they are deflated for taxes. This beguiling notion is wrong in two respects: (a) In order to apply tenable acceptance standards such as the company's outside cost of capital, it is necessary to measure rate of return after taxes, rather than before taxes. (b) The impact of taxes differs depending on the time shape of the project; and the after-tax ranking of proposals will differ significantly from their before-tax ranking if taxes are correctly taken into account in computing rate of return. For example, the tax effects of accelerated amortization can convert a borderline project into a highly profitable investment opportunity.

Positive Concepts

Having looked at these ten fallacies, we are in a better position to formulate positive concepts of what needs to be estimated in measuring project earnings and project investment.

A correct estimate of earnings must be based on the simple principle that the earnings from a proposal are measured by the total *added* earnings or savings from making the investment as opposed to not making it. The proper bench mark for computing earnings on a project is the *best alternative* way of doing the job; comparison therewith will indicate the source and amount of the added earnings. Project costs should be unaffected by allocations of existing overheads but should cover all the changes in total overhead (and other) costs that are forecasted to result from the investment, but nothing else—nothing that will be the same regardless of whether the proposal is accepted or rejected.

The value of a proposed investment depends on its future earnings. Hence, the earnings estimate should be based on the best available projections of future volume, wage rates, and price levels. Earnings should be estimated over the economic life of the proposed facilities. Because project earnings vary in time shape, and because this will affect the rate of return, the earnings estimates should reflect the variations in the time trend of earnings.

In estimating economic life of an investment, consideration must be given to (a) physical deterioration, (b) obsolescence, and (c) the possibility that the source of earnings will dry up before either of the first two factors becomes operative.

Interest on investment should not be deducted from project earnings. Charging interest increases the complexity of the rate-of-return computation without adding to the information it provides. Earnings should be stated after corporate income taxes, for only in such form are they relevant for capital attraction and for dividend payment.

The appropriate investment base for calculating rate of return is the added outlay which is occasioned by the adoption of the project as opposed to rejecting it and adopting an alternative which requires less investment. The entire amount of the original added outlay should be included in the investment amount, regardless of how it is treated in the books. Any tax benefit which results from expensing certain items rather than capitalizing them should be reflected. Those repairs which would be made whether or not the proposal is adopted should be excluded from the investment amount, because they are not caused by it.

If the proposal involves a transfer of facilities from another part of the company, the opportunity cost of these facilities (the amount foregone by using them this way rather than another) should be added to the amount of investment. If the opportunity foregone is merely to sell the facilities for scrap, then this will indicate the value to set on the transferred assets.

The amount of the investment should also include the amount of any additional necessary investment in working capital or other auxiliary facilities. Research and promotional expenses to get new products rolling or to develop new methods or to expand business are no less investments than plant and equipment.

Calculating Rate of Return

Once the basic estimates of project earnings and investment have been made, there are two major ways of combining them into a rate-of-return measurement. One way—which can be called the "accounting method" because it is closely related to many of the concepts used in conventional accounting procedure—computes rate of return as the ratio of (a) the project's earnings averaged over the life of the proposition to (b) the average lifetime investment. The other—which can be called "discounted cash flow"—computes rate of return as the maximum interest rate which could be paid on the capital tied up over the life of the investment without dipping into earnings produced elsewhere in the company.

Accounting Method

A characteristic of the accounting method is that it has many variants, each of which produces a different rate-of-return figure for any one investment proposal. One set of variants comes from diverse concepts of the investment amount (e.g., the original outlay, $100,000, versus the average amount tied up in the facility over its life, $50,-000). Another source of variants is the diverse concepts of the project earnings. Earnings can be either gross or net of depreciation, either before or after taxes. They can be the average for several years or for the first year only. This variety of alternatives produces a tremendous range of rate-of-return results. But they all fall into the category of accounting method, provided the final result is a ratio of earnings to investment.

This shortcoming can be minimized only by arbitrarily standardizing on one variant of the method and making all computations according to this standard.

A more serious drawback to the use of the accounting method is that it is insensitive to variations in the time pattern of investment outlays and earnings. By taking an annual average of earnings over the life of a project this method ignores the earning trends, which may be quite important.

The economic worth of an investment will be affected by the time shape of its lifetime earnings, because near money has greater economic value than distant money. For example, an oil well has a strikingly different time shape than a service station. A well which comes in as a gusher trails off to a pumper. In contrast, a service station in a new area has a rising curve of earnings and is likely to show post-operative losses in the first year or so. Failure to reflect these time-shape disparities in the index of investment worth leads to unprofitable capital-expenditure decisions.

The effect of time shape on economic worth is especially great when the company's cost of capital is high or when the foregone earnings on projects that are passed up are high. Only a company whose investment projects are roughly similar in time shape and in economic life can ignore this feature. For such a firm the added accuracy of the discounted-cash-flow method probably does not justify the transitional pain and effort required to install the system. But any company which has projects that vary significantly in either time shape or longevity has an important stake in using the most sensitive rate-of-return method available.

Discounted Cash Flow

The mechanics of the cash-flow method consist essentially of finding the interest rate that discounts future earnings of a project down to a present value equal to the project cost. This interest rate is the rate of return on that investment. Exhibit II illustrates the way in which rate of return can be determined under the cash-flow method for a cost-reducing machine which costs $2,200 and has an anticipated life of five years with no salvage value at the end of that time. In this case, an interest rate of 20% is found to make the present value of the

Exhibit II. Cash-Flow Method of Computing Rate of Return Illustrated
(Machine costing $2,200 with anticipated life of five years and no salvage value at the end of that time)

Year	Gross earnings before depreciation	Present value of earnings discounted at		
		18%	20%	22%
1	$200	$184	$182	$180
2	600	458	446	432
3	800	510	486	462
4	1,200	640	596	556
5	1,200	534	488	448
Total	$4,000	$2,326	$2,198	$2,078

future earnings stream equal to the present cost of the machine, so this is the rate of return.

Conceptually, this method is based on the principle that in making an investment outlay we are actually buying a series of future annual incomes—ranging in the example in the exhibit from $200 the first year to $1,200 by the fourth and fifth years. We have an investment in each of those incomes, an investment which compounds in value through time until its own year arrives and it materializes in cash earnings. Thus, for example, the $596 present value of the fourth year's earnings at 20% is the amount that would have to be invested at 20% now to yield $1,200 gross earnings during the fourth year ($596 compounded at 20% for 3½ years—since the $1,200 would begin to come in at the beginning of the fourth year).

The basic simplicity of this method is brought out by this illustration. Earnings are stated as gross cash receipts (not figuring depreciation). Therefore, it is not necessary to allocate the cost of the machine over its life before computing return. Depreciation is allowed for automatically because the interest rate that discounts the sum of present values to zero is the rate of return on the investment after annual provisions for repaying the principal amount. We are not, as in the accounting method, watching the write-off of original cost; we are watching instead the growth of our investment outlay as we compound it through time.

The method is simplified by the fact that there is no need to make a decision as to which earnings base to use (e.g., original outlay, average investment, and so on), nor is there any need to enter interest as a direct cost of the project. Once the data are gathered and set up, there is only one rate-of-return answer possible, and it can be arrived at by straightforward working of charts and interest tables.

Net Superiority of Discounted Cash Flow. The accounting method does have the advantage of familiarity and transparency. Although education would be necessary to get everyone to standardize on one method of averaging earnings and investment, the idea of computing a simple ratio by dividing one number by another is familiar to anyone who went beyond the second grade.

The discounted-cash-flow method admittedly is less familiar. While a method essentially similar to this has been widely used throughout the financial community for computing bond yields, insurance premiums, and rates on leased facilities where accuracy is important and even small errors may cause serious loss, it is new in its application to the measurement of productivity of individual capital-expenditure projects in industry. Hence the job of explaining it to the bookkeeper and the clerk will require time and effort. But its appearance of complexity is deceptive. Once the basic method is understood, it is actually simpler and quicker to use than the accounting method.

Another deterrent to its use is the fact that it does not correspond to accounting concepts about the recording of costs and revenues, so that special analysis is necessary to compute a post-mortem on an investment made in the past. But this seems minor in comparison with its imposing superiorities:

(1) The discounted-cash-flow method is economically realistic in confining the analysis to cash flows and forgetting about customary book allocations. The books, although very valuable for other purposes, are irrelevant for the task of measuring investment worth.

(2) The use of this method forces guided thinking about the whole life of the project and concentration on the lifetime earnings.

(3) It weights the time pattern of the investment outlay and the cash earnings from that outlay in such a way as to reflect real and important differences in the value of near and distant cash flows.

(4) It reflects accurately and without ambiguity the timing of tax savings, either from expensing part of the investment outlay or from writing off capitalized costs over the life of the investment—something quite difficult to do by the accounting method.

(5) It permits simple allowances for risks and uncertainties and can be adapted readily to increasing the risk allowance over time.

(6) It is strictly comparable to cost-of-capital ratios so that decisions can be made quickly and safely on the basis of the relationship between indicated rate of return and the value of money to the company.

Conclusion

Examination of the capital-expenditure policies and procedures of some 50 well-managed companies shows that top management is forced to a distressing degree to rely on intuition and authority. Management lacks the skilled analysis and the scientific control needed for sound judgment on these intricate, vital capital decisions. The pivotal problem of capital-expenditure management is the measurement of the investment worth of individual proposals. Project evaluation needs to be integrated into a comprehensive program of capital management composed of the ten elements listed in Exhibit I.

Systematic exploration to assure that investment opportunities are ferreted out and objectively analyzed is a prerequisite for the measurement of investment worth. Long-range capital plans and projections enable management to appraise projects in better perspective and to fit them into broader patterns. The comprehensive short-range capital budget which forecasts the timing of probable cash outlays for investment and the timing of cash inflows is essential for determining cut-off points by cash-generation criteria.

For orderly operation of rate-of-return rationing, management needs not only good management of capital productivity but also objective and defensible standards of minimum acceptability. These should generally be based on the company's cost of capital. Candid and economically realistic post-completion audits are indispensable incentives for measuring project profitability accurately; they also provide the systematized experience for improving project measurement in the future.

Special forms and procedures to implement these capital-expenditure management principles also need to be tailored to the particular conditions of the individual company. Above all, good capital-expenditure management must operate in an enlightened intellectual environment throughout the company; all the personnel concerned should understand the economics of capital expenditures and of the measurements and controls which a sound program entails.

For most companies, productivity of capital should be measured by rate of return, rather than by payback or degree of necessity. Estimates of a project's rate of return should be based on concepts of capital investment and project earnings, which are indicated by what would happen if the company were to go ahead on the project instead of selecting some alternative which requires a smaller investment.

Prediction is essential; project worth depends solely on future earnings—the added earnings that will result from the added investment. These future earnings need to be forecasted over the whole economic life of the facility. Project costs should be unaffected by allocations of existing overhead, but should include all increases in overhead (and in other costs) that will be caused by the project. Earnings should be deflated for taxes. The investment base should be the entire added outlay regardless of bookkeeping—adjusted for corporate income taxes.

The discounted-cash-flow method of computing rate of return is demonstrably superior to existing alternatives in accuracy, realism, relevance, and sensitivity. Acceptance of rate-of-return capital budgeting should not hinge on willingness or reluctance to go this far in breaking with traditional methods.

21 Management Techniques for Stimulating Productivity*

By Joseph M. Juran

Summary

WITHIN a single century, the form of industry has evolved from primitive handicrafts to a very complex technology. Techniques for stimulating productivity have changed drastically in order to keep pace with the changing form of industry. Necessarily, the application of the new techniques lags behind the potentialities. Many managers are unwittingly applying, to today's problems, techniques designed to solve the problems of yesterday.

Management techniques for productivity have to date emphasized productivity of the individual production worker. To solve the problems of tomorrow, management must not only extend these techniques to include the non-production worker; it must give far more consideration to the productivity of the enterprise as a whole.

This new emphasis will find expression in improved coordination between departments, in extension of the concept of management controls, and in a planned selection and training of managers.

Characteristics of Simple Enterprises

The more primitive forms of industry were (and still are) characterized by:

(a) A simple product devoid of precise quality characteristics

(b) A simple process involving use of elementary tools to fabricate elementary materials

(c) Use of unskilled human labor for the fabrication and materials-handling operations

---

* Reprinted from *Industrial Productivity* (Industrial Relations Research Association, 1951, pages 76-93), by permission of the editor.

(d) A small shop in which the owner-manager directly supervised all workmen as well as carrying on the commercial function of the enterprise.

Under these conditions, the costs of materials and of overhead were relatively small. The chief costs were the wages of the workmen. It is entirely understandable, therefore, that the emphasis of the managers of such enterprises, was (and still is) devoted to increasing the productivity of the workmen.

Manifestly, it is unit cost of production which is vital in the enterprise. Where labor was the dominant cost, the "solution" for the owner-manager was "obviously" to make the wages as low as possible, the while securing from the workman as great a day's work as possible.[1]

Early Management Techniques

Following this primitive reasoning, the early managers did in fact keep wages low the while exhorting workmen to high production. The stimuli used by the managers varied with the form of civilization in vogue, but the effectiveness of the stimuli was always based on the compelling needs of the workman. The workman had no recourse under the then existing forms of society.

Wages were placed at that minimum required to sustain the lives of the slaves, serfs, or by whatever other title the workmen were called. The day's task was evidently based on past performance. The toil and the weariness associated with completion of the day's task were preferable only to the consequences of failure. Tasks were subject to arbitrary increase, again with no recourse on the part of the workman.[2]

The early days of the Society of Contract brought forth very little change in the conditions which had prevailed in the Society of Status. The early Lancashire mills operated under standards of a day's work and of wages which we now regard as appalling. Curiously and tragically, the same workman who had fought his way out of political bond-

---

[1] These two, the day's work and the day's wage, are often coupled in slogans. But it is well to avoid confusion here. Actually, two different dimensions are involved. Determination of a "fair day's work" is a problem in measurement through engineering and biometrics. Were we able to define and apply a unit of human work with precision, the problem of how much is a day's work could be laid to rest just as effectively as the problem of how much is a bushel of wheat has been laid to rest. On the other hand, the fair day's pay is a problem in economics just as is the price of a bushel of wheat.

[2] Exodus 5 (Bricks without straw).

age became forced by circumstance to contract himself, "voluntarily," into economic bondage.

It is important to note incidentally that the application of these blind stimuli *placed on the workman the burden of solving many problems in productivity.* The concepts of finding the best way, and of selection and training, were a long time in developing. Until they had developed, the workman was, in the main, left to solve his problem unaided.

Taylor's Principles of Productivity

A number of managers of the 19th century experimented with means for improving the productivity of the individual workman. It remained for Frederick W. Taylor to give clear expression to four management principles for securing productivity. Use of these principles has become widespread indeed. Taylor's principles may be restated as follows:

1. The *method* for performing each job is to be determined by scientific study, not by rule of thumb.

2. For each job there is to be established, through scientific study, *a standard of a day's work.*

3. For each job, the workman is to be *selected* on a basis of general fitness, and then is to be *trained* in the best method.

4. An *incentive* is to be established to urge the selected and trained workman to use the best method and to meet the standard of a fair day's work.

Much improvement in productivity has been achieved through use of these principles. However, much mischief has also been done. In part this is due to misapplication of these principles by men unqualified, over-zealous, or unscrupulous. But in part the principles themselves were limited in their validity.

Taylor's principles will now be considered individually.

The Best Method

The concept of replacing human effort by mechanical effort had already been well developed when Taylor arrived on the scene. But Taylor dramatized the principle that the use of *the human body as a machine for work* likewise warranted study. In his studies of materials handling (shoveling, carrying pig iron) he came up with scientific determination of size of shovels, percent of resting time required, and related measures.[3]

---

[3] Frederick W. Taylor, *Scientific Management* (New York: Harper & Bros., 1947).

It remained for Frank and Lillian Gilbreth to devise the techniques for putting the principle of the best method into practice. This they did through development of what is generally known as Motion Study. Their methods included the techniques of motion picture study, the definition of elemental motions (therbligs), a system of codes and symbols, flow charts, and numerous others. The techniques of the Gilbreths have been widely applied in industry.[4]

Within the last decade, the question "Who shall determine the method to be used?" has received much discussion in industry. It was Taylor's view that the method must be left for scientific determination by experts. The workman was to be given detailed instructions on what to do and how to do it.

Experience since Taylor has raised several objections to so rigorous a view, on the following counts.

(1) It is simply uneconomic for an expert to establish all methods, since many operations involve relatively little production time.

(2) The foreman and the workman resent adapting themselves to changes originated by someone else.

(3) It is desirable to enlist the *mind* of the workman, not merely for his specific contribution of ideas, but for the vital sense of participation created thereby.

Out of this experience, the following appears to be evolving:

(a) On major questions of method, i.e., plant layout, purchase of machinery, etc., the basic study is made by the engineer.

(b) On minor questions of method, i.e., layout of the individual work-place, the foremen and workmen are trained in the psychology and the techniques of methods improvement, and are stimulated to find new ways in old surroundings.

(c) In any event, the foremen and workmen have a voice before a change is made effective.

The Standard of a Fair Day's Work

Taylor not only stated this principle; he developed the use of stop watch time study as a technique for establishing the standard. Thereby he generated a storm which has at this writing not yet subsided.

It is easy enough for engineers and Union stewards to agree on how long a workman in fact *did take* to perform a given job. The

---

[4] See Ralph M. Barnes, *Motion and Time Study,* Third Edition (New York: John Wiley & Sons, Inc., 1949).

difficulty is in converting this record of actual performance into an estimate of how long it *should take* a trained workman to perform the job. Implicit in this conversion are two principal sources of error:

(1) The "rating" or estimate of the effectiveness of the workman under observation. This rating is made to a subjective standard carried in the mind of the observer.

(2) The fatigue factor added in the (usual) case that the study was conducted over a short period of time rather than a full working day.

Taylor[5] and those who came after him have generally overstated the precision attainable in measuring the fair day's work. Until the last few years, industrial engineers have avoided publication of results of independent studies by engineers on identical jobs. This reluctance has undoubtedly slowed down the development of a solution.

A recent research study[6] has generated much new data on the precision of measuring a fair day's work, as well as making available motion picture films of various common operations to serve as objective standards.

Another development has been publication of time values[7] for "elemental" operations on the theory that a job can be analyzed to discover which of these "elements" it contains. These elements can then be summed up to yield a time value for the total job. In the absence of comparative data on results arrived at independently by practitioners, the precision of the method cannot as yet be appraised objectively.

The precision of any device for establishing standards of a day's work is measured by the uniformity of the results obtained when the device is used independently by a number of engineers (or Union stewards). Such data as have been seen by the present author would indicate that the best of the existing means, if tested independently by a group of engineers, would find at least a third of them differing by more than ten per cent from the average of the group.

On the face of it, such a result, if attained universally, would not be too bad. Certainly it is far more precise a measure than that derived by perpetuating past history. Considering the errors inherent in many

---

[5] Frank B. Copley, *Frederick W. Taylor, Father of Scientific Management* (New York: Harper & Bros., 1923), Volume 2, Chapter VI.

[6] Conducted by the Society for the Advancement of Management.

[7] See for example, Harold B. Maynard, Stegemerten and Schwab, *Methods-Time Measurement* (New York: McGraw-Hill Book Co., Inc., 1948).

engineering computations, the present attainable precision of measuring the fair day's work is not unreasonable. (In designing a bridge, or a vehicle, the fine precision of theory of stress and strain is grossly diluted by an arbitrary factor of safety which may run to several hundred percent.)

Nevertheless, the industrial engineers are not happy over present precision of measuring a fair day's work. In part this is due to the fact that the results touch a sensitive nerve of the workman. In part it is due to the fact that so long as any subjectivity remains in the measure, so long will there continue to be accusations to the effect that the slack is all taken up in favor of management.

Moreover, it is surprising to industrial engineers that the unions have not made more of an issue of the matter. Evidently union engineers are fully aware of the limitations.[8] Yet the fair day's work problem is but one of a whole series in the entire complex of union-management relationships. To date, at least, the unions have generally been more concerned with other problems in the collective bargaining group.

Selection and Training of the Workman

The selection principle has run squarely into a series of limitations of union origin. From the viewpoint of the manager, three of these limitations are particularly unsavory:

(a) Hiring. In some instances, employee nepotism, former length of service, or other form of employee determination becomes part of the basis for choosing new employees.

(b) Upgrading. It is now a widespread requirement that notice of higher grade jobs be published so that employees may bid for such jobs. The point is that the management is precluded from appointing that employee which it thinks most qualified. It must appoint, at least on a trial basis, that employee of longest service who wants a trial.

(c) Layoff. The seniority rule has come to compete quite successfully with the rule of merit in sequence of layoff.

Running through these and other elements of the selection problem is the clear evidence of development of "rights in the job." These rights are rapidly becoming a new form of property, and are prevailing against the historical management "prerogatives."

The principle of training of the workman was dramatically

---

[8] William Gomberg, *A Trade Union Analysis of Time Study* (Chicago: Science Research Associates, 1948).

demonstrated in World War II as a result of the Training Within Industry[9] program. There can be no doubt of the important role played by this training in the productivity of the United States.

The comparatively wholesome acceptance of the training principle suggests extension of its use to offset the limitations imposed on the selection principle. Management has far to go to apply even existing knowledge on usefulness and techniques of training.

Taylor's Principle of Incentives

Taylor's principles of the best method, the fair day's work, selection and training have proven sound, though lacking complete mechanisms for applications. However, Taylor's version of the principle of incentives has been demonstrated to require fundamental modification.

Underlying Taylor's system of incentives were the concepts:

(1) The prime concern of the workman is money.

(2) The lure of added money is a sufficient incentive to induce the workman to increase production.

These considerations may well have been vital in Taylor's time. When one is at or below the subsistence level, money becomes the basis of liberation from a budgetary prison. The dominant concern is indeed to secure liberation from this perpetual poverty.

But it is another thing to conclude that preoccupation with money continues even though the workman has risen above the subsistence level. On the contrary, the gathering evidence indicates that the higher the workman's standard of living rises above the subsistence level, the less is the relative importance of any money increment, and the higher becomes the relative importance of other incentives. Moreover, there are widespread instances in which the workman has restricted his production notwithstanding his clear need for higher income. His reasons? Simply that there are things in life more important than increments of money.[10]

The lesson of these recent researches is that money, as an incentive for productivity, is no longer the paramount incentive, even granting

---

[9] *Training Within Industry Report,* 1940-45 (U. S. Government Printing Office, 1945). U. S. War Manpower Commission, Bureau of Training.

[10] For examples see:

F. J. Roethlisberger and W. J. Dickson, *Management and the Worker* (Cambridge: Harvard University Press, 1939).

William F. Whyte, *Pattern for Industrial Peace* (New York: Harper & Bros., 1951).

that it might have been so in other years, or that it may be so today in other countries.

Currently much is being done to establish an up to date principle (if not an enduring principle) of incentives to worker productivity. The final result is by no means clear, though rough outlines have begun to emerge.

Certainly the concept of *participation,* the idea of being on the team, is bound to play an important role.[11] This is not restricted to financial participation in a form such as profit sharing; it is essential that the workman have a voice in the shaping of events as well.[12]

The Shift from Emphasis on Production Worker Productivity

The foregoing has dealt with principles of *production worker* productivity. In the handicraft industries, this production worker productivity is the main variable; no vital gains in productivity can be made unless production worker productivity is improved. However, other aspects of productivity, of minor importance in the handicraft industries, become of substantial or even leading importance in the larger, more complex enterprises.

In particular, management emphasis has been revolutionized by the advent of mass production of precision goods. The very nature of such mass production suggests the direction of the new emphasis. Mass production of precision goods is characterized by:

(1) A product design adapted to interchangeable manufacture. This requires engineering effort, not merely for the basic functional design, but to an even greater extent for the specification of the standardized, interchangeable components essential to mass production.

(2) A manufacturing process of sufficient precision and digestive capacity to meet the needs of quality and quantity. This requires engineering effort to specify machines and processes, to design tools, fixtures and gauges, to lay out the plant for economic flow of materials and to specify the necessary operations and division of work for production operators.

(3) A swift, sure flow of large quantities of materials. This requires increased effort in purchasing, expediting, storing, materials-handling, packaging and shipping.

---

11 See James F. Lincoln, *Lincoln's Incentive System* (New York: Mc-Graw-Hill Book Co., Inc., 1946).

12 See Sir Charles Renold, *Joint Consultation Over Thirty Years* (London: Allen Unwin, 1950).

(4) Timely maintenance of the physical buildings, machines, tools, etc. This requires a new force of skilled workmen, which in some enterprises (certain chemical process plants) exceeds, in number, the production force.

The foregoing, plus still other services (such as employment of workmen, inspection of the product, etc.) were once performed, if at all, by the foreman. In the large enterprise of today such functions must be performed by special auxiliary departments. These auxiliary departments are vital organs in the enterprise. Not only must each perform its function; in many instances the size of these auxiliary departments is such that *their* productivity is likewise important to the enterprise. For example, a large office force for customer billing (certain public utilities) not only must perform this vital function correctly; it must perform it efficiently as well. Thus it can lower the productivity of the enterprise in two ways, either through failure to carry out the billing function, or through carrying out this function at a waste of manpower.

Nor is this all. The functions of finance and sales, usually performed by the proprietor of the small enterprise, likewise grow in size and complexity as the enterprise grows. The sales function, especially, has grown broadly to include sales promotion, advertising, sales service and still other complications. The efficient functioning of these departments is secondary only to their basic performance.

Finally, the growth of the enterprise gives rise to the need for a whole series of management controls. These are of the utmost importance. It is no exaggeration to state that *in the larger enterprises, the limiting factor in productivity lies in the management controls.*

A rudimentary example may be in order here. Consider the simplicity of regulation of pedestrian traffic in the village market place or on a country lane. However, as the traffic multiplies, is mechanized, bears great loads, and moves at high speeds, controls become essential as to right of way, speeds, loads, and many other characteristics. The limiting factor in the successful movement of this complex traffic lies not in the skill of the drivers or in the excellence of the vehicles; it lies in the traffic *controls.*

It follows that early management emphasis on production worker productivity is out of date in the large complex enterprises. It does not follow that managers have fully grasped the implications or even the presence of these changes. On the contrary, there are many enterprises in which management attention is focused on trivia of worker productivity (talking on the job, personal time-out, etc.) when there is no clear definition of organization, no table of delegation, no clear channels of communication, no system of reports for executive control. Such situations are not surmises. Not only do they exist; they abound.[13]

Manifestly, the productivity of the individual production worker is now of no less numerical importance than it has been. However, the importance relative to total productivity is decidedly less. Sole preoccupation with production worker productivity is in many enterprises the application of yesterday's management solutions to the vastly different problems of today.

Consequences of the Shift in Emphasis

Manifestly, Taylor's principles—the best way, the fair day's work, selection and training, and the incentive—apply with equal force to all employees, whether production worker, office worker, supervisor, engineer, or any other. But economic application of these studies to improve productivity presupposes that the thing to be controlled is large relative to the cost of exercising the control. The large gangs of unskilled labor of Taylor's time have disappeared to be replaced by the more variegated production and auxiliary tasks of modern enterprise. Thereby the economics of extensive time study and motion study has shifted.

In a measure, these new problems have suggested their own solutions. Study of methods of doing work is no longer asserted to be the sole province of the industrial engineer; the foreman and the workman are trained to aid in such determinations. Individual time studies are giving way to tables of standard times based on prior studies. Individually designed piece rates are giving way to group incentives.

But these adjustments relate only to the economics of controlling worker productivity. The new and often greater problem of management controls is of a different character. It requires not merely an adaptation of former solutions; it requires new solutions in place of or in addition to the old solutions.

In part, the new solutions involve fundamental changes in managerial attitude. Foremost of these is the change in the manager's basic loyalty. This loyalty, originally devoted primarily to the interests of the owner, must now be devoted primarily to the interests of the enter-

---

[13] A wag has labeled such situations as "Polishing brass while the ship is sinking."

prise. This change has become simplified as a result of the separation of ownership from management.

A second change in managerial attitude is that with respect to employee relations. At the dawn of the Industrial Revolution, the basis of employee relations was the Anglo-Saxon law of contract, a sale of the services of a human being for money. But as more and more human beings have become involved, it has become increasingly evident that this relationship includes a private regulation of the daily lives of a sizeable segment of the population. Wherever human beings live, whether on the farm or in the factory, there human rights spring up.

As these new human rights develop form and substance, there arises the need for enforcement of the new rights. On the industrial scene, the managers failed generally to recognize the existence of these new rights, let alone attending to their enforcement. In consequence a new agency, the labor union, arose to represent the industrial citizenry in redress of grievances and in codifying of the industrial law.

A further shift in emphasis arises from the growth of organization to a point that communication and coordination become serious limitations on productivity. Such problems exist only in rudimentary form, if at all, in the small enterprise. In the large enterprise, much management effort is required to develop lines of communication and methods of coordination.

A corollary to growth of organization is the need for a supply of intermediate supervisors and of technical personnel. The selection and training of men to fill these posts is again a serious new problem for management.

Summarizing, it is seen that for the modern enterprise, the former emphasis on production worker productivity must now be extended to include all workers. Moreover, the basic attitudes of management must be re-examined, both as to management loyalty and as to industrial relations. Finally, the new problem created by size must also be solved. These new problems include establishment of means for communication and coordination within the enterprise and for the selection and training of the management hierarchy.

Productivity of Non-Production Workers

The early handicraft industries featured a high concentration of manpower in the direct productive operations—not only the skill, but the energy was supplied by human beings. Because the human being is such a feeble source of energy, it required many human beings to generate any respectable amount of energy.

With the advent of mechanical sources of energy, the productivity of the production shops rose sharply. The collateral advent of mass production processes still further increased the productivity of the shops.

As the production of the shops rose, both through greater productivity and through expansion, the numbers of service personnel rose sharply. The flood of goods needed to be inspected, counted, packed, stored, sold, shipped, invoiced, etc. Furthermore, in the service industries (merchandising, insurance, government, banking, etc.) the numbers of employees also rose sharply. Much mechanization[14] has taken place in these industries, with the collateral need for machine operation and machine maintenance.

Taylor's principles for doing work are admittedly applicable to non-production operations, even though the applications are special. But the pace of application lags decidedly behind that in vogue in the production shops. In the United States, serious charges of inefficiency continue to be leveled at the government agencies, the railroads, the building industry and many others. In contrast, great strides are being made in merchandising, and in farming.

The modifications necessary to apply Taylor's principles to non-production jobs are beyond the scope of this discussion. The main point

---

[14] *Note on Productivity Through Mechanization*

There is much debate over whether mechanization is a problem in engineering or in management. This may be a good place for some clarification.

Engineering is generally understood to consist of utilization of the forces of nature (as discovered by the scientist) for the benefit of man.

The distinction between engineering and management lies in the fact that the latter coordinates the forces of *people,* also for the benefit of man.

Of course, the engineers who design machines, the craftsmen who build them and the workmen who operate and service the machines are all people. In this way, management, through directing the activities of these people, makes vital decisions regarding mechanization. But the distinction made between engineering and management is of great importance.

Management, in its prime loyalty to the enterprise, must strive for higher productivity through all means available. One of these means is through mechanization. Management's role is to sense those situations which might economically be mechanized, to have studies conducted by the experts, to consider the findings of the experts in the light of the surrounding circumstances, to find ways of financing the mechanization, and finally, to put the mechanization into practice in a way which avoids any serious disruption of the lives of the human beings affected.

is rather, that progressive management cannot afford continued pre-occupation with production worker efficiency. This is placing continued emphasis on a problem of diminishing size, the while neglecting the greater and growing problems of non-production worker productivity.

Departmental Productivity

As the enterprise grows, there arises the necessity to create departments for the more effective performance of the work. This development parallels the development of organs in the biological organism. Thereby a new unit of industrial life, the department, comes into being and requires management techniques for productivity.

The principles of the best method, and of measure of a fair day's work, apply to the department as well as to the individual workman. "Method" as applied to the department more usually is designated as "procedure" or "routine." The standard of a fair day's work for the department is often called the "production capacity."

"Selection of the workman" takes on a new connotation, for it implies selection of mutually compatible associates for the department. Training in working together as a group is no less important. Often the training time in group collaboration exceeds in length the time required for training the individuals to carry out their individual tasks.

The incentive for the group is often more forceful than the incentive for the individual. The individual wants to be part of a team, and his desire "to belong" generates a corresponding desire to perform in a way which does not let the team down. Industry has far to go to exploit this team-work form of incentive.

The system of management controls requires measures of departmental productivity both as a measure of the effectiveness of the departmental performance and of the departmental supervisor's performance. However, carried to extremes, high departmental productivity comes at a prohibitive price. A perfect record by the credit department normally means that too many sales have been lost. A demand, by the inspection department, for flawless appearance of the product, usually raises the cost of production needlessly.

The emphasis on departmental performance is far more complex than mere productivity. The urge to develop the department into an independent, self-sufficient industrial community is ever present. Rivalry and even hostility can develop respecting other departments. "Iron curtains" are not unheard of between departments.

Such over-emphasis on departmental importance can become a serious drag on the productivity of the enterprise. The necessary means for communication, coordination and control must be developed. At times these rise spontaneously from below. In the absence of such spontaneous leadership, top management itself must step in to fill up the gap.

Coordination to Aid Enterprise Productivity

The concept that top management can effect all necessary coordination is simply naive. The enterprise has need for numerous reflexes over and above the conventional coordination through the central nervous system, i.e., the top management hierarchy.

Coordination is the antidote to many of the ills of departmentalization. An example, one of many, can be cited from a company fabricating metal parts. The productive organs consisted essentially of a large foundry and a large machine shop. Each of these departments was well equipped with modern machinery. Each was manned with sincere, able people. Yet the organization was suffering serious losses due to numerous parts being defective beyond repair.

Closer scrutiny disclosed that while each department was devoting much effort to improving its own operation, the basic scrap problem was interdepartmental. The bulk of the scrap, turned up at machining, was of foundry origin. Under the circumstances, no solution was possible unless, through coordination, the fabrication conditions at the foundry could be correlated with the troubles discovered during machining. In this instance, coordination was through a staff department which could, by investigation, discover relationships between cause and effect.

Such situations abound in industry. Production lags because the equipment maintained by another department fails repeatedly. Yet the repeated failure might be designed out of existence were the facts known. Again, seriously unbalanced inventories may result from failure of communication between sales and production.

In contrast to the bits and pieces improvement derived through greater worker productivity, instances such as the foregoing can mean much at one stroke. The recognition of the presence of these situations, and their solution through staff department or higher management intervention, constitute a fruitful field for improving productivity.

The devices for securing coordination include, over and above the appeal to the common boss:

Conferences—a spontaneous form of meeting for discussion of problems.

Committees (for discussion)—a more formal group, with legitimacy as to the agenda and as to the right to publish minutes.

Committees (for decision)—a relatively new management development, differing from the conventional committee through having a delegation of power to make binding decisions. Sometimes called Junior Boards.[15]

Committees (for consultation)—a discussion group which is adjunct to the presiding executive. It appears to retain the usefulness of group deliberation while retaining also the unbroken chain of command.[16]

Staff departments—a device of great flexibility, used to collect facts, to make analyses of facts, to draft recommendations, and to secure approval for joint action.

As the enterprise grows in size and in complexity, the need for devices for coordination rises in geometric proportion. This trend is equally evident in the biological organisms. But management has far to go to develop means for coordination which approach, in effectiveness, the nervous system of the biological organism.

Management Controls

The amazing parallel which exists between the enterprise and the biological organism suggests the need for far greater development of the concept of "management controls." The biological organism achieves control by:

(a) Sensing what is going on, through a marvelous number and variety of sensory organs,

(b) Analyzing the resulting data through the integrating mechanism of the nervous system,

(c) Issuing orders to effector organs to take action based on the results of analysis,

(d) Sensing the results of the action, which starts the cycle of events over again.

The development of the servo-mechanism has gone far to adapt these biological principles to solution of engineering problems. Many production processes are now equipped with instruments which meas-

---

[15] See Charles P. McCormick, *Multiple Management* (Clinton, S. C., Jacobs Press, 1938).

[16] See Sir Charles Renold, *op. cit.*

ure a phenomenon, and compare the results of measurement with a standard. In the event of disparity, the servo-mechanism sets into motion the means for regulating the process to meet the standard.

A related problem faces the manager. Expressed in more appropriate terms, the need in management controls is to:

(1) Decide on what are the essential facts required to regulate the enterprise,

(2) Define units of measure for these facts,

(3) Design management instruments to measure the facts in terms of those units of measure,

(4) Connect the instruments to the source of the facts,

(5) Summarize and present the facts in relation to standards of performance,

(6) Focus managerial attention on those situations in which performance fails to meet standard.

The resulting collection of facts is sometimes called the "Executive Instrument Panel."

The idea of steering an enterprise by instruments is in its early stage of acceptance by managers. For the small enterprise, most essential facts are within the direct observation of the manager, and the need for an instrument panel is small. The larger the enterprise, the more acute becomes the need for the instrument panel.

The instrument panel is but a technique for aiding management control. Management control includes not only the sequence of events discussed above; it includes also the definition of the objectives of the enterprise. It includes defensive policy in discovery of what are the perils of the enterprise, and planning to avoid these perils. It includes aggressive policy planning for the growth of the enterprise.

Much remains to be done in clarifying the concept of management controls and in perfecting techniques for accomplishing the controls. The parallel between the problem of engineering control with that of biological control has given rise to a new word[17] to identify the generic character of these controls.

The Supply of Managers

The know-how of productivity is only of academic value unless the managers on the job possess this know-how and have the deter-

---

[17] See Norbert Wiener, *Cybernetics* (New York: John Wiley & Sons, 1948).

mination to put it into practice. The supply of such managers constitutes one of the limitations in achieving productivity.

The problem is not merely one of quantity of managers; the quality is equally a problem. There is increasing awareness that neither general knowledge of life, nor special knowledge of technical processes, suffice to make a man a manager. The need is for skill and experience *in the managerial process,* which is quite a different thing.

Training of managers poses new problems in education. For such training, the laboratory is not to be found in the schools; the laboratory is industry itself. Thus far, management training has been restricted to the locale of the laboratory, i.e., on the job. Men have learned to be managers through being apprenticed to practicing managers. The advantage has been that in practice one deals with real situations as they arise. The limitation has been in the extent of empiricism which prevails among practicing managers.

Within the last decade a relatively new form of management training has arisen—the seminar.[18] This is essentially a meeting of not more than (about) 20 practicing managers, under skilled leadership. Through multi-lateral discussion these practitioners not only learn techniques from one another; what is far more important, they develop a keen awareness of the existence of universal principles of management.

In the large enterprises there has been development of long range planning to insure adequate supply of managers. Inventories are taken of the number and kind of managerial vacancies which are coming up on the horizon. Paralleling this, inventories are taken of the available candidates for these openings and of the extent of further training and experience needed by these men. Thereupon a long range program of rotation and training is established to close the gap.

A final problem in supply of managers is the question of professionalism for managers. The responsibilities of the manager, both as to the life of the enterprise and as to the many people whose well-being depends on the life of the enterprise, have grown greatly. In this way, while the decisions of the manager appear on the face of it to be private in character, these decisions strongly influence the lives of many people and can properly be regarded as tinged with a public interest.

Those who as a class make important decisions affecting the pub-

---

[18] Seminars offered by American Management Association currently exhibit the broadest variety of subject matter.

lic interest must solve the problem of competence, ethics, etc., if they are to avoid regulation by the public. The doctors and lawyers solved this problem through creation of professions. At the other extreme the railroads failed to solve the problem and found themselves heavily regulated by public laws.

The attributes of a profession are well known. They include the rendering of an essential public service, a codified body of special knowledge, selection of the candidates on the basis of fitness, cultural and special training, examinations as to proficiency, subscription to a code of ethics, and finally, licensing by the public.

Analysis discloses that as yet, management has moved only partly in the direction of professionalism. But if interchangeability of managers is to expand, there will have to be a change in the manner of appointment of managers. The present system of apprenticeship must give way to professionalism.

22 Employee Attitudes and Productivity*

By CHARLES C. GIBBONS

RECENTLY a large ship ran aground in a well-charted harbor. The man at the helm had brought ships into that harbor many times without difficulty. At the board of inquiry into the accident, the helmsman testified that he knew he was steering the ship aground. When asked why he did not alter his course, he said that he was following orders from the captain. The helmsman was then asked why he did not ask the captain to alter the course of the ship. His reply was, "It wasn't my business to give orders to the captain and, besides, the captain was busy."

Incidents similar to this one happen frequently in business and industry. Millions of men and women who work in factories are giving their jobs only part of what they have to give. They are going through the motions, they are getting by, but they are not as productive as they could be. Business managers are often disappointed that workers do not seem willing to contribute more to their jobs. Workers, in turn, often find their jobs lacking in interest and basic satisfactions.

Business managers face the challenge of getting workers to participate fully in achieving the goals of their firms. Up to the present time, managers have failed to recognize fully the benefits of this greater participation. Managers have failed to recognize that workers have hearts and heads, as well as hands, which they will gladly contribute to the business if they are encouraged to do so. If workers are to participate more fully, managers must adopt such participation as a conscious goal. Conditions must be set up which will encourage and facilitate participation.

* Reprinted by permission from the November, 1953, issue of the *Michigan Business Review,* published by the School of Business Administration, University of Michigan.

The Dynamics of the Relationship

Before managers can influence the worker to contribute more to his job, they must understand more fully the worker as an individual and the nature of the relationship between the worker and his company. A man's behavior is directed toward the satisfaction of his biological needs such as hunger, thirst, and sex; and toward the satisfaction of his social needs such as security, recognition, and approval. A worker will adopt the company's goals as his goals only if he feels that by so doing he can satisfy his own needs.

The basic human relationship in industry is the one between the worker and his supervisor. Before this relationship can be thoroughly sound, the worker must gain the insight that the "boss" is not the supervisor but that the real controlling factor is the need for achieving the goals of the organization.

In a manufacturing firm, for example, the real "boss" is the customer. When the worker understands this fact, he can accept orders from his supervisor without feeling subservient and without feeling that the supervisor alone is responsible for achieving the goals of the business. If workers understand how their efforts contribute toward achieving the company's goals and, very directly, toward achieving their own goals, the whole relationship becomes more intelligent and satisfying. Workers who have this insight are motivated to contribute their full energies to their jobs.

Insight for the Worker

The problem might be restated then as: What can be done to help the worker achieve insight regarding his relationship to his supervisor and fellow workers?

The first step is for the manager to recognize and accept the antagonisms and hostilities which the worker often feels toward his supervisor and his company. It is not surprising that such feelings exist, for work is regarded by many workers as a burden to be endured in order that they can enjoy certain satisfactions away from the job. The work itself may have no appeal. It is quite normal for individuals to have both favorable and unfavorable feelings toward the same person or situation.

The manager should not be surprised, then, to find that workers have both favorable and unfavorable feelings toward their supervisors, toward their company, and toward the work which they are required to do. He can do much to help the situation by simply recognizing and accepting the unfavorable feelings which workers express. Only when the working relationship is such that the worker feels free to express his feelings—favorable and unfavorable—can he gain insight into his relationship to his supervisor and to his fellow workers.

The next thing which the manager must do if he wishes workers to identify themselves with the company and its goals is to keep them informed. Workers must know the goals of the organization, the major problems, and the plans which the managers and supervisors have for solving the problems. This process of explanation should start the first day the worker is on the payroll. There must be a thorough and well-planned program of orientation which will acquaint the new worker with the situation, with his supervisor and fellow workers, and with the relationship which his work has to the work of the entire organization.

Frequent interviews between the worker and his supervisor are perhaps the most effective means of keeping the worker informed. The manager should give information regarding the company's activities to the supervisors who, in turn, should pass the information on to the workers.

Although these interviews are basic, other channels may also be used to keep workers informed. A company may hold meetings at which policies are discussed with workers. Bulletins and booklets may be distributed. The medium used to convey information to workers will depend upon the type of information and other circumstances.

The important thing is for management to recognize that one way of getting workers "on the team" and keeping them "on the team" is to keep them informed.

Wider Participation

Keeping workers informed constitutes just one half of the process of communications. The other half of the process is giving the workers an opportunity to express their ideas regarding the operation of the company.

In the past, managers have done a better job of keeping workers informed than they have of getting and using workers' ideas. If managers wish workers to feel like a part of the company, they must solicit workers' ideas and they must use the good ones. By contributing their ideas to the operation of the business, workers not only help to solve problems but also, by participating, become identified with the goals of the organization in such a way that their motivation is increased.

The basic channel for the flow of such ideas should be through the supervisor. Every supervisor, at whatever level, should encourage the people under him to think independently about the processes and methods used on their jobs and about possible improvements.

The interviews between workers and their supervisors should permit a two-way flow of ideas. At the same time the supervisor is giving the worker information regarding the plans and needs of the organization, the worker should feel free to suggest any ideas that occur to him regarding the work to be done. There should never be any question as to whether the supervisor would welcome suggestions for improvement. One of the greatest challenges of this whole process is to change the attitudes of workers and supervisors and the spirit of their interviews so that such a two-way flow of ideas will occur. Even though this supervisory relationship is basic, it is usually desirable to provide additional channels through which ideas may flow from workers to management. There are several special procedures which companies may use for this purpose.

Suggestion Systems

Many companies use a suggestion system as a means of stimulating and collecting workers' ideas for the improvement of the business. There is much to be said for such a system, for companies that use suggestion systems properly find that the number of constructive suggestions coming from workers is much greater than would otherwise be the case. It is easy to show that the ideas collected through a suggestion system save the company a great deal of money. Perhaps even more important is the fact that workers who submit suggestions and see them put into effect get a real feeling of participation in the running of the business. This feeling that they are part of the company may go far toward motivating them to do their best on their jobs.

Some companies use morale surveys as a means of finding out what workers are thinking. These surveys help to remove some of the guesswork from decisions affecting employee relations. Such surveys are most effective when they are limited to a specific topic of immediate interest to both management and workers. When workers are allowed to express their opinions regarding matters that affect them, they feel more like a part of the company.

Communications Among Management Personnel

The process by which rank-and-file workers can participate in solving some of the problems of the company has been described. There is often a need, also, for better utilization of the ideas of supervisors and staff members. The basic channel for the flow of ideas is, of course, through the regular organization structure. Special methods are often useful, however, in facilitating the flow of ideas. Some companies have daily meetings of men representing production, sales, engineering, and other phases of the business. These brief daily meetings make a great contribution toward coordinating the activities of supervisors and staff men and toward stimulating and utilizing the ideas of the entire group of employees.

It is common, however, to find companies where persons responsible for closely related functions do not see one another from one week to the next.

Another way to get the ideas of supervisors and staff members is for a trained investigator to hold a private and confidential interview with each of them. The purpose of these interviews is to stimulate these individuals to think critically and constructively about the company's operations and to collect their ideas for consideration by management. The ideas are then presented to management without identifying the persons who proposed the ideas. In companies where such interviews have been held, dozens of useable ideas have been suggested regarding operating efficiency, sales administration, product development, employee relations, and the organization and coordination of efforts. Supervisors and staff members, as well as rank-and-file workers, appreciate an opportunity to present their ideas to management.

Leadership in Process

It takes real leadership from managers and supervisors to get workers to feel and act like members of the team. Such leadership requires a thorough understanding of workers as human beings, and an understanding of the type of relationship that should exist among the members of the group.

Workers will be fully motivated only if they have insight into their relationships with supervisors and fellow workers. They must understand that, in working to achieve the company's goals, they will also be accomplishing their own goals. Only if this identity of interests exists, and only if workers understand it, can there be a fully productive and satisfying working relationship. Building such a relationship should be one of the major goals of every business manager.

Managers can help workers to understand their relationships within the company by making them feel free to express their feelings—both favorable and unfavorable—toward their jobs, their supervisors, and other factors in the work situation. Only after the worker has expressed his feelings can he proceed to deal with the more intellectual aspects of his relationship.

Managers can further help workers to understand their relationships within the organization by keeping them informed regarding the goals, problems, and plans of management. Interviews, meetings, and printed material provide workers with the facts they need for sound understanding.

Workers will feel that they are an integral part of the company only if they have an opportunity to express their ideas. Managers should encourage workers to present their ideas to their supervisors, and to submit them through suggestion systems and attitude surveys. Ideas coming to managers through these channels should receive careful attention.

If a manager or supervisor is to be an effective leader of men, he must understand men—their needs, their motives, and, most of all, their feelings. He must also know how to facilitate the two-way flow of ideas between management and workers. Acquiring such knowledge, attitudes, and skills is an essential part of the development of a business manager.

IV. THE GUARANTEED ANNUAL WAGE AND BUSINESS
STABILIZATION

23 Labor's New Victory: Threat or Promise?*

By SUMNER H. SLICHTER

1

No SETTLEMENT in union-employer negotiations since the dramatic agreement of 1937 between John L. Lewis and the United States Steel Corporation has aroused so much comment from editors, economists, and business leaders as the recent agreements between the United Automobile Workers and Ford and General Motors. Although the provision for the payment of supplementary unemployment compensation represents only one third of the cost of the companies' concessions, it is this feature of the agreements that is entirely responsible for the widespread comment.

The president of the National Association of Manufacturers charged that agreements to pay men for not working "could have seriously damaging effects on the American economy, perhaps leading to a socialistic state and a controlled economy," and the N.A.M. called an emergency conference to discuss the danger. Many papers and some economists questioned whether small employers would be able to do what Ford and General Motors are doing and suggested that small companies would be squeezed out of existence and the concentration of industry accentuated. Still others asserted that the higher labor costs represented by supplementary unemployment compensation would start an inflationary spiral of costs and prices.

A few commentators forecast that such payments would accelerate "automation"—taking it for granted that this would be bad. Many businessmen expressed the fear that employees would be discouraged from working. A frequently expressed fear was the possibility that supplemen-

* Reprinted by permission of the editor, from *Atlantic Monthly*, 196 (September 1955), 63-66. Copyright 1955, by the Atlantic Monthly Company, Boston 15, Massachusetts.

tary unemployment compensation would lead managers to plan less boldly for expansion—that, in the words of the Baltimore *Sun,* the characteristic adventurousness of American industry would fade away.

Supporters of the Ford and General Motors agreements are as numerous as the critics. The agreements have been hailed as evidence of the ability of American employers and unions to defy tradition, to work out their own arrangements for dealing with problems by bargaining—a method superior to the European practice of relying upon social legislation. A thoughtful article in the *Christian Science Monitor* described the Ford agreement as proving "that labor and industry are working out a new social system in the United States." Supporters of the new agreements stress their influence in encouraging managements to work out more stable year-round production schedules, and argue that additional unemployment compensation, by helping to maintain the demand for goods in periods of business recession, will strengthen the resistance of the economy to contraction.

Both the critics and the supporters of the Ford-General Motors agreements assume that provision for supplementary unemployment benefits will be added to many union-employer contracts during the next few years —just as supplementary pension schemes spread rapidly after the precedent-setting agreements in the steel industry in 1949. This assumption is correct, subject to the important qualification that these unemployment benefits will meet far more resistance from employers than supplementary pensions and thus will spread more slowly. But if there is a considerable spread of supplementary unemployment compensation, what will be the results to business and the economy and who will turn out to be right—the critics or the supporters of the Ford-General Motors agreements? Before attempting to answer these questions, let us see briefly what the agreements provide.

The agreements are long and detailed because they cover many technical points. In essence, however, both Ford and General Motors have agreed to contribute 5 cents for each hour worked by hourly-rated employees to a trust fund from which supplementary unemployment compensation shall be paid. No matter how small the amount in the trust funds, the obligation of the companies to make contributions shall not exceed 5 cents an hour. Furthermore, when the funds exceed a certain size in relation to the number of employees, the contributions of the employer are to cease.

The payments will not begin until June 1, 1956. After that date employees with at least one year's seniority who are laid off will be paid supplementary benefits sufficient, when added to state unemployment compensation, to give them 65 per cent of their weekly after-tax straight-time wage for the first four weeks of unemployment, usually after a one-week waiting period, and 60 per cent for the next twenty-two weeks, but in no event less than $25 a week. After twenty-six weeks the employees shall cease to draw supplementary unemployment benefits. Since the average benefits under state unemployment compensation schemes have been only about 35 per cent of average straight-time earnings after taxes, the Ford and General Motors schemes nearly double the unemployment compensation received by the employees of those companies.

2

Are the Ford and General Motors agreements a radical innovation in industrial relations embodying an important new principle: namely, that employers have an obligation for the welfare of workmen whom they lay off? I think not. The very fact that the Ford and General Motors agreements provide only for *supplementary* unemployment benefits shows that they were not setting up a new principle. The new principle that employers have the duty to provide income for laid-off employees was established first by the state of Wisconsin in 1932 when it set up a state scheme of employer-financed unemployment compensation, and later by the federal government in 1935 when Congress, through a special payroll tax, virtually forced the states to set up unemployment compensation schemes. The Ford and General Motors agreements simply attempt to make up for the inadequacy of benefits under the state laws—an inadequacy that was pointed out by President Eisenhower in his economic reports for 1953 and 1954.

Will the spread of agreements of the Ford and General Motors type squeeze the small and less successful employers out of business? No criticism of the Ford and General Motors agreements has been made more frequently than this one. The charge naïvely assumes that large concerns are better able to keep down layoffs than small concerns. The spread of the Ford-General Motors type of agreement would obviously help those companies which are best at keeping the number of layoffs low in relation to the number of workers on the payroll. This means that the Ford-General Motors type of agreement, if widely adopted, would confer advantages (1) on those companies which are growing rapidly and (2) on those which are good at limiting the seasonal and cyclical fluctuations in their output. The agreements would add to the difficulties of the enterprises which for any reason are not able to keep layoffs low—firms in declining industries or high-cost and inefficient companies.

In short, the spread of unemployment compensation agreements would help the most efficient companies (large or small) and all enterprises in expanding industries and would hurt the less efficient concerns and all firms in contracting industries. In some industries success in keeping down layoffs may be associated with largeness, in other industries with smallness, and in still other industries it may be quite independent of size. Hence, it is wrong to suggest as a broad generalization that the widespread adoption of unemployment pay will tend to squeeze out the "little fellow."

The extent to which the spread of supplementary unemployment compensation tends to concentrate production and employment in the hands of those firms (large or small) that are best at keeping down layoffs will depend upon the bargaining policy of unions. Unions must decide whether to insist on different rates of contribution to the trust funds by different employers in order to make possible the same scale and duration of supplementary benefits regardless of the employer's layoff rate, or whether to accept differences in the scale and duration of unemployment pay in order to keep uniform the contribution rates of different employers.

Long experience has taught unions that they get into trouble both with employers and with their own members if they go very far in imposing more onerous terms on some concerns among a group of competitors than on other enterprises in the group. Hence, one is reasonably safe in predicting that unions will not vary the rate of contributions made by various competing employers. It follows that the spread of the Ford-General Motors type of agreement would have only a moderate tendency to concentrate production in the hands of firms that are best at keeping down layoffs. Some advantage, however, would still accrue to the firms with low layoff rates because contributions are made by the employer to the trust fund only when the fund is less than a specified ratio to payrolls. The lower the layoff rate, the smaller the proportion of the time that the employer would be contributing.

The tendency for the spread of the Ford-General Motors type of agreement to concentrate production in the firms with the lowest layoff rates will be limited by the fact that unions will not be able to negotiate such agreements with the very weakest firms and in the declining industries where the shrinkage of employment has been greatest. Thus the failure of supplementary unemployment compensation to extend to some of the weakest and least efficient firms will help these firms to survive.

Will the spread of the Ford-General Motors type of agreement encourage the use of machines to run machines—so-called automation? The answer to this question is "Yes." Hand methods have the advantage over machine methods, from the standpoint of employers, that they entail fewer fixed costs. When business falls off, the employer who uses hand methods can get rid of a considerable part of his payroll by dropping men, but most machine costs (interest on the investment, depreciation, obsolescence, insurance) go on whether or not the machine is running. Unemployment pay makes hand-method costs more like machine-method costs because it lessens the savings that employers achieve in slack times by making layoffs. To that extent, supplementary unemployment compensation will encourage the shift to machine methods.

But so strong are the present incentives for employers to shift to machine methods that the practical effect of the spread of supplementary unemployment compensation will be small. Cutting tools in recent years have become so efficient that slow and cumbersome hand methods of loading and unloading machines greatly limit machine capacity and keep machines idle a large part of the time. Hence, enormous gains are to be made from the development of (1) machines for loading and unloading other machines and (2) machines that perform several operations on a part without being reloaded. Unemployment pay would add only a small amount to the gains from automation.

3

Will the spread of the Ford-General Motors type of agreement add substantially to the stability of the economy by increasing the incomes of unemployed workers during recessions? A moderate gain in stability may be expected. Obviously, the laid-off workers who receive supplementary unemployment compensation will be greatly helped in maintaining their demand for goods since, as I have pointed out, their unemployment benefits will be almost doubled. But the effect of the supplementary unemployment compensation will be limited by the fact that, even after it has spread to the fullest practicable extent, it will reach only a small fraction of all employees. It will not extend to any important degree beyond union members, of whom there are about 16 million in private industry. But many union members are in industries in which for one reason or another it is either not necessary or not feasible to negotiate supplementary unemployment benefits. Hence, unless union membership grows quite rapidly in the next few years, supplementary unemployment compensation is not likely to cover more than about 10 million workers, less than one fourth of the non-agricultural employees in American industry and only about one fourth the number covered by the various government unemployment compensation schemes.

On the other hand, supplementary unemployment compensation agreements are likely to be concentrated in manufacturing, mining, transportation, and construction—the industries in which the cyclical ups and downs of employment are greatest. Hence, even if supplementary unemployment compensation covers less than one fourth of the non-farm employees, it will raise the incomes of a much higher proportion of the unemployed.

What substance is there to the charges that unemployment pay will make men unwilling to work and that it will be an important inflationary influence in the economy? Paying men unemployment benefits of 60 per cent or 65 per cent (or even 75 per cent) of their straight-time earnings after taxes is not likely to deter many men from working. In the first place, wives do not care to have idle husbands around the house when jobs are available, and the influence of the wives is not to be overlooked.

In the second place, consumption in the United States is rather competitive, and the family with only 65 per cent of its usual income after taxes cannot live in the way that it has been accustomed to live and in the way that the neighbors are living. A drop of 35 per cent in income means postponing the buying of many things that the family would like to have, cutting down on recreation and trips, and perhaps changing plans for the education of children. People who fear that American workers will be content with $50 or $60 a week unemployment benefits when jobs are to be had paying $20 or $30 a week more are not aware of the enormous unfilled wants of most families.

To the extent that unemployment pay sustains incomes in periods of recession and thus limits the drop in the demand for goods that accompanies recessions, it will be an inflationary influence. In fact, *any* arrangement that limits the severity of recessions is inflationary because such arrangements tend to prevent prices from falling sufficiently during recessions to offset the rise in prices that accompanies most booms. But supplementary unemployment compensation will not be a *major* influence determining the long-run movement of the price level in the United States.

Since various anti-recession measures (of which supplementary unemployment compensation is only one) will prevent much of a drop in the price level during recessions, the long-run movement of prices will depend upon how much prices rise during booms. The principal determinants of the movement of prices during booms will be (1) the strength of trade unions, (2) the willingness and ability of employers to resist the demands of unions, and (3) the rate of technological change. These three conditions will determine the movement of labor costs to which the price level must adjust itself.

A widely expressed fear is that unemployment pay will weaken the spirit of adventure that has always characterized American industry. If adding new employees to the payroll imposes heavy obligations on the employer, will not enterprises be reluctant to expand?

This argument is without merit. Employers who have orders or who expect orders are going to hire enough employees to fill them. Failure to receive good service would cause customers to take their business elsewhere. It would take a very high rate of unemployment benefits to make employers prefer to lose customers rather than to add workers who may be needed only temporarily.

In two ways the spread of more liberal unemployment pay will encourage industry to expand. In the first place, as I have pointed out, the broad adoption of the scheme will confer advantages on the firms that through expansion and other means are able to keep down the rate of layoffs. In the second place, to the extent that supplementary unemployment benefits limit the severity of recessions they reduce the risks of expansion. On the whole, one must conclude that the widespread adoption of supplementary unemployment compensation would strengthen rather than weaken the dynamic influences in the American economy.

Up to this point the survey of the pros and cons yields a verdict in favor of agreements of the Ford-General Motors type. Such agreements, if widely adopted, would tend to concentrate production and employment a little more in the enterprises (large or small) which are most efficient, would stimulate in small measure the spread of automation (surely a desirable result), would add modestly to the resistance of the economy against recessions, and would stimulate moderately the expansion of industry. The fears that generous unemployment benefits would undermine men's willingness to work do not seem to be well founded. To a small extent supplementary unemployment compensation would be an inflationary influence, but this criticism can be made of any arrangement or policy which mitigates the severity of recessions.

But I have yet to present the most important criticism of supplementary unemployment pay. It is a criticism which, despite its importance, is rarely made either by employers or by union leaders. The criticism is that supplementary unemployment compensation, even if widely adopted, is not a satisfactory substitute for adequate normal unemployment benefits. In other words, it does not give the country what it needs—an adequate system of unemployment compensation.

I have pointed out that, at the best, supplementary unemployment compensation agreements could be expected to reach only about one out of four of the workers now covered by government unemployment compensation schemes. Furthermore, in the very spots where unemployment is most serious, in declining industries and among weak firms, unions will have the greatest difficulty in negotiating agreements of the Ford-General Motors type.

There is no doubt that the unemployment benefits provided by the present state unemployment compensation laws are inadequate. President Eisenhower in his last economic report pointed out that the ratio of benefits to the average weekly wages of covered employees is only 34 per cent— in some states below 30 per cent. Back in 1938 the ratio was 43 per cent. President Eisenhower recommended that benefits be raised so that the great majority of covered workers will be eligible for payments that are at least half their regular earnings. He also recommended broadening the coverage of these laws.

President Eisenhower's recommendations received far less publicity than the Ford-General Motors agreements; yet their adoption would do far more to give the country an adequate system of unemployment compensation than can be expected from the spread of supplementary unemployment compensation. Undoubtedly, the provisions in the Ford-General Motors agreements calling for total unemployment benefits (regular and supplementary) equal to 65 per cent of wages after taxes for the first four weeks will help the state legislatures raise their conception of what are "adequate" benefits. Surely President Eisenhower's recommendation of half of "regular earnings" is too low—though not far below 60 per cent of straight-time earnings after taxes as provided in the Ford-General Motors agreements between the fifth and the twenty-sixth weeks of benefits.

An important characteristic of an adequate scheme of unemployment compensation is that it costs less than nothing—it is an asset to the community, not a burden. The test of whether any economic or political arrangement is a burden or an asset is whether it tends to add to or to subtract from production—whether it makes for a higher or a lower standard of consumption. Adequate unemployment compensation, if properly managed, does not subtract from production and consumption in times of boom, and it does help check the drop in production and employment in times of recession. Hence, over the entire business cycle it tends to increase production and consumption.

An adequate system of unemployment compensation would not only add to the security of workers—it would also add to the security of business enterprises and would enhance the value of the investment in American industry and the value of every farm. It is amazing that the businessmen and farmers have not sought to stabilize their markets by insisting that the government provide an adequate system of unemployment compensation.

24 Stabilization of Employment Is Good Management*

By CHARLES C. GIBBONS

WHAT I have to say in this paper can be summarized in five simple statements:

1. A company can do much to stabilize its employment.

2. Steady jobs result from steady sales and production.

3. Steady sales and production result, in turn, from good management in all phases of the business.

4. The personnel manager can make an important contribution to the stabilization of employment.

5. A company can guarantee employment only after it has been successful in stabilizing its sales and production.

I shall make no attempt to prove that stabilization of employment is desirable. Most personnel managers, I believe, recognize the desirability of providing steady jobs for employees. Those who are interested in proof will find it in the many books, articles, and reports published on this subject during the past 15 years.

How Much Can One Company Do?

There are some who question how much a company can do to stabilize its employment. Such persons believe that a company's employment is determined primarily by general business conditions. Although general business conditions do exert a powerful influence on the operations of a company, most firms can do much to reduce fluctuations in their sales, production, and employment. The American Legion Employment Stabilization Service proved the truth of this state-

* Reprinted from *Planning for Worker Security and Stability*. Personnel Series No. 152 (1953), by permission of the American Management Association, copyright holder.

ment by a study[1] of 74 companies that had made efforts to stabilize their operations. Before stabilization, these companies had provided jobs throughout the year for only 58 per cent as many workers as they employed during their peak periods. By their stabilization efforts, they increased this figure to 89 per cent.

The success that a company has in stabilizing its operations depends largely on the attitude which top management takes toward the problem. If much is to be accomplished, management must regard stabilization as an important objective. Three companies are best known for providing steady work or wages: the Procter & Gamble Co., the Nunn-Bush Shoe Co., and Geo. A. Hormel & Co. In each of these three companies, the stabilization program was sponsored with evangelistic zeal by the top man—Col. William Procter and Mr. Richard R. Deupree at Procter & Gamble, Mr. H. L. Nunn at Nunn-Bush, and Mr. Jay C. Hormel at Hormel. Real progress in stabilization can be made only if management attacks this problem with the same determination and ingenuity which it applies to other business problems.

Influence of Sales and Production

My next point is that stabilization of employment is not achieved independently but is the result of stabilization in other phases of the business, especially in sales and production. Before companies like Procter & Gamble, Nunn-Bush, and Hormel could offer steady work or wages to their employees, they had to reduce sharp fluctuations in sales and production. Frequent layoffs in a company indicate that something is wrong—usually not in the personnel department but in the sales department, the production department, or some other place in the company.

Since all areas of the company are involved, employment stabilization calls for the combined efforts of everyone from top management to rank-and-file employees. Real progress toward stabilization can be made only if most of these individuals have a sincere wish—even a determination—to achieve stabilization.

Countering the Effects of Recession

There are two types of instability with which a company must be concerned: (1) instability associated with a general recession in business and (2) instability due to seasonal or other short-run fluctua-

---

[1] American Legion Employment Stabilization Service. *To Make Jobs More Steady and to Make More Steady Jobs.* St. Paul, Minn.: Webb Publishing Co., 1942, p. 3.

tions in demand. In both cases, stabilization depends on good management in all areas of the business more than it depends on special techniques of stabilization.

Consider first what a company can do to weather a recession. Interesting information on this point is found in the experience of companies which had difficulty during the depression of the 1930's. Robert Roosa studied 1,300 of these firms—small companies in financial distress which had applied for emergency loans from the Federal Reserve Bank of New York.[2] Roosa states that these companies had one great weakness in common—spotty management. The companies possessed one kind of management skill to a high degree but were weak in other areas. One firm might have an excellent sales program but be weak on production methods. Another might be strong in production but have poor control over its finances. Companies with such spotty management had been able to survive, and even prosper, during good times. Spotty management was not able, however, to carry the companies through the rigors of depression.

My own experiences of the past five years are in line with Roosa's findings. I have studied several companies in order to recommend changes that would result in stabilizing their operations. Always the story has been the same: The important changes needed are improved policies and procedures in production, sales, research, personnel, control, and finance; and the importance of changes in these areas far outweighs the importance of measures aimed *directly* at stabilization.

If, as all this suggests, the best way to sail through a storm is to enter it with a sound ship, we should remember that a sound ship is not built in a day. Nor is it easily built during a storm. It must be built and made strong during the good weather which precedes the storm. The ships which are going to enter whatever economic storms the future may bring will be strong or weak, depending on what business men do in the good weather which is still ahead. Thus it is very timely for us to be considering employment stabilization now—more timely by far than it would be for us to consider this same topic in some future year, after the bad weather has begun.

Combating Short-Run Fluctuations

We have been discussing what a company can do to prepare for a general business recession. Let us consider now what a company can do

---

2 Roosa, Robert V. "Small Business and Depression," *Harvard Business Review*, January, 1948, pp. 58-62. (See page 134 of this book.)

to reduce seasonal and other short-run fluctuations in employment. Many workers find their jobs unsteady, even in good times. In an average month at the present time, 1.4 per cent of workers in manufacturing are laid off for lack of work.[3] This percentage may sound insignificant, but it is equivalent to more than 200,000 cases of layoff a month in manufacturing alone.

Many books and articles on employment stabilization deal with special techniques that may be used to stabilize employment. It is customary to describe such techniques as production for stock, selling in off seasons, transfer of employees, and dovetailing of products. My emphasis is different, for I believe that such an approach to the problem is too narrow. A close look at the special stabilization techniques reveals that the basic ingredient in each of them is good management.

1. *Production for stock* can be undertaken safely only if the company has good inventory control, accurate sales forecasts, sound financing, and a durable product.

2. *Selling in off seasons* must be supported by an aggressive sales force, by sound pricing policies, and by effective advertising.

3. *Transfer of employees* is feasible only if the company's employees are able and willing to perform jobs other than their regular ones.

4. The development of new products for *dovetailing* purposes depends on an active research department.

A well-managed company will employ these stabilization techniques, whenever their use is appropriate, to reduce seasonal and other short-run fluctuations. A company will reduce fluctuations, however, not so much by concentrating on these special stabilization techniques as by improving its policies and procedures in production, sales, research, personnel, control, and finance. In short, the best stabilization technique of all is good management.

Role of the Personnel Manager

In view of the fact that stabilization of employment involves all areas of management, we should recognize that contributions can be made by the sales manager, by the production manager, and by the research director. In this discussion, however, I shall emphasize the contribution that the personnel manager can make to stabilization of employment.

It seems to me that there are three ways in which the personnel

---

[3] This figure is based on Bureau of Labor Statistics reports for the 60 months prior to October, 1952.

manager can contribute to stabilization in his company:

1. He can perform the regular personnel functions so as to maximize their contribution to the efficiency of operations.

2. He can use certain personnel techniques that contribute directly to stabilization of employment.

3. He can spearhead a stabilization program in his company.

Since a company can offer steady jobs only if it is in a good competitive position, personnel procedures that contribute to operating efficiency are also contributing to employment stabilization. Employment, training, communications, employee benefits and services, and other phases of personnel work all make a contribution to efficiency of operations and to the stability of employment that can exist only in a well-run company.

Specific Stabilization Techniques

Several personnel procedures that can contribute directly to stability of employment deserve our consideration. Two of these which I wish to discuss here are transfer of employees and communications.

Transfer of employees is the personnel procedure which has the most direct effect on stabilization of employment. In 1940, the National Industrial Conference Board reported on the stabilization programs of 203 companies.[4] Forty-nine per cent of these companies used transfer of employees as a method of stabilizing employment. Experience has shown that, if a program of transfer is to be successful, the following conditions must be met:

1. Employees must be versatile, in the sense that they must either have skills to perform several different jobs or have the ability to learn those skills easily.

2. A thorough study should be made of the jobs in the factory to determine which ones are similar enough to make transfer of employees feasible.

3. Employees must be willing to accept transfer and must cooperate in learning the new work.

4. There must be a satisfactory training program for each job.

5. Seniority provisions in union contracts must be flexible enough to permit transfer from one job to another and from one department to another.

---

4 Brower, F. Beatrice. *Reducing Fluctuations in Employment; Experience in 31 Industries.* Studies in Personnel Policy No. 27. New York: National Industrial Conference Board, 1940.

6. A policy regarding pay for transferred employees must be worked out and accepted by the employees.

In spite of the difficulties to be overcome in working out a transfer program, the efforts of many companies have been successful. Transfer of employees has played a large part in the successful stabilization programs of such companies as McCormick & Co. and Spiegel, Inc.

The communication of ideas between employees and managers is a second area of personnel work which can contribute directly to the success of a company's stabilization program. Employees must be kept informed regarding management's efforts to stabilize operations and regarding some of the difficulties involved in stabilization. If employees recognize the efforts management is making to provide steady jobs, they will be more willing to cooperate on matters like transfers and technological changes. Employees must recognize that they, as well as management, have a responsibility for achieving stable operations.

Importance of Leadership

The personnel manager can contribute much toward stabilization of employment through regular personnel procedures and through special stabilization techniques. He can make his greatest contribution, however, by spearheading a drive within his company for the stabilization of sales, production, and employment.

Because he is involved in the layoff of workers, the personnel manager is often more conscious than anyone else in the company of the need for stabilizing the company's operations. He sees clearly how fluctuations in sales and production—often preventable ones—result in frequent layoff and rehiring of workers.

Each company must develop a stabilization program to meet its own needs. Experience has shown that some one person in each company must enthusiastically and persistently sponsor the idea of stabilization if much progress is to be made. Top management must give its support, and all departments must cooperate, but a single individual is usually the driving force behind stabilization. It is possible for the personnel manager to be this person.

A personnel manager who is conscious of the need for greater stability can do several things to promote a stabilization program in his company. He can:

1. Point out the magnitude of the problem with facts about fluctuations in sales, production, and employment.

2. Show what other companies have done to reduce fluctuations.

3. Cooperate with others in developing a stabilization program for the company.

4. Arrange meetings at which department heads can discuss the problems they encounter in stabilizing their operations.

5. Evaluate the results of the stabilization program and report these results to top management and department heads.

Achieving Guaranteed Employment

A company can guarantee employment or wages only after it has been successful in stabilizing its sales and production. In 1945, after a study of annual wages, Ernest Dale of AMA concluded that "an annual wage plan can be best applied, when it is least needed; and when it is most needed, it can be least applied."[5]

I believe that labor and management would be putting the cart before the horse if a union should demand and management should grant a guarantee of employment or wages before the operations of the company had been stabilized. No company has the resources to fulfill such a guarantee if its sales and production are unstable. In the cases of both Hormel and Procter & Gamble, management offered guarantees of work and wages to employees only after years of effort to stabilize operations.

Of 61 employment guarantee plans studied by the Conference Board in 1946,[6] 32 had been discontinued—two-thirds of them after less than five years of operation. These plans were discontinued for a variety of reasons: employee attitudes, wartime conditions, depression, and others. This experience shows that fulfilling an employment guarantee is difficult under the best conditions. The minimum requirement is a fair amount of stability in sales and production. Achieving a reasonable degree of stability comes first; the guarantee of employment comes later.

Many companies have not made any serious efforts toward achieving stabilization. The opportunities for improvement, therefore, are great. If a few companies succeed at stabilization, they will be the ones

---

[5] Dale, Ernest. *Annual Wages and Employment Stabilization Techniques*. Research Report No. 8. New York: American Management Association, 1945, p. 55.

[6] Brower, F. Beatrice. *Annual Wage and Employment Guarantee Plans*. Studies in Personnel Policy No. 76. New York: National Industrial Conference Board, 1946.

to benefit. If many companies could succeed at this job, the entire economy might become more stable. The significance of employment stabilization goes beyond the particular companies involved, for steady jobs will go far toward keeping America sold on the free enterprise system.

If we are to develop effective stabilization programs to benefit our companies and our country during the hour of need, now is the time to start working toward this goal.

25 Methods of Company Employment Stabilization*

By Samuel M. Wilson

DURING the last half century the American people have been faced with a growing problem of insecurity due to industrial unemployment. Relief and other social security devices have been adopted at the Federal and State levels as one means of meeting the problem; and, considerable attention has been devoted to the possibilities of developing programs for employer participation in reducing the onus of the problem. Similarly, increasing emphasis has been given to the development of specific internal or managerial employment regularization programs within specific companies. Since the early 1920's, for example, much thought has been given to the idea of production planning with a view to the elimination of peak and trough employment periods and reducing the amount of casual employment in manufacturing firms. It is the purpose of this article to review the history of some of these management devices which have been evolved as a means of increasing plant efficiency and incidentally of regularizing employment in specific companies. Although the study is general, the experience of 25 non-durable consumer goods industries in the Philadelphia area was investigated.[1] These findings have been used both to illustrate

---

* Reprinted from *Economics and Business Bulletin*, 3 (December 1950), 19-29, by permission of the Bureau of Economic and Business Research, Temple University.

[1] The types of firms surveyed for employment stabilization techniques include: Petroleum Refining, Transportation, Communications, Publishing, Department Store, Chemical Products, Ice Manufacturing, Can Container Manufacturer, Drug & Pharmaceutical Mfg., Pharmaceutical Manufacturing, Milk Products, Milk Processing, Food Processing, Wholesale Foods Products, Meat Packing, Confectionery (2 companies), Chewing Gum Manufacturer, Cigarette Manufacturing, Cigar Manufacturing (2 companies), Greeting Cards Publisher, Laundry & Dry Cleaning, Brewing, and Carbonated Beverages.

and to test the general thesis developed by industry management theorists during the past half century—that a high degree of employment stabilization can be achieved by specific company efforts in that direction.

The History of Company Stabilization

Employment regularization as a problem of business management was virtually unrecognized at the beginning of the 20th century. All industrial countries regarded unemployment accompanying major economic recessions as an unavoidable social phenomenon.[2] The problem was considered one of maladjustment of the labor supply rather than one caused by economic forces over which businessmen could exert control. During the first decade of the 20th century, reports of several committees created especially to examine the causes of and suggest remedies for irregularity totally ignored the possibility of using improved methods of business management as one means of meeting the problem.

A report prepared by an engineering committee, appointed by Mr. Herbert Hoover, the President of the Federated American Engineering Societies, and published in June, 1921, attributed 50 per cent of business waste of industrial operation to the management of industrial enterprises. The responsibility of management for reducing the controllable waste of unemployment was the dominant note of this report. Similarly, employment stabilization programs to be developed by businessmen was an important recommendation of the Unemployment Conference of 1921 called by President Harding.[3] Even more impetus to the development of individual company regularization programs was given by the report, "Business Cycles and Unemployment," prepared by the President's Committee.

Public interest in stabilization plans subsequently subsided with the return of economic prosperity during the later 1920's, but the principles of employment regularization continued to gain acceptance from a constantly increasing number of business organizations. The Industrial Relations Committee of the Philadelphia Chamber of Commerce in 1928 recommended that an institute be established to study regularization of employment.[4] By 1930 more than 200 concerns had already undertaken

---

[2] American Section of the International Chamber of Commerce, "Employment Regularization in the United States of America," Washington, D. C., April, 1931, p. 7.

[3] Julia E. Johnsen, Compiler. "Stability of Employment," *The Reference Shelf.* The H. W. Wilson Company, New York, 1931, p. 3.

[4] *Ibid.,* p. 3.

systematic programs to provide for a maximum continuity of employment.[5] In that same year, the Governor of New York called for the establishment of a committee for the stabilization of industry for the prevention of unemployment.

Interest in these programs was revived; and the number of companies undertaking regularization experiments during the 1930's increased rapidly, a condition which may be attributed to the increase in the volume of unemployment resulting from the depression of 1929-34. Further, the passage of unemployment compensation laws by the federal and state governments stimulated a considerable continuing interest in regularization programs. Moreover, various taxing schemes designed to charge employers with the cost of their own instability have focused much attention on the problem. One such program, the merit rating plan in effect in the State of Wisconsin under the Huber Bill, has been the basis for much national review. Some think this plan has had an influence on employers in that State in stimulating the adoption of stabilization methods.

Irregular Employment

Irregular employment and unemployment are essentially the same problem. The principal causes involved include technological change, casual or naturally intermittent employment, seasonal fluctuations, and business cycles. Many other minor causes such as changes in supply and demand, changes in population, legislation, strikes, wars, natural disasters, and all the multitudinous variations of modern industrial life may cause irregularities.

The importance of the problem on our social and economic structure has been indicated by former President Hoover who said:

> There is, to my mind, no economic failure so terrible in its impact as that of a country possessing a surplus of every necessity of life with numbers, willing and anxious to work, deprived of those necessities. It simply cannot be if our moral and economic system is to survive.[6]

The Wainwright Commission subsequently cited in its report the effects which unsteady work may have on the employee, stating,

> . . . From the being unable to get steady work, the unemployed often

---

[5] American Section of the International Chamber of Commerce, *op. cit.,* p. 10.

[6] The Industrial Relations Committee of the Philadelphia Chamber of Commerce. "Program for the Regularization of Employment and the Decrease of Unemployment in Philadelphia," n.d., p. 29.

become unable to do steady work—unreliable, inefficient, "good for nothing." During long periods of unemployment, good workmen degenerate into tramps. They become habituated to a life of idleness and uncertainty, so that when at last employment is once more to be had, they are unfit for continuous labor. The mere unemployed have become unemployable.[7]

Recognizing this to be the case, programs which combat irregular employment have a sound business basis from the employer viewpoint. A stable work force tends to reduce inefficiency, decrease labor turnover, and increase employee morale. Moreover, the view expressed by Mr. Herman Feldman in the late 1920's has come to have wide acceptance. He pointed out that:

. . . An investigation of industrial operation is sure to show that the chief cause of irregular employment in the past has been the indifference of management. The particular technique of various firms which have regularized employment is important, yet it is only second in significance to the fact that their principle in doing business has been to keep employment regular.[8]

Thus, the problem is clear. Stability of employment has become a necessary measure and should be one of the major responsibilities of the employer.[9] Insecurity is a growing personal as well as social problem and unemployment, one of the chief causes of it, is of far-reaching importance. One real question, then, is whether the problem of irregularity in industry can be solved as one phase of any program ameliorating insecurity.

The Nature of the Problem

It has been noted that some measure of control over the economic forces which produce irregularity of employment can be exerted by management, a fact proven by the regularization experiments and programs of employers. The economic forces vary in nature and intensity in each type of business. The manufacturers of cigars are confronted with obstacles to continuous operations entirely different from those confronting the manufacturers of automobiles. There are very few industries or companies which are not affected by seasonal variations and business cycles. There is, however, scarcely an industry in which some company has not effected an appreciable reduction in the irregularity of its operation.[10]

---

[7] Johnsen, op. cit., p. 66.

[8] Herman Feldman. "Newer Methods in the Stabilization of Employment." American Labor Legislation Review, 16:47-56. March, 1926, p. 55.

[9] Johnsen, op. cit., p. 10.

[10] American Section of the International Chamber of Commerce, op. cit., p. 29.

Executive commands will not guarantee continuous operation or employment for any particular company. If a company is to remain in a competitive business, work can be provided only when there is work to be done. Philanthropic methods used by a company to prevent its workers from financial impoverishment are of little use. The real remedy is management's constant attention to the innumerable factors of ordinary business operation which tend to cause fluctuations and the development of systematic efforts to remove the causes of such intermittent employment and production.

An examination of some of the techniques adopted makes it clear that methods used by a company in one line of industry may not be applicable to companies in other industries, nor even in the same industry. However, there are some basic considerations in the development of such a program which must be understood and variously applied by virtually every type of industrial enterprise. First, the problem of employment stabilization is primarily one for the principal executives of the company. Second, its solution involves formulation and continuous application of broad policies. Third, it involves constant attention to minute details. Fourth, the solution may be found in any or all of three approaches including (a) distribution methods; (b) production methods; and (c) personnel methods. Fifth, absolute stability is neither practical nor economically desirable. Such a condition would insure inflexibility of management and stagnation of progress. However, relative stability is desirable. Sixth, it is desirable to reduce employment and production fluctuations to a minimum.

The stabilization problem is all-embracing and it involves every company in the industrial system. It is not a problem of protecting one group of workers but rather one of maintaining full employment and constant work for the entire working force. The solutions range from those developed by and for the individual company to those designed for the entire industrial system; and, frequently, they are not easily established.

In this industrial system, many have contended that labor tends to work itself out of a job. While this is not true, generally, fluctuations can be minimized by the adoption of a well-balanced program. Program-making, therefore, must be kept well ahead of program executing since forward planning is the basis for any company employment regularization program.

General Limitations to the Solution of the Problem

Even though an employer has done all of the things in his power to solve his problem of irregular employment, the ultimate success of the program may depend on forces outside of his control.[11] Some companies may be prevented from stabilizing their operations by the vivid realities of immediate competition and possible loss of sales. This is especially true in extremely fluctuating businesses. Furthermore, if one employer uses a certain method, conditions in another company or branch of industry may become unsettled or worse than before. The introduction of a side-line may stimulate progress in stabilizing one company for a while but the new product may upset the business of other companies whose main product is the "side-line." If diversification is used to stabilize a company, extreme care in the selection of the side-line product is essential.

Another limitation grows out of the fact that extra capital is required to initiate almost any company stabilization program. Many companies are unable to meet this extra capital requirement under present conditions. Thus, until stabilization programs become more general, and hence, a factor in securing employees, it is likely that this requirement will impair the program.

The progressive employers are still in the minority. . . . They have the problem of stabilizing their operations while competing with the majority of employers who are engulfed by tradition and habit. The problem is complex, and individual, uncoordinated programs seem unable to solve the whole problem, but these individual solutions indicate what can be done with success if every company in every industry initiates a program to achieve general stabilization.[12]

Stabilization of Employment: Distribution Methods

Distribution techniques are commonly studied with a view to reorganization by firms seeking to reduce their costs due to fluctuations in all levels of operation. One such cost results from irregular employment, both of labor and equipment. As one means of reducing this cost, a number of specific practices have been adopted. To analyze the basic acceptability of each, some 25 Philadelphia firms were studied. The following is a summary discussion of the results of this work so far as primary distribution methods used are concerned.

Sales Forecasts

The attempt to forecast sales on an annual, periodical, and monthly basis is so much a part of the practice of many concerns that such a tech-

---

[11] Carroll R. Dougherty. *Labor Problems in American Industry.* 15th ed. Houghton Mifflin Company, New York, 1941, p. 590.

[12] *Ibid.,* p. 590.

nique can be considered essential to stabilizing employment.[13] The first step in forecasting sales is to analyze and estimate the future demand for the total amount of a given product through intelligent and scientific market research. After the demand has been ascertained, the amount which the particular company can reasonably expect to sell in the following period should be determined. This involves the interpretation of the past, present, and future sales' trends of the product generally as well as the specific company's market position. After analyzing all data, rational sales forecasts can be made. This forecast must not be "frozen" over the period because fluctuations during the period should be reflected in current modifications of the forecast.

Price Concessions During Dull Periods

Many companies use several methods of reducing prices to increase customers' demand during slack periods. A department store cuts selling prices of goods after the peak season. The meat packer has a flexible price system whereby the demand for the cuts of meat is kept in line. The petroleum refining company delivers fuel oil during the summer at a reduced price, or makes deliveries in the summer with an understanding that the bills can be paid in October. The food processing company gives discounts to its jobbers during the peak period, thereby reducing its own need for extra handling and storeroom personnel.

The publisher of greeting cards uses dated shipments and anticipated discounts during slack periods. Bills of spring shipments on Christmas cards are dated for collection on the first of December. In addition, a cash discount of 2 per cent-ten days is frequently offered to the customers. In this way, the customer is influenced to pay his bill in advance of December 1 to gain the advantage of the cash discount (anticipated discount) for each month he pays his bill in advance. This method has proven to be excellent in the case of one publisher studied.

Sales Promotions During Off-Peak Periods

Sales promotions during dull seasons include the breaking down of traditions, expanding into other areas, developing new products, increasing advertising, and consignment selling. A milk processing company, for example, has broken down the traditional habits of the consumer by influencing him to eat ice cream throughout the year. When sales declined, several of the companies studied expanded their sales into other areas. Ex-

---

[13] Herman Feldman. *Stabilizing Jobs and Wages.* Harper and Brothers. New York, 1940, p. 27.

pansion of this type may be either temporary, as was the case with the publishing company, or permanent, as was true in the case of a cigar manufacturing company. If such a program is undertaken, however, the expansion areas should be well-defined in advance; and, if they are new areas, the company will need to conduct market research before expanding into the unknown.

Consignment selling involves the distribution of goods to the consumer but waiting for payment until the goods are sold. The drug and pharmaceutical manufacturing company studied, for example, made considerable use of this selling technique. Early deliveries are promoted by selling to the distributors on consignment. The distributors do not pay for the products until they are sold; and if they are unable to sell them, the manufacturing company will take them back.

Production Diversification

Research in sales possibilities may result in more than simply establishing the fact that the demand for the company's products is inherently fluctuating. Such analysis may show demand for additional or related products and lead to a rounding out of the line. Similarly, the new products may, and frequently can, be fitted into the seasonal or cyclical slack periods as "fillers." This study showed that the milk products, food processing, wholesale food products, and drug and pharmaceutical manufacturing companies are all examples of producers who have a diversified line of products. It also showed that diversification may be the result of a fluctuating supply of raw materials, as with the food processing company, or that it can be used to counteract the fluctuations in the demand for the manufactured product. In the case of the milk processing company, the fluctuation of both the supply of raw material and the demand for the product resulted in an even greater desire for diversification.[14]

Diversification of the product line is one of the most extensive methods used to stabilize the operations of a company. Numerous advantages are to be received from diversification. It promotes greater financial stability and a higher degree of continuity of operation. Labor costs are decreased because of lower labor turnover. Fixed charges and overhead costs are spread over a greater volume of production. The production capacity is

---

[14] The problem of stabilization in this industry was intensified because there is a two-sided seasonal variation. Both the raw material and the demand for processed milk products have seasonal peaks which did not coincide. The largest quantity of raw materials is produced in the spring. In contrast to this peak, the peak demand for the products comes in July and August.

utilized to a greater degree. Salesmen are busy the entire year and there is a constant flow of money into the company. It may even be possible to use by-products and scrap in the new products.

Market diversification is a further method whereby a company may extend its distribution. It may involve coverage of a larger geographical territory, thus extending its markets over several types of industries. The wholesale food products, milk processing, and other companies made some use of diversified markets to increase their stability.

Production Methods

All of the companies studied have a demand for their goods or services which fluctuates to some extent. These fluctuations may be daily, weekly, seasonal, or cyclical. Thus, the principal function of any program designed to promote stability must be to provide a means of obtaining steady production despite fluctuations. The method most used by the companies covered herein was leveling production on an annual basis.

Producing for Stock

During seasons of low sales demand, many companies produce for stock, which is used to fill orders during the rush seasons. By using this technique, the companies can produce at a steady monthly rate throughout the year. There are numerous examples of companies which produce for stock in the slack seasons. The chemical products company, for example, has a seasonal sales variation amounting to 1600 per cent from the lowest to the highest month; however, there are practically no variations in the number of employees throughout the year. The primary method used to accomplish this phenomenal stability is to manufacture for stock during a large part of the year.

The ice company is another example of a company which must manufacture for stock to obtain steady employment. Ice is a perishable product and must therefore be placed in cold storage if it is to be kept for a long period. Even so, the company elects to store the ice rather than have the additional capital investment and expenses necessary to produce all the ice required by the market during the peak demand season. Thus, it achieves constant yearly operation by producing and storing ice during the cool months for the increased summer demand. Adequate storage facilities exist for reasonably regular annual manufacturing. Other examples are the cigar manufacturer, where humidified and cold storage is used, and the can container manufacturer who produces certain parts for stock during the off-season. The food processing company manufactures the stable products for stock. This is done so that the employees can be transferred from departments processing stable products into the seasonal products' department. There must be an adequate supply of the stable product to cover customers' orders for the two month period when the employees are working in the seasonal line.

Although production for stock regularizes employment demands, it occasions many problems for the manufacturer. For example, adequate storage space is a necessity. Failure to provide for this can only limit this technique of adjustment. Similarly, in some cases, the cost of storage may be too great to permit this. However, even if the costs are high for the assembled unit, component parts may be assembled and produced for stock and later assembly. Some products, such as can containers, for example, are much too bulky to be stored and, moreover, the value of the product is too low for the storage costs required. Companies which produce such products may make some parts or sub-assemblies for stock. When it is impossible to make any storage arrangement, other methods of stabilization should be used.

Prices may vary sharply over short or long periods of time. A downward swing in prices could spell defeat to a stabilization program if there were a large volume of finished goods on hand. The non-durable goods' producers are influenced more by the seasonal price fluctuations than the cyclical variations. The products are mostly perishable and production estimates are generally made on an annual basis with frequent modifications.

There is considerable danger of obsolescence during a period of storage. Changing style factors leading to an immediate change in the consumer's demand, new product development, and legal restrictions, are also risks associated with producing for stock. The non-durable consumers' goods include many necessities of life, and obsolescence is not as large a risk in these cases as in the durable and industrial goods industries.

Large amounts of additional capital may be required to permit the firm to produce for stock. These costs include both storage facilities, inventory, and other working capital requirements, and the risk factor cost noted above. One company interviewed reported that an additional annual capital requirement of $2 million was necessary in its program to produce for stock. Thus, the capital costs involved in manufacturing for stock for several months in advance of the demand must be considered.

The danger of deterioration poses a constant problem in storage. Even the most durable products will deteriorate to some degree. The non-durable consumers' goods usually have a high rate of deterioration. Milk sours, cigars dry out, meat and vegetables perish, and chocolate melts unless special provisions are made for the necessary type of storage. Many methods have been developed and constant research is being carried on to increase the durability of goods. This limitation is both technical and physical, and, depending on the type of industry, may be so great as to supersede all others.

The question concerning the quantity of production necessary to meet future needs depends, of course, on a market forecast. To be successful, production for stock should be based on accurate sales forecasts for a future period. Although sales forecasts are questionable, sound techniques have been developed which result in a high degree of accuracy. Properly protected against contingencies, the use of the device permits considerable planning and production programming without danger of serious loss.

Postponement of Maintenance Work to Slack Seasons

When production is planned, it is often possible to postpone certain activities, such as special construction work, repairs, cleaning, painting, and machine adjustments to the time when this work is most useful in filling a slack in production. The ice manufacturing company studied, for example, uses employees to do maintenance work during the winter months. The regular workers do construction work, make repairs or install new machines, and paint the facilities during the slack season.

Proper use of preventive maintenance results in steady operations. Production will not be disrupted by current machine breakdowns and much temporary idleness can be avoided by using intensive, scheduled, preventive maintenance. The petroleum refining, transportation, and communications companies are examples of companies which control and schedule their maintenance work to such an extent that little time is lost because of major break-downs.

The petroleum refining company's employment stabilization program is enhanced through planned maintenance operations so designed as to average out the maintenance load. To stabilize still further the work load of maintenance mechanics, a back log of minor construction work is kept available for them to perform when not engaged in maintenance work. Although maintenance work can be deferred to slack seasons in many cases, some maintenance work, especially that of construction, should be done during the warm months. Thus, since some companies' peak production season is in the summer months, there is some difficulty in using maintenance and construction activities to stabilize the work force.

Labor unions will frequently restrict the use of regular production employees for maintenance work. The trade unions, in particular, resist the policy of using regular production employees for several different jobs about the plant. Some companies have no problem with the unions while others must restrict the use of their regular employees for maintenance work.

It is practically impossible in most plants to plan the maintenance work to fit into the production schedule. Preventive maintenance work must be carried on to avoid major break-downs, and it cannot always be dovetailed into the production schedule; however, constant coordination between the production and maintenance departments will assist in planning the most perfect maintenance and production schedules. Several companies, for example, do maintenance work at night or on the weekends. When a company operates only one shift, the maintenance work can only be performed while the production employees are off their jobs and hence offers no means of stabilizing employment. However, preventive and corrective maintenance during the off-hours provides steadier operating during the main shift.

Other Production Methods

A number of other programs have been devised to aid in stabilizing employment. One company keeps a raw material inventory which is used as a cushion if its supplier should temporarily discontinue operations. Research is carried on in this company to increase the durability of the raw materials and finished products. Standardization of products is used by the can container corporation. If the product can be standardized, then the parts can also be made to standard. Both product and parts can be manufactured for stock during the dull seasons.

Some companies accumulate extra work during the rush season to be done during slack periods. When the slack comes, these extra banks of work are used to reduce the employee lay-offs. Other companies contract for additional work during the slack seasons and contract out work in rush periods. This technique provides level production which normally means steady employment.

Methods Used By Personnel Departments

In addition to the production planning and control devices discussed in detail above, the firm may develop an integrated personnel policy which will supplement its work schedule in stabilizing the demand for labor. Many of these devices appear insignificant but, as a part of a total pattern, they are effective morale builders as well as physical contributors to stability.

Vacation Policy

The postponement of vacations to slack periods of the year is an obvious aid to balanced operation. More companies use the method of having the vacation period during the lowest weeks of the production year than any other personnel technique. The department store, transportation company, pharmaceutical manufacturer, cigarette company, wholesale food products company, and milk products company are some examples of those who use this method. Concentration of vacations also avoids running the plant with a force constantly disorganized by the unavailability of key or skilled men because they are on vacations at intervals throughout the year.

There are some individuals who want to take additional time as non-paid vacations or leaves of absence when they are sure that being away will not weaken their relationship with the firm. Scrupulous care in this matter will encourage such requests for non-paid vacations during dull seasons, perhaps relieving management of some of the burden of maintaining a normal work force during those times.

Varying the Hours of Work

After all other efforts and techniques have been used and fluctuations of employment have not been wholly eliminated, stability is still possible by providing for flexibility in the company's hours of work. If it is engaged in only during seasonal fluctuations, this method is different from part-time work or spreading the work. The reason for the difference is that in peak periods the regular employees will work over-time to make up for the slack periods. Varying the hours of employment is the second most used personnel technique for stabilizing employment used by the companies included in this study. In the meat packing company, for example, any change in the immediate demand for meat, such as the pre-Easter rush for hams, requires additional work. This work is accomplished by increasing the hours worked by the regular employees. A confectionery manufacturer normally works its employees forty hours a week; however, when the need arises, the hours worked per week are increased. Additional employees are hired only after this increase in operation proves to be a long-run situation. The reverse is also true when the company faces slack periods.

While varying the work time per week may aid in stabilizing employment, it occasions several problems. Chief among them is the standard work week with a requirement for extra pay beyond that minimum. The National Fair Labor Standards Act of 1938 established a maximum work week to be paid at the regular hourly rate, with time and half time for all work in excess of this standard. The Act partly exempts companies in some seasonal industries and in certain other cases.[15] The higher pay rate for over-time work has obviously hampered the use of over-time as a method of stabilizing employment because it increases labor costs; but, labor turnover is also costly. Pennsylvania, for example, has a merit rating system whereby companies with a low labor turnover pay a lower employers' unemployment compensation tax. This study showed that many employers preferred to pay the higher over-time rate rather than to have an increase in their labor turnover.

Centralized Personnel Department

A centralized personnel department is a primary prerequisite in the use of personnel techniques to stabilize employment. Lay-offs are caused by some conditions over which the personnel department has control. The techniques used in selection, training, placing, transferring, and retraining of employees influence the results of a stabilization program.

One of the most important duties of a centralized personnel department is to effect transfers among the departments of the company. One department may have a temporary surplus of workers while another department needs additional temporary help. Many times the jobs are of such a nature that the employees can be transferred satisfactorily to several different jobs. The department store, for example, has a centralized personnel control system which assists in creating flexibility among the departments by transferring employees from one section to another. The can container manufacturer not only transfers employees from one job to another and from one department to another, but it has some highly skilled employees who are transferred between plants located over a thousand miles apart.

Other Personnel Procedures

The communications company uses an "over-lapping of tours" arrangement to stabilize the daily employment peaks. The shifts are so arranged that there is an over-lap for approximately a two-hour period during the daily peaks.

"Split-shifts" are used by the transportation company. Under this

---

[15] The Act exempts a concern from the payment of over-time rates if the worker is employed under certain annual or semi-annual contracts made by representatives of employees certified as bona-fide by the National Labor Relations Board.

arrangement the same employees work at two different times each day. They usually receive higher hourly wages for the split-shift work.

The department store used surveys and research for a period of three years to determine the number of regular employees required. After the number of "regular" employees was established, a list was made of those who were classified as regular and these were assured steady employment from year to year.

One company which has an excellent stability record retains older workers longer because it is believed that they help in holding the labor turnover to a minimum. This is true both because of their influence in keeping the younger workers from leaving a secure job and because of the difficulty of finding new employment at older ages.

Many companies employ temporary employees. Some have the policy of using only those employees who are interested in a job of short duration. In the summer months, high school and college students are available for many types of temporary employment; and several companies use them for the major part of their seasonal work.

The meat packing company trains its workers for versatility. This training permits transfers between jobs with the least friction possible. They are also more proficient on each and every job on which they have been trained.

Management's Responsibility for Employment Stabilization Plans

Although the managements of some concerns have not realized the need for stabilized employment, there has been a steadily growing interest in securing employment stability. Company executives do not usually become interested in the techniques of assuring greater stability of employment until they come to recognize the need for it. Once it is known that such programs will result in increased efficiency of plant as well as labor use, the desirability of such programs is at once apparent. Before deciding to establish a stabilization program, as such, the company executives will have to come to recognize some of the advantages of employment stability. Regular employment may afford greater production efficiency through utilization of facilities to their fullest extent, and production may be scheduled at a steady rate of flow which usually means better material handling and plant layout. Job security may increase the output efficiency of employees. It usually results in better employee morale, lower labor turnover, and higher loyalty of the employees. There are also other tangible and intangible advantages. Some can be measured by dollars and cents but many cannot.

Management can recognize the need for stabilizing employment by analyzing the following data:

1. The periodic fluctuations in the number of man-hours worked and in the total number of employees;

2. The periodic fluctuations in output and sales volume;

3. The causes of employees' grievances; and

4. The causes of labor's demand for a guaranteed annual wage.

Management must be responsible for the stabilization program which may determine the success or failure of the company. The authority for a regularization program stems from top management, the initiator of the policies, plans, and procedures.

There are several steps which management must take to reach the goal of employment stability. First, it must recognize the need for stability and decide to act. Second, it should define the objective of a company stabilization program and formulate the policies necessary to carry it out. Third, management must plan the program in advance of its execution and control it through comparisons and evaluations.

Conclusion

As a result of this survey of the employment regularization programs adopted by 25 Philadelphia firms, a summary of the specific devices in use was obtained. Although reference has been made to companies making primary use of each of the general devices discussed in this article, the findings indicate that each firm studied has adopted at least one distribution, production, or personnel method designed to stabilize employment. The distribution of the specific techniques used, however, showed wide variation. Twenty-four firms, for example, made use of advertising and sales programs to enlarge slack season activity while only five made any use of the sales forecasting devices to improve distribution. Sixteen firms manufactured for stock during the slack season but only ten deferred maintenance to slack seasons. Similarly, 19 firms attempted to schedule vacations during slack periods, 13 varied hours of work, while only seven actually attempted to transfer personnel within the firm to meet minimum and peak employment requirements. (See Table I.)

On the basis of this study it may be concluded that a number of intra-company methods are now available to management and, in fact, are used for improving general plant efficiency which may also be used to assist in stabilizing employment levels. Management has given evidence of its willingness to make use of these programs, as has been shown herein, but additional methods and devices are available and may be tested by firms to determine their possibilities. While no accurate data can be obtained to permit any real evaluation of the efficiency of these techniques on the general level of employment, it would appear that considerable regularization may be accomplished as a result of continued management efforts in the case of specific companies.

TABLE I

THE NUMBER OF COMPANIES USING THE MOST COMMON EMPLOYMENT
STABILIZATION TECHNIQUES

Methods	Number of Companies
Distribution Methods	
Improving Sales in Slack Seasons 24	
Diversification of Product 8	
Sales Forecast 5	
Total Distribution Methods Frequency ..	37
Production Methods	
Manufacturing for Stock 16	
Deferring Maintenance to Slack Seasons 10	
Total Production Methods Frequency	26
Personnel Methods	
Permitting Vacations in Slack Periods 19	
Varying Hours of Work 13	
Transferring of Personnel 7	
Total Personnel Methods Frequency	39

26 Coordination Between Production Management and Distribution*

By R. E. Brooker

A GOOD production executive can and will assert himself vigorously in the development of product lines and the methods of distribution. Indeed, he has an important part to play in achieving an economic balance between these two great factors of industry.

The time is most appropriate for the recognition of this responsibility. Market analyses of most items of consumer goods will show that the pent-up demand for these items, accumulated during the war years and expanded during the postwar years, has been satisfied or nearly satisfied and that the demand factors from this point on will be based on the growth of population, improved standards of living, and replacement sales of individual items. While the facilities to produce the basic raw materials may not have been over-expanded during this period, through better long-range planning of raw material production with its higher capital investment and slow pay-out, it is evident that the facilities to produce consumer goods may and probably do exceed the demand in many lines and that the marginal plants, which compete today because of material control, will be hard-pressed to compete in a free market. Many branches of industry, particularly the textiles, have faced a buyer market for more than a year, and this will become more general with unrestricted production.

A Problem of Costs

I want to make it clear that, in discussing the problem of correlation of production and distribution, I do not imply that distribution

---

* Reprinted from *Planning for Efficient Production.* Manufacturing Series No. 206 (1953), by permission of the American Management Association, copyright holder.

has no other problems than this. To quote from a recent talk made by Mr. T. V. Houser of our organization, who has achieved national recognition as a merchant, at a Boston conference on distribution:

> If we will start with raw material as the manufacturer knows it, the textile mill, the shirt manufacturer, the plumbing goods, foundry or rug manufacturer, it can be established that more costs are incurred, more individuals employed in distributing the products from the point of manufacture to the ultimate consumer than were involved in the manufacture of the articles in the first place. For example, I took a group of important items of wearing apparel, home furnishing, home building and sporting goods, and the average of these items would indicate that the amount paid by the consumer, omitting the value of raw materials purchased by the factories, would divide as follows: 31 per cent for the cost of producing these goods, including factory profit, and 69 per cent for distribution cost, including distributor profit. If we include the value of raw materials purchased by the factories, the division would still be 47 per cent for the cost of the production versus 53 per cent for the cost of distribution.

While we recognize that retail distribution must find ways to improve its efficiency, and while we ourselves see many avenues for research on this subject, we know, and can demonstrate with examples from our own experiences (I am going to cite only our experiences so that I can use factual evidence), that the coordination between the system of distribution and the manufacturing sources has brought us savings in many lines of merchandise not available to other distributors who have been unable or unwilling to correlate their distribution with the manufacturers' production. In this discussion, I want to make the point that production management must be ever alert to the problems of distribution.

Planning the Rate of Production

What is the concept of this correlation and where does production management take a part? Where the manufacturing processes in any one industry are fairly well standardized, the cost of operations in one well engineered plant will be about the same as in another equally well engineered plant. Then distinct advantages in cost can be achieved only through a closer correlation between the manufacturing of the product and its distribution.

It is often said that volume is the cure for many evils. This is fundamentally true, but there are elements that create volume at a consistent rate that can be predetermined by manufacturing and sales. Consumer acceptance of a product is created through its basic value, which is a function of quality, serviceability, and design, and by the effectiveness of its channels of distribution.

The elements that control the basic value of a product are in most cases controlled or greatly influenced by both manufacturing and distribution, and where the planning of a product line is a joint venture the effect of each element on basic value can be carefully considered.

I am sure that the buyers in our company and the sales departments or distribution outlets in other companies are well aware of the cost savings resulting from consistent high levels of volume which fully absorb overhead burdens, but I wonder how many companies have fully explored the possibility of maintaining a consistent planned production through 12 months of operation.

In the staple lines a competent sales department will be able to project consumer demand with a fair degree of accuracy for a 12-month period, including the seasonal variation in demand. An expected volume having been established, the rate of production is then influenced by warehouse space and/or working capital limitations, but each of these factors can be weighed in the decision.

Examples of Saving

As a simple example of this type of correlation, the battery industry has projected unit sales of 23,500,000 *batteries* for 1953. Its projections are based upon car registrations, the number of older cars, and the historical replacement cycle. Our percentage of the national market should vary but slightly between years, which allows us to use a normal historical percentage of industry.

In normal years not affected by restrictions or other factors which might distort demand, 35 per cent of the battery business is done in the spring and 65 per cent is done in the fall. Because batteries cannot be stored for long periods, the manufacturer cannot increase his stocks in the spring to take care of the fall selling. It is possible, however, to build plates and assemblies prior to the peak season and thus relieve the fall schedule on these parts and also spread employment over the slow months. We have not attempted to interpret the savings effected by the spreading of the peak in this case, as this is the fundamental approach that any manufacturer would use with the same results.

There are, however, many cases where the correlation between production and distribution is just as simple but depends on converting the long-range demand of distribution into long-range production planning and backing up the planning with firm contracts for definite quantities of goods at firm prices. In many of these cases the actual savings can be determined.

For example, we have a source in Rutherford, Tennessee, which makes *mackinaws and outer jackets*. These products are not shipped into retail stores until the middle of July or the first of August. The season is over by the middle of November. Prior to the establishment of this plant, our sources of these products planned their production to begin in the spring, producing the orders for fall shipment. By the first of September production was reduced to take care of the fill-in orders, which in this business are usually small. With the establishment of the Rutherford plant, we calculated the demand for the year and divided this demand into a 50-week production period. The plant has now been running on this basis for more than 10 years. We do have unusual sales in some years, and the plant may work six or eight Saturdays to keep up with the demand. We also have had several years when the demand did not equal our estimates and we had an additional two-week shutdown beyond the inventory period. However, in the main there has been fine correlation between the distributor and the manufacturer, and we believe that, in addition to better values in these lines, this correlation has resulted in a saving in costs of approximately 12 per cent on these garments. This saving is computed after taking into consideration the cost of providing warehouse space and the interest on the money invested in this build-up of inventory.

I should make it clear at this point that, in building so far ahead, the manufacturer takes no risk on the product, as we provide the manufacturer with a contract covering the goods to be produced and the shipping dates that these goods are to move from his warehouse. Where it is necessary for the manufacturer to finance the inventories, we have a standard form of repurchase agreement with the banks to make this financing possible, and all the costs of financing and warehousing are included in our cost of products.

Another example of correlation is found in the line of *shotguns and rifles* manufactured for us by a source in New Haven. Guns are a very seasonal item. In 1951, for instance, 73 per cent of factory shipments were made in four months, August through November. In order to give the factory a uniform production schedule, estimates of the year's sales were made early in December and a 12-month sales contract was negotiated with the buying department. This takes courage and good judgment on the part of the buyer. The estimates are not always achieved; in November, 1951, at the end of the selling season, the finished goods inventory was $400,000 higher than the previous year, which, in this case, was par. This is serious, but in the long run it is better than adopting an over-cautious attitude and thereby creating a loss in sales.

In this particular instance, the inventory carry-over consisted of 22-caliber rifles. The 1951 sales for this product fell below the estimates. The buyer reduced the 1952 selling price for this model and increased his advertising budget, thereby selling the carry-over inventory and the 1952 production early in the season and increasing the dollar sales volume.

The success of this factory is due mainly to concentrating on the most popular items, keeping the line as simple as possible. As an example, one competitor has 135 models in the 12-gauge pump shotgun line, while we have only four. This, of course, permits the factory longer runs for each part with many economies due to fewer setups as well as the opportunity to use the most efficient manufacturing methods. A comparison of the retail prices for two of the products may be of interest: The Sears catalogue price for the Model 50 high-powered rifle is $89.95, while competition is currently selling a comparable model at $120.95. Sears' price for the 12-gauge pump shotgun is $61.50, while competitive models are selling for $93.85.

Further Means of Cost Reduction

These examples show correlation between selling and production scheduling where the potential savings are self-evident. Our concept of this correlation must go further to a point where production men, realizing the elements of cost affected by method of distribution, design, and breadth of product line, initiate proposed changes which will benefit the product or its cost or its consumer acceptance.

For the purpose of illustration, I should like to take the line of gas ranges which we sell, as it follows a pattern repeated many times in other lines of merchandise and other departments of our business. In 1939 our catalogue listed four models of gas ranges, priced from $32.95 to $71.95, each of which was available for either regular or bottled gas. By the fall of 1952 our catalogue listing showed seven illustrations of gas ranges, each model again available either for natural gas or bottled gas, and three of the models furnished either with lamp and timer or without, priced from $73.95 to $199.95. A review of the sales and potential sales of gas ranges showed that the demand had jumped on a national basis from 1,500,000 units in 1939 to 3,100,000 units in 1950 but that a more normal projection would show a consumption for the years ahead based on expanding population, new homes, and replacement in the neighborhood of 2,200,000 units annually. Present factories in the industry have a capacity to produce from two to two and one-half times this volume.

The potential competition for this market was equally obvious to both the buyer and the manufacturer, and they decided on a well-coordinated plan of action to secure and strengthen each other. The buyer and merchandising supervisor, working with the production design and production engineering departments of this particular factory, an outside firm of industrial designers, and the production management, made a thorough study of all our present models, including unit sales, the cost of deluxing the merchandise, installation, and the customer service after installation. In addition, a study of the competitive lines of merchandise in this field was made to determine the essential features to be included in gas ranges based on consumer demand.

There were certain fundamental conceptions of aesthetic *design and utility* which had been accepted when our 42-inch de luxe range was brought out in 1947 but which were now questioned by the buyer and manufacturer in view of field experience and the competitive market ahead. At this point, production management recommended the elimination of the top covers and presented a clear-cut case of the savings which could be realized through the elimination of this design. The service department was quick to perceive that the elimination of the top covers would reduce their problems in the field: the chipping of enamel parts, the adjustment of the hinges, and deluxing and installing the ranges. The buyer agreed that the merchandising value of the covers could not be justified if substantial savings would result from their elimination. Production management also recommended the elimination of the curved surfaces on the end panels and door fronts, which had resulted in excessive service costs in the field while this product was in service. Further, it was recommended that tolerances on enameled parts assembled on the frame be loosened up to permit a normal manufacturing flow. The buyer, interested in improving the quality and adding additional features to the product, was willing to reduce the number of models and effect standardization between models, which could be accomplished with no penalty to the aesthetic design or to the merchandising breadth of the line, and which would result in longer production runs of additional parts and assembled ranges. As a result of these conferences between buyer and manufacturer, the new line of ranges was conceived.

The most startling change in the range *construction* from a manufacturing standpoint is in the cooking surface. The number of parts has been reduced from 28 to 7. This reduction in parts has cut the number of press and shear operations from 122 to 53. In the Welding Department, nine operations originally were performed; now none will be performed. In the Enameling Department, a reduction has been made from 53 operations to 30 operations. The reduction of these operations and additional savings in the Assembly Department show a total direct labor saving of $80.54 per 100 ranges. To this must be added the saving in material cost of approximately $70 per 100 ranges. In the top alone the total saving, then, in material and direct labor is approximately $1.50 per range at cost. To this, of course, must be added overhead, administrative costs, and profit.

The 1953 line will consist of eight basic models as compared with 10 in the 1952 line. However, the real saving in cost has been brought about because of a reduction in the number of basic frames used. The 1952 line consisted of four basic frames, while in the 1953 line this has been reduced to two. Furthermore, a complete program of standardization of parts has been accomplished for the two basic frames. To illustrate, a comparison of the front panels required for the entire line shows a reduction from 12 in the 1952 line to five in the 1953 line.

A new positive clamping arrangement for the backguard eliminated the necessity of custom-adjusting each backguard to the range. Now it is possible to assemble and package each backguard separately on a completely separate assembly line.

While it was agreed at the start that lower cost was an objective and that the quality was to be improved through sturdier design and greater utility, further new selling features were needed. Let us take a look at a few of the *new or improved features* of the 1953 line: They include 125 per cent more insulation, de luxe cast iron grates, wire oven-rack supports, porcelain-enameled main front, one-piece main top, built-in lamp, and several others which I shall not mention. The buyer and the merchandise supervisor were very enthusiastic and estimated that the new features equaled a $15 increase in value, based on competitive ranges.

So far I have commented only on the savings in cost of producing the ranges. I should also point out that this simplification in line, in addition to resulting in a *better-quality product* with additional features, will also contribute to *lower cost of distribution*. In the first place, the stores will have to stock fewer numbers. Consequently, they will enjoy a better turnover. In the second place, a study of our deluxing service —whereby the ranges are received into a store warehouse in carload quantities, unpacked, inspected, and set up for delivery into the customers' homes—shows that the deluxing time per range will be reduced from 50 to 35 minutes, resulting in a saving of approximately $1 per range. Also, the trend of our service calls will show a decided drop in servicing in the field. All these savings—a saving in original cost of manufacture because of the elimination and simplification of parts, better production, reduction of work in process, and finished goods inventory, plus the reduction of costs in the field—will result in the saving to the consumer of $30 a range, or 15 per cent, on this de luxe model. We are convinced that, by bringing the consumer a better value, we can expect to sell to a larger percentage of the existing market than heretofore, thus benefiting both ourselves and the manufacturer.

Basic Role of Production

While it is the usual procedure in our company to conduct these joint meetings (and I assume it is more or less general procedure in manufacturing, where the buyer is represented by the sales department), I have seen many such sessions where the production men were outsold. Either the aesthetic designer made such a strong presentation, so brilliantly illustrated and presented, that production design and production engineering were awed and overpowered, or the representative of the sales department presented such a strong plea as to the features that must be incorporated into the line to meet so-and-so's competition that production supported broadening of the line which it knew or should have known would reduce production efficiencies and greatly complicate all the problems of production flow. In these cases the representatives of production, either through a feeling of inadequacy due to the superior presentation or through a resignation to the fallacy that the sales end of the business, was dominant, agreed to everything that sales and aesthetic design asked for with no full disclosure of the effects on the economics of production.

I believe that we realize and recognize the importance of salesmanship, advertising, and promotion and their contribution to our general over-all business and growth. However, salesmanship, advertising, and promotion are not the only elements necessary to a successful system of distribution. Equally important are the convenience of retail facilities, the completeness of merchandise lines, and the service and installation facilities, but fundamental to the success of any distribution and back of all of these is the product value it brings to its customers. Perhaps Henry Ford oversimplified the correlation between manufacturing and distribution when, with his Model T Ford, he gave them anything they wanted as long as it was black and in either of his two models! Consumer demand, plus some improvement in distribution, proved that Mr. Ford had gone too far in the simplification of his line; and, by the time he made the correction by the introduction of his Model A, his principal competitor, Chevrolet, had far outdistanced him.

The problems of correlating production with distribution are not as simple today, with our multi-plant setups and competition for consumer markets with improvements, added features, and changing styling, as they were in the 1920's or even the 1930's. However, the necessity to solve the problem of correlation of production and distribution is as pressing or more pressing than it was during these periods; and, in our experience, our greatest successes have resulted from an association with good production management which has had the initiative to bring up problems of production and, where we have then been willing to coordinate our distribution, to simplify the production runs and maintain a constant level of production by planning and buying ahead during the slow seasons so that an adequate inventory is accumulated and by guaranteeing a distribution of the product produced.

The field of production must be credited with a great achievement in reducing the cost of producing goods. The challenge today is to project our knowledge of production costs into the field of distribution through our great sales departments and through our outlets of distribution, whether wholesale or retail, so that the methods of distribution will work hand in hand with the methods of production to produce a better value for the consumer—or, in reality, a better standard of living.

27 Prerequisites for a Guaranteed Annual Wage*

By HENRY C. THOLE and CHARLES C. GIBBONS

THE purpose of this paper is to discuss some of the more important methods of stabilizing the sales, production, and employment of a company. The achievement of stability now looms larger than ever as a problem confronting American business. The recent trend for industry to supplement unemployment compensation makes it clear that planning for stability of sales, production, and employment will be one of the greatest challenges facing management in the years ahead. An analysis of recent contracts providing supplementary unemployment compensation reveals that the number of contracts containing such provisions is increasing rapidly. Contracts providing supplementary unemployment compensation have already been negotiated in the following industries: automobile, automobile parts, rubber, motor trucks, steel containers, farm equipment, aviation, and plate glass.

Two companies in the steel container industry, American Can Company and Continental Can Company, already have signed contracts providing 52 weeks of supplementary unemployment compensation benefits to their employees. These benefits, including unemployment compensation, in both cases amount to 65 per cent of take-home pay. While the payments to be made to employees are supplements to unemployment compensation, and while there is a maximum limit to the funds, these plans are closely related to traditional guaranteed annual wage plans. Plans similar to those of Continental Can and American Can may become the goal of organized labor in the future. Such heavy obligations would be a burden to companies which could not provide steady em-

* Reprinted from *Advanced Management*, 21 (June 1956), 25-29, by permission of the editor of *Advanced Management*.

ployment. To meet this challenge many companies will have to search intensively for a successful approach to stabilization of sales, production, and employment. In this paper we shall outline an approach that can profitably be used by managers to increase stability in their firms.

The traditional approach in studying the possibilities for stabilization within the individual firm is to investigate several so-called stabilization techniques. The following techniques are the ones proposed most often for the stabilization of employment: producing for stock, developing a new product to fill in during slack seasons, training for versatility, transfer of workers, and making seasonal buying habits more regular. These techniques are useful and every well-managed corporation should apply them to its operations wherever such techniques are applicable.

We believe, however, that limiting the search for stabilization measures to such techniques is too narrow an approach to the problem. Most companies will find it more profitable to emphasize management improvement in all areas of the business rather than to use only the standard stabilization techniques. Even the traditional stabilization techniques depend for their success on excellent management in those areas where they are to be applied. Transfer of workers, for example, depends on good union relations to gain labor acceptance and on employment procedures which secure workers able and willing to perform jobs other than those for which they were hired. Production for stock depends on sound sales forecasts and on good inventory control. Production for stock without sound procedures in these areas would be unworkable and might even endanger the survival of the company. The development of a new product to fill in valleys caused by seasonal demand likewise depends on good management. Research and engineering must work closely with sales so that the new products developed will conform to consumer preferences.

Another limitation to the traditional stabilization techniques is that they emphasize what management can do to level out short-range fluctuations in the existing level of sales, production, and employment. Production for stock results in smoothing out the existing level of production. Making customer buying habits more regular through such techniques as stimulating advance orders results in regularization of the existing level of sales. Flexible hours, sharing work, and deferring work likewise result in dividing up the existing amount of employment. Such techniques are defensive measures aimed at adapting the firm to conditions as they exist.

On the other hand, the approach to stabilization which emphasizes better management in all areas of the business considers that expansion of the enterprise is basic to the achievement of stability. This approach considers offensive as well as defensive measures to increase stability and, as such, is valuable in combating cyclical as well as seasonal fluctuations.

It would be impossible to improve simultaneously every important area of management. For best results management should select areas in its business which hold the greatest promise for improving company stability. The areas selected may be different for firms in different industries. Creating new markets, for example, may be the most important problem of a firm in the chemical or mass production industries, which are characterized by high overhead costs; but design and consumer preferences may be most important in an industry such as women's clothing. Problems may vary also among firms in the same industry. In attempting to expand markets, one company may choose to expand by extending the geographical area in which goods are sold and another may choose to expand by reducing costs so that prices may be reduced. Each company must decide which factors are most important to it, considering its industry and the major characteristics of its business.

While the approach to company stabilization will vary among different companies, there are several key areas which are likely to offer the greatest promise for improving stability. The remainder of this paper will be devoted to a discussion of these key areas, leaving the job of determining the proper emphasis to the individual reader. The following are considered by the authors to offer the greatest promise for increasing company stability: (1) long-range planning, (2) research on products and productivity, and (3) expanding and stabilizing sales.

Long-Range Planning

Long-range planning is essential to healthy growth and development of a company. It enables a company to balance important objectives in the various phases of the business. Future requirements must be balanced against present-day needs. Often sacrifices need to be made today in order to assure long-run continuity of operation. There are many examples of long-range company planning which illustrate this point. The United States Steel Corporation purchased the Mesabi Range 30 years prior to actual needs in order to assure itself of ore reserves important to the continued operation of the company. The Crown Zellerbach Corporation has replanted thousands of acres of forest land so that the supply of wood pulp 50 years hence will be assured. The American Pulley Company has established a funded reserve to offset the effect of cyclical fluctuations on its business. Years before television became popular, the American Telephone and Telegraph Company started to provide the facilities required to service the television industry. Such long-range plans as these are fundamental to long-run company prosperity.

The successful solution to many business problems requires long-range planning. Developing a new product, for example, often takes 10 to 15 years from the initial planning stage to finished product. Constructing a new plant certainly involves long-term planning, since the useful life of the plant may easily extend to 20 or 30 years. Advertising is often more effective if continued over a long span of time. Even building an effective dealer organization is likely to take 5 or 10 years. On such problems, managers are constantly making long-range decisions, whether they are making them consciously or unconsciously. To make sounder decisions on these important matters, management needs to place greater emphasis on long-range planning.

Achieving growth while maintaining reasonable stability necessitates a thorough plan covering the major elements of the business. Major emphasis must be placed on developing new products and services, increasing productivity, and expanding and stabilizing sales. Other important areas which must be covered by long-term plans are finances, facilities, personnel requirements, and organization. While emphasis will differ with each company, all of these areas are important for most companies. Omitting any one element may cause weaknesses which will retard the growth of the enterprise.

To be effective, long-range plans must make provision for change. Long-range planning without a high degree of flexibility would be useless. No company can accurately make plans for five or ten years ahead. Plans must be restudied constantly, and revised as conditions change. Plans made with provision for change are possible of attainment, but those made without subsequent follow-up are likely to be abandoned.

A company's plans must be flexible enough to meet emergencies as they arise. In a dynamic economy there is always the possibility of sudden change. Since the beginning of World War II, there have been almost constant demands to increase production. Wars and threats of war, combined with high consumer demand, have placed stress on manufacturing, engineering, and related activities. Along with a readiness to increase production, there must also be a readiness to change product lines. It now appears that cold war may last indefinitely. Such a situation requires constant readiness to switch from civilian to defense production and back again. Many companies are now producing both "guns and butter"; others must be ready to change in the event of an emergency.

Flexibility in planning must, finally, take into account the emergencies that may arise from sudden decreases in demand. A dynamic economy is characterized by rapid growth and subsequent readjustment, and there is always the possibility of a sudden drop. In an economy where the consumer is king, there is always danger of a decline in the sales of an individual firm.

Research on Products and Productivity

One of the firm's best resources for growth and stability in a changing world is an active product research department. Many companies have invested heavily in research to promote steady growth in their sales and profits. In a dynamic economy with growing population, changing age distribution, increasing per capita income, and rising standards of living, there will be constant change and improvement in products.

As a result of increased efforts in research by aggressive firms, there is sure to be an accelerated rate of technological innovation in the future. New products, new services, new processes, and new materials will undoubtedly be marketed in increasing numbers. Established products of today will become obsolete tomorrow. Survival and growth will depend on the ability of the individual company to develop new and improved products and services.

The importance of developing new products has been illustrated in a study by Brookings Institution entitled "Big Business in a Competitive Society." The following quotation from a summary of this study compares lists of the 100 largest corporations in 1909 and 1948 and suggests some of the factors that enabled 31 firms to remain in this select group during the entire period of study:

> What stands out from the two lists—and the reader may develop variations on the theme merely by inspection—is the way in which the financial resources of Big Business have constantly shifted. The companies that have grown are those that have been able to convert technological progress into customer preferences. Few that have stuck to their traditional product lines—and none that have retained traditional methods—have grown in stature either within the family of the 100 largest or in the economy as a whole. There is

no reason to believe that those now at the top will stay there except as they keep fully abreast in the race of innovation, i.e., of competition.[1]

Increased productivity has been responsible for much of the expansion which has taken place in the U. S. economy during the past 50 years. Numerous small changes in equipment, methods, processes, and management techniques enable firms to produce the same amount of goods with less manpower and equipment or to expand production using the same amount of manpower and equipment. The net effect of each change is small, but the cumulative effect of hundreds and thousands of such changes is considerable. These changes keep a company healthy, ever ready to expand. Consequently, in seeking methods of expanding and stabilizing operations, measures to increase productivity should be among the first ones considered.

Crawford H. Greenewalt, president of E. I. du Pont de Nemours and Company very aptly describes the role of research in increasing productivity:

We like, of course, to think about research in terms of the startling new product that springs from the test tube to the accompaniment of lyric headlines. At du Pont we like to talk about moistureproof cellophane, about neoprene, and about nylon. In addition to being fodder for good publicity, these developments have certainly contributed largely to our corporate prosperity. In retrospect, however, I doubt that such individually spectacular accomplishments would account for as much as half of our growth over the last twenty-five to thirty years.

It is easy to overemphasize the new and in so doing to pay insufficient tribute to what might be called "bit-by-bit" research. By this I mean the day-to-day effort that produces results which over a short period seem inconsequential, but which over the long run are extraordinarily important. It would be my guess that the average research man in the du Pont Co. would have to work for two or three lifetimes before being associated with a development that hit the headlines. He pays his way not by the spectacular but by the bit-by-bit process of incremental accomplishment.

To be more specific, let me mention the progress of cellophane. We enjoyed headlining the invention of the moistureproofing process that for the first time put cellophane on its commercial feet. That was a spectacular and quite extraordinary development. On the other hand, during the last twenty-five years the output of a cellophane-casting machine has been increased six-fold, the output per man-hour fifteenfold, and the pounds produced per dollar of investment have been increased sevenfold. And it is these results that have made cellophane the important product it has become today, that have put

---

[1] Kaplan, A.D.H., and Alfred E. Kahn. "Big Business in a Competitive Society," *Fortune*, Section 2, 47 (February 1953). Pp. 14.

its price at a sufficiently low level to make it generally useful. During any given year, process and product improvements, while solid and sure, are likely to be completely unspectacular. Over the long term, however, they make the difference between a static and a burgeoning economy.[2]

While Mr. Greenewalt's remarks deal with improvements in products and processes, they apply equally well to improvements in all areas of the business. Every company can assure itself of increasing productivity by carrying on a continuous management improvement program. Such a program will emphasize research in its broadest sense and should cover all facets of the enterprise. Increasing productivity depends first of all on the competence and skill of management. It depends on efficiency of capital plant, equipment, and on good plant layout and flow of work. Increasing and stabilizing sales are important also because they enable a company to utilize capacity. Production planning and control are essential to productivity inasmuch as they contribute to the best and cheapest method of production. Sound financial administration is necessary, for without the proper type and amount of financing, new plant and equipment would be unobtainable. And, finally, sound personnel administration is essential to increased productivity because it makes possible a more effective utilization of human resources.

Expanding and Stabilizing Sales

One of the best methods of obtaining company stability in a dynamic economy is through continual expansion of the business. Growth companies are seldom beset by problems of unemployment, idle capacity, and unprofitability. More often the managers of growth companies are concerned with obtaining enough resources and manpower to keep the company growing. The dynamic American economy provides opportunities for continuous growth for the majority of business firms. Increasing population, increasing per capita income, new methods, and new processes provide almost unlimited opportunities for expansion.

Planning for stability, therefore, should place much emphasis on the function of marketing. The climax in the industrial process is the sale of the product to a consumer. All the planning, product development, production, and merchandising are steps toward this end. Unless the product can be sold at a profit, the other phases of a company's operation must be curtailed or even terminated. These obvious truths in-

[2] Greenewalt, Crawford H. "The Slow, Steady Way of Progress," *Fortune*, 51 (May 1955), 100-101, 198ff.

dicate the importance of selling in enabling a company to survive and grow. Specifically, the sales management of a company has two important contributions to make: (1) to increase the volume of sales, and (2) to provide reasonable stability in the level of sales.

While creativity is needed in all areas of management, nowhere is it needed more than in marketing. With the rise in the standard of living, more and more purchases are falling within the range of consumer choice rather than in the category of necessities. Competition, therefore, is not only among producers of the same articles, but increasingly among producers of widely different products. Television sets compete with dishwashers, power mowers compete with automatic washers, and all of these compete with the consumer's desire for a second automobile. By effective promotion, therefore, a manufacturer can expand significantly the market for his products.

In the difficult job of expanding and stabilizing the sales of a company, management should be guided by an active market research program. Factors such as population trends, the marriage rate, and the redistribution of purchasing power, should have an influence on the development of marketing plans. Market research can make a contribution in these broad areas as well as in specific areas such as market potentials, consumer preferences, and distribution channels.

In addition to raising the level of sales, management must be concerned with reducing fluctuations in sales to a minimum. A factory using mass production methods cannot operate efficiently with marked fluctuations in volume. Heavy capitalization, high break-even points, loss of skilled workers, and pay for laid-off workers are some of the factors which make fluctuations in production costly.

In spite of efforts to increase and stabilize the level of sales, there will be periods in the experience of most companies when sales decline considerably. A wise management will be prepared for such periods. There should be advance planning as to what level of expenditure for sales promotion is appropriate during such periods. There is a tendency among many companies to reduce drastically expenditures for sales promotion during periods of business decline. Although such curtailment may be necessary in many cases, it may in other cases be quite unwise, since it results in reducing expenditures for sales promotion at the very time when it may be most useful. In the recession of 1949, for example, many companies were successful in combining increased promotion with lower prices to maintain and even raise the level of sales.

Creative Management

The degree of growth and stability achieved by a company depends to a great extent on the caliber of management personnel. The intense competition which characterizes American industrial activity puts a premium on creative management. Managers must be cognizant of the ever-changing nature of the economy, and must be able to adapt company operations to these changing conditions.

The need for creative management is sure to increase in the years ahead. The pace of change, particularly as it affects the business manager, seems certain to be accelerated in the future. Automation, increasing expenditures for research, the application of atomic energy, and new management techniques will increase the rapidity of change.

There are many important factors that influence the creativity of individuals: the free flow of information on company problems, opportunity to explore new ideas, some freedom from pressure of everyday work, and opportunity for the individual to have a voice in planning his work. The authors would like to emphasize one aspect of developing creativity, that of increasing the participation of management and other employees in the search for new and creative ideas. In our work with individual firms we have found that efforts to increase participation are likely to lead to substantial improvement in the firm's operations.

Achieving growth and stability of company operations requires good ideas: ideas for new products and services which will create new markets; ideas for cost reduction which will enable the company to lower prices; ideas for increasing efficiency which will increase profits and stimulate investment. These ideas, of course, are supplied by the employees of the business.

An important aspect of planning for stability, then, is to increase the flow of ideas regarding improvements in basic operations of the company. One of the ways in which this can be accomplished is to encourage greater participation by employees at all levels. Few managers now obtain the degree of participation which is desirable. There is great potential for increasing the profitability and stability of a company by adopting such participation as a conscious goal. To do this, management must establish and maintain a climate which is favorable to the stimulation of ideas.

One important aspect of stimulating participation is to encourage suggestions from employees. The chief executive and others high in the management hierarchy should encourage subordinates to make suggestions for improvements in the company. Executives of many companies have been successful in creating a high level of participation by informally seeking out and listening to suggestions from subordinates. If it is generally known that employees are rewarded for their ideas, and if there is no fear of criticism or recrimination, a favorable climate for obtaining the best thinking of the entire organization will be established.

Officers and other key people are more likely than rank-and-file employees to contribute important ideas for improving company operations. An effective means of obtaining ideas from key people is to have a trained investigator conduct interviews with each of them. A program of interviews to stimulate key people to contribute their ideas regarding improvements needed has been carried on by the authors in several companies. Broad questions concerning all phases of operations are used to stimulate management people to contribute ideas that have not been proposed through the regular organization channels. After the ideas are collected, a report containing the major ideas is prepared and presented to the head of the department studied and to the chief executive. Identities of persons making the suggestions are not disclosed. Providing the opportunity for management personnel to express their ideas improves the climate of the organization in addition to providing worth-while suggestions for improvements in operations.

Summary

The guaranteed annual wage is the latest in a series of pressures on the American business firm, pressures which make production cutbacks extremely costly and hazardous. Management action to reduce fluctuations cannot be confined to the traditional techniques of business stabilization. It must extend, rather, to improvement in the functioning of management itself, in all phases of the company's business.

We suggest three areas in which most companies are likely to find promising opportunities for improvement: (1) long-range planning, (2) research on products and productivity, and (3) expanding and stabilizing sales. The foundation of improvement in these three areas— and, indeed, in all other areas—is the creativity of management personnel. Managers who appreciate the importance of creativity will encourage employees at all levels to contribute their ideas for the improvement of the company's operations.

While a dynamic economy creates uncertainty and risk for enterprises, it also creates opportunity. Growth in population, increasing per capita income, new ways of living, and new technology provide opportunities for aggressive firms to expand. Wise managers will seize these opportunities to achieve growth and stability for their enterprises.

Bibliography

I. CHANGES FACING THE MANAGER OF TOMORROW

Bober, William C. "Thinking Ahead: Changing Geography of Industry," *Harvard Business Review,* 32 (November-December 1954), 159ff.

Clark, J. M. *Guideposts in a Time of Change.* New York: Harper & Brothers, 1949. Pp. 210.

Daugherty, Carroll R. "Some Labor-Management Trends and Their Implications," in *What's New on the Labor-Management Front?* Personnel Series No. 161. New York: American Management Association, 1955. Pp. 3-19.

Dewhurst, J. Frederic and Associates. *America's Needs and Resources.* New York: The Twentieth Century Fund, 1955. Pp. 1148.

Diebold, John. *Automation.* New York: Van Nostrand Co., Inc., 1952. Pp. 181.

Ewell, Raymond H. "Role of Research in Economic Growth," *Chemical and Engineering News,* 33 (July 18, 1955), 2980-2985.

Furnas, C. C. "Energy Sources of the Future," *Industrial & Engineering Chemistry,* 46 (December 1954), 2246-2457.

Hirsch, Julius, Editor. *New Horizons in Business.* New York: Harper & Brothers, 1955. Pp. 134.

Humphrey, George M. "The Future: Sound as a Dollar," *Fortune,* 51 (April 1955), 116-118.

Jacoby, Neil H. "How Public Economic Policies Affect Business Capital Expenditures," *Advanced Management,* 20 (March 1955), 5-8.

Kaplan, A. D. H. "The Current Merger Movement Analyzed," *Harvard Business Review,* 33 (May-June 1955), 91-100.

Kuznets, Simon, Editor. *Economic Change: Selected Essays in Business Cycles, National Income, and Economic Growth.* New York: W. W. Norton and Co., Inc., 1953. Pp. 333.

Lane, Frederick C. and Jelle C. Riemersma, Editors. *Enterprise and Secular Change.* Homewood, Illinois: Richard D. Irwin, Inc., 1953. Pp. 556.

Learned, Edmund P. "Thinking Ahead: Trends in Administration," *Harvard Business Review,* 29 (July 1951), 127ff.

Meany, George. "What Labor Means by 'More'," *Fortune,* 51 (March 1955), 92-93, 172ff.

Moore, G. H. *Statistical Indicators of Cyclical Revivals and Depressions.* Occasional Paper 31. New York: National Bureau of Economic Research, 1950. Pp. 95.

Newman, William H. and James P. Logan. *Management of Expanding Enterprises.* New York: Columbia University Press, 1955. Pp. 125.

Samuelson, Paul A. "Built-in Stabilizers of Our Economy," *Reporter,* 8 (February 17, 1953), 13-15.

Sarnoff, David. "The Fabulous Future," *Fortune,* 51 (January 1955), 82-83, 114ff.

Smyth, H. D. "Industrial Application of Atomic Energy," *Journal of Business,* 27 (October 1954), 312-320.

Snyder, Richard M. *Measuring Business Changes.* New York: John Wiley & Sons, Inc., 1956. Pp. 382.

von Neumann, John. "Can We Survive Technology?" *Fortune,* 51 (June 1955), 106-108, 151ff.

Weston, J. F. *The Role of Mergers in the Growth of Large Firms.* Berkeley: University of California, Bureau of Business and Economic Research, 1953. Pp. 159.

II. ADJUSTING TO CHANGING CONDITIONS

"Adjusting to That 'Readjustment'," *Fortune,* 49 (February 1954), 95-96.

Alderson, Wroe. "Survival and Adjustment in Organized Behavior Systems," Chapter 4 in Part I, *Theory in Marketing.* Homewood, Illinois: Richard D. Irwin, Inc., 1950. Pp. 65-87.

Brozen, Yale. "Adapting to Technological Change," *The Journal of Business,* 24 (April 1951), 114-126.

Bursk, Edward C. and Dan H. Fenn, Jr., Editors. *Planning the Future Strategy of Your Business.* New York: McGraw-Hill Book Co., Inc., 1956. Pp. 302.

Copeland, Melvin T. "Survival in a Changing World," Chapter VI in *The Executive at Work.* Cambridge: Harvard University Press, 1951. Pp. 100-124.

Cresap, Mark W., Jr. "Long-Term Planning," *Advanced Management,* 18 (January 1953), 34-36.

Dale, Ernest. "Centralization Versus Decentralization," *Advanced Management,* 20 (June 1955), 11-16.

Dale, Ernest. *Planning and Developing the Company Organization Structure.* Research Report No. 20. New York: American Management Association, 1952. Pp. 232.

Drucker, Peter F. *The Practice of Management.* New York: Harper & Brothers, 1954. Pp. 404.

Friend, Irwin. "What Business Can Do to Prevent Recession," in *Problems in Anti-Recession Policy.* New York: Committee for Economic Development, 1954. Pp. 1-11.

Hoffman, Paul G. "Role of Businessman in Dynamic Economy Defined," *Factory Management & Maintenance,* 105 (August 1947), 230ff.

Hopf, Harry A. "Adapting the Industrial Organization to Changing Conditions," *The Management Review,* 36 (February 1947), 68-70.

Juran, Joseph M. "The Anatomy of Industrial Habits," in *Adjusting to a Competitive Economy—The Human Problem.* Manufacturing Series No. 214. New York: American Management Association, 1954. Pp. 34-39.

Kelley, Pearce C. "The Technique of Management Required to Meet Rapidly Changing Conditions," in *Handbook of Business Administration.* New York: McGraw-Hill Book Co., Inc., 1931. Pp. 159-165.

Knauth, Oswald W. *Managerial Enterprise—Its Growth and Operation.* New York: W. W. Norton & Co., Inc., 1948. Pp. 224.

McGregor, Douglas. "Leadership and the Conditions of Organizational Effectiveness," *Public Health Reports,* 67 (January 1952), 42-46.

McKinsey, James O. *Adjusting Policies To Meet Changing Conditions.* General Management Series No. 116. New York: American Management Association, 1932.

McLean, John G. and Robert W. Haigh. "How Business Corporations Grow," *Harvard Business Review,* 32 (November-December 1954), 81-93.

Mitchell, William N., Editor. *Management's Adjustment to the Changing National Economy.* Chicago: The University of Chicago Press, 1942. Pp. 61.

National Bureau of Economic Research. *Policies to Combat Depression.* Princeton: Princeton University Press, 1956. Pp. 417.

National Bureau of Economic Research. *Regularization of Business Investment.* Princeton: Princeton University Press, 1954. Pp. 513.

Olson, James C. "Is Your Company Prepared for Rough Weather?" *Harvard Business Review,* 25 (Autumn 1947), 595-608.

Reilley, Ewing W. "Planning the Strategy of the Business," *Advanced Management,* 20 (December 1955), 8-12.

Sampson, Robert C. *The Staff Role in Management. Its Creative Uses.* New York: Harper & Brothers, 1955. Pp. 226.

Tead, Ordway. "Business Leadership in the Decade Ahead," *Advanced Management,* 20 (February 1955), 5-9.

Thole, Henry C. *The Adaptation of the Individual Firm to Economic Change.* Kalamazoo: Unpublished Master's Thesis (Kalamazoo College), 1949. Pp. 104.

Whyte, William F. "Organization and Motivation of Management," in *Industrial Productivity.* Madison: Industrial Relations Research Association, 1951. Pp. 94-109.

III. MANAGEMENT ACTION IN SPECIFIC AREAS

Product Research

Andrews, Kenneth R. "Product Diversification and the Public Interest," *Harvard Business Review,* 29 (July 1951), 91-107.

Blough, R. M. "Guided Research Essential to Economic Strength and Stability," *Commercial and Financial Chronicle,* 181 (May 19, 1955), 2303ff.

Borden, Neil H. "Development and Marketing of New Consumer Products," in *Twenty-Sixth Boston Conference on Distribution.* A National Forum for Problems of Distribution. Boston: Retail Trade Board, 1954. Pp. 65-70.

Brozen, Yale. "Research, Technology, and Productivity," in *Industrial Productivity.* Madison: Industrial Relations Research Association, 1951. Pp. 25-49.

Bush, George P. and Lowell H. Hattery, Editors. *Scientific Research: Its Administration and Organization.* Washington: American University Press, 1950. Pp. 190.

Dooher, M. J., Editor. *Getting the Most from Product Research and*

Development. Special Report No. 6. New York: American Management Association, 1955. Pp. 149.

Ewell, Raymond H. "Role of Research in Economic Growth," *Chemical & Engineering News,* 33 (July 18, 1955), 2980-2985.

Furnas, C. C., Editor. *Research in Industry.* New York: D. Van Nostrand Co., Inc., 1948. Pp. 574.

Greenewalt, Crawford H. "The Slow, Steady Way of Progress," *Fortune,* 51 (May 1955), 100-101, 198ff.

Marvin, P. R. "Developing Strong Product Lines," *Machine Design,* 26 (May 1954), 116-122.

National Industrial Conference Board. *New Product Development. II. Research and Engineering.* Studies in Business Policy No. 57. New York: National Industrial Conference Board, 1954. Pp. 52.

Standard Oil Development Co. *The Future of Industrial Research.* New York: Standard Oil Development Co., 1945. Pp. 173.

Walton, Charles W. "Today's Research—Tomorrow's Profits," in *Critical Areas in Top Management Responsibility.* General Management Series No. 166. New York: American Management Association, 1953. Pp. 10-18.

Sales Management

Alderson, Wroe. "Marketing Services and Business Stability," in *Problems in Anti-Recession Policy.* New York: Committee for Economic Development, 1954. Pp. 41-53.

Burck, Gilbert. "Who'll Buck a Trend?" *Fortune,* 46 (October 1952), 134-135, 209ff.

Colley, Russell H. "Needed: A Marketing Preparedness Program," *Harvard Business Review,* 30 (March-April 1952), 106-118.

Converse, Paul D. "What's Going to Happen Is Already Happening," *Current Economic Comment,* 13 (November 1951), 57-66.

Crisp, Richard D. *How To Reduce Distribution Costs.* New York: Funk & Wagnalls in association with Modern Industry, 1948. Pp. 390.

Dean, Joel. "How Much to Spend on Advertising," *Harvard Business Review,* 29 (January 1951), 65-74.

Gruber, Lewis. "Marketing Strategy and Changing Consumer Trends," in *Twenty-Sixth Boston Conference on Distribution.* A National Forum for Problems of Distribution. Boston: Retail Trade Board, 1954. Pp. 43-47.

Harper, Marion, Jr. "Advertising in an Adjustment Period: A Program for Action," *Advertising and Selling* 42 (April 1949). Pp. 35.

Hollander, Sidney, Jr. "A Rationale for Advertising Expenditures," *Harvard Business Review,* 27 (January 1949), 79-87.

Huegy, Harvey W. "A Continuous Audit of Distribution Policies," in *Twenty-Seventh Boston Conference on Distribution.* Boston: Retail Trade Board, 1955. Pp. 58-61.

Jeuck, John E. "Is Selling a Key to Sustain Prosperity?" *Commercial and Financial Chronicle,* 179 (February 11, 1954), 16, 38-39.

Knauth, Oswald W. "Distribution: The Keynote of Today's Economy," *Dun's Review,* 57 (May 1949), 14-15, 50-54.

Lebow, Victor. "Our Changing Channels of Distribution," *The Journal of Marketing,* 8 (July 1948), 12-22.

MacGowan, T. G. "Assignment for Tomorrow," Part I and Part II, *Dun's Review*, 60 (August 1952), 30-31ff; 60 (September 1952), 25ff.

National Industrial Conference Board. *New Product Development, III. Marketing New Products.* Studies in Business Policy No. 69. New York: National Industrial Conference Board, 1954. Pp. 48.

"The Product That Sells," *Fortune*, 47 (March 1953), 110-112, 188ff.

Wales, H. G., Editor. *Changing Perspectives in Marketing.* Urbana: University of Illinois, 1951. Pp. 292.

Financial Management

Beckett, John A. "Preparing for Times of Economy," *The Controller*, 22 (April 1954), 155-158, 188ff.

De Chazeau, Melvin G. "Can We Avoid Depression in a Dynamic Economy?" *Harvard Business Review*, 32 (July-August 1954), 37-44.

Dewing, Arthur S. *The Financial Policy of Corporations.* New York: The Ronald Press Company, 1948. Pp. 1538.

Dobrovolsky, S. "Capital Formation and Financing Trends in Manufacturing and Mining, 1900-1953," *The Journal of Finance*, 10 (May 1955), 250-265.

Gross, Walter H., David D. Jacobs, and Stanley O. Sargis. "Management of Business Under Inflation," *The Management Review*, 41 (May 1952), 313-317.

Johnson, Norris O. "The Trend of Interest Rates with Relation to Future Planning," in *Sharing in Our Expanding Economy*. Financial Management Series No. 107. New York: American Management Association, 1954. Pp. 22-29.

Miller, Stanley R. "Recent Trends in Corporate Finance," in *Industrial Development at Home and Abroad—Problems and Prospects*. Financial Management Series No. 101. New York: American Management Association, 1952. Pp. 7-14.

Silverman, Herbert R. "The Changing Financial Pattern in Company Growth," in *Guides to Modern Financial Planning*. Financial Management Series No. 104. New York: American Management Association, 1953. Pp. 22-31.

Snider, Joseph L. "Funds for Stability," *Harvard Business Review*, 30 (July-August 1952), 86-96.

Soule, George. "Business Finances a New Autonomy," *Challenge*, (January 1955).

Ulmer, Melville J. "Long-Term Trends in the Financing of Regulated Industries, 1870-1950," *The Journal of Finance*, 10 (May 1955), 266-285.

Production and Personnel Management

Aronson, Robert L. *Layoff Policies and Practices.* Princeton: Industrial Relations Section, Princeton University, 1950. Pp. 55.

Barkin, Solomon. "Trade-Union Attitudes and Their Effect Upon Productivity," in *Industrial Productivity*. Madison: Industrial Relations Research Association, 1951. Pp. 110-129.

Bowden, Gordon T. "The Adaptive Capacity of Workers," *Harvard Business Review*, 25 (Summer 1947), 527-542.

Burck, Gilbert. "The American Genius for Productivity," *Fortune*, 52 (July 1955), 86-87, 159ff.

Burck, Gilbert and Sanford Parker. "Productivity: The Great Age of 3%," *Fortune*, 52 (November 1955), 102-105, 241ff.

Coch, Lester and J. R. P. French. "Overcoming Resistance to Change," *Human Relations*, 1 (August 1948), 512-532.

Gitlow, Abraham L. "An Economic Evaluation of the Gains and Costs of Technological Change," in *Industrial Productivity*. Madison: Industrial Relations Research Association, 1951. Pp. 172-193.

Golden, Clinton S. "Management-Labor Relations in a Changing Economy," *The Annals of the American Academy of Political and Social Science*, 274 (March 1951), 171-178.

Golden, Clinton S. and Virginia D. Parker, Editors. *Causes of Industrial Peace Under Collective Bargaining*. New York: Harper & Brothers, 1955. Pp. 369.

Lagemann, John K. "Job Enlargement Boosts Production," *Nation's Business*, (December 1954), 35-37, 79.

Lawrence, Paul R. "How to Deal with Resistance to Change," *Harvard Business Review*, 32 (May-June 1954), 49-57.

Lester, Richard A. *Adjustments to Labor Shortages*. Princeton: Industrial Relations Section, Princeton University, 1955. Pp. 89.

Lewyt, Alexander. "Pinch-Hitters in Production," *Dun's Review*, (June 1953), 30-32, 34ff.

Ronken, Harriet O. and Paul R. Lawrence. *Administering Changes*. A Case Study of Human Relations in a Factory. Boston: Harvard University, Division of Research, Graduate School of Business Administration, 1952. Pp. 324.

Selekman, Benjamin M. "Resistance to Shop Changes," Chapter 6 in *Labor Relations and Human Relations*. New York: McGraw-Hill Book Co., Inc., 1947. Pp. 111-137.

Tripp, L. Reed, Editor. *Industrial Productivity*. Madison: Industrial Relations Research Association, 1951. Pp. 224.

Walker, Charles R. "Adjustment, Individual and Social, to Technological Change," in *Industrial Productivity*. Madison: Industrial Relations Research Association, 1951. Pp. 194-211.

Walker, Charles R. and F. L. W. Richardson. *Human Relations in an Expanding Company*. New Haven: Yale University Press, 1948.

Zander, Alvin. "Resistance to Change—Its Analysis and Prevention," *Advanced Management*, 15 (January 1950), 9-11.

IV. THE GUARANTEED ANNUAL WAGE AND BUSINESS STABILIZATION

Allen, James L. and C. Wilson Randle. "Challenge of the Guaranteed Annual Wage," *Harvard Business Review*, 32 (May-June 1954), 37-48.

American Management Association. *Management Planning for Employment Stabilization*. General Management Series No. 135. New York: American Management Association, 1945. Pp. 23.

Dale, Ernest. *Annual Wages and Employment Stabilization Techniques.*

Research Report No. 8. New York: American Management Association, 1945. Pp. 96.

Deupree, Richard R. "Management's Responsibility Toward Economic Stability," *Dun's Review,* 56 (August 1948), 11-12, 74ff.

Feldman, Herman. *Stabilizing Jobs and Wages Through Better Business Management.* New York: Harper & Brothers, 1940. Pp. 334.

Kaplan, A. D. H. *The Guarantee of Annual Wages.* Washington: The Brookings Institution, 1947. Pp. 269.

Latimer, Murray W. *Guaranteed Wages.* Washington: Government Printing Office, 1947. Pp. 473.

National Industrial Conference Board. *Annual Wage and Employment Guarantee Plans.* Studies in Personnel Policy No. 76. New York: National Industrial Conference Board, 1946. Pp. 55.

National Industrial Conference Board. *Reducing Fluctuations in Employment (Experience in 31 Industries).* Studies in Personnel Policy No. 27. New York: National Industrial Conference Board, 1940. Pp. 60.

Rukeyser, Merryle S. "Help Yourself to Stability," *The Management Review,* 42 (September 1953), 496-497.

Slichter, Sumner H. "Managements Can Help Prevent the Depression That They Fear," *Manufacturing & Industrial Engineering,* 31 (May 1953), 20-26.

Smith, Edwin S. *Reducing Seasonal Unemployment.* New York: McGraw-Hill Book Co., Inc., 1931. Pp. 296.

Snider, Joseph L. *The Guarantee of Work and Wages.* Boston: Division of Research, Graduate School of Business Administration, Harvard University, 1947. Pp. 191.

Society for Advancement of Management. *Proceedings of Guaranteed Annual Wage Conference.* New York: Society for Advancement of Management, 1955. Pp. 153.

Index